The Law of the Somalis

The Law of the Somalis

A Stable Foundation for Economic Development in the Horn of Africa

Michael van Notten

Edited by
Spencer Heath MacCallum

The Red Sea Press, Inc.
Publishers & Distributors of Third World Books

P.O. Box 1892
Trenton, NJ 08607

P.O. Box 48
Asmara, ERITREA

The Red Sea Press, Inc.

Publishers & Distributors of Third World Books

P.O. Box 1892

Trenton, NJ 08607

P.O. Box 48

Asmara, ERITREA

Book design: 'Damola Ifaturoti
Cover design: Roger Dormann

Library of Congress Cataloging-in-Publication Data

Notten, Michael van, 1933-2002.
  The law of the Somalis : a stable foundation for economic development in the Horn of Africa / Michael van Notten; edited by Spencer Heath MacCallum.
      p. cm.
  Includes bibliographical references and index.
  ISBN 1-56902-249-6 (cloth) -- ISBN 1-56902-250-X (pbk.)
  1. Customary law--Somalia. 2. Law reform--Somalia. I. MacCallum, Spencer Heath. II. Title.

KTK46.7.N68 2005
340.5'26773--dc22

                            2005018531

To the rightfully proud and independent people
of Somalia

The Horn of Africa

Shading shows approximate area inhabited by Somali people

0 Miles 500

0 Kilometers 500

SAUDI ARABIA

Arabian Peninsula

OMAN

Red Sea

★ Khartoum

Asmara
ERITREA ★

YEMEN

SUDAN

White Nile
Blue Nile

Suqutra

DJIBOUTI
★ Djibouti

Gulf of Aden

WESTERN AWDAL
AWDAL Berbera
Borama
SOMALILAND SANAAG
Dire Dawa Harar Hargeisa
Burao SOOL
Bossaso
PUNTLAND

Addis Ababa ★

ETHIOPIA

OGADEN

Shabelle River
Juba River
Webi Dhusa

SOMALIA

Lake Rudolph

INDIAN OCEAN

UGANDA

KENYA

Merka
Mogadishu

Kampala ★

Lake Victoria

Nairobi ★

Kismayo

Tana River

Kilimanjaro

Mombasa

TANZANIA

Zanzibar Island

Dar es Salaam ★

ATLANTIC OCEAN

INDIAN OCEAN

MAP BY CARTIFACT, LOS ANGELES

Contents

Editorial
Preface

This important and highly original work, outlining Somali customary law and pointing the way to a practical synthesis between the modern world economy and the traditional institutions of the Somali people, was interrupted by the untimely death of its author on June 5, 2002. Nevertheless, its message is clear. It addresses Somali customary law not only as it is, but also as it has been and may yet become.

A practicing lawyer in the Netherlands, Michael van Notten married into and lived as one of the Samaron Clan during the last twelve years of his life. His libertarian cast of mind was an asset in understanding the culture and institutions of this people whom he adopted and who received him as a kinsman. It enabled him to gain a deeper understanding of traditional African institutions than he might have otherwise. Readers need not share his personal libertarian philosophy in order to find enormous value in this descriptive account and assessment of traditional Somali law, economics, and politics.

At first, this book might seem to straddle two horses—law and commerce. But each presupposes the other. Economic development presupposes law, and the growth and development of the law proceeds largely from the hustle bustle of economic activity. In a stateless setting especially, these are two aspects of a single phenomenon. Hence the author's emphasis on economic development, in which he envisions freeports playing an important catalysing role. Economic development will have the capability of stimulating the growth of the customary law into a full body of common law capable of meeting the complex needs of a developed society. Such growth is essential if, as seems likely, Somalia is to continue without a central government.

The question as to whether significant economic development is even an option in a region lacking a legislative authority is squarely addressed in this book. The last chapter contains innovative thinking on how, in the absence of a central government, freeports might be designed to operate in the world economy while being fully compatible with traditional Somali institutions. Such tradition-friendly development could enable Somalis to assume a respected place in the world by leaving aside their colonial legacy and building on their indigenous institutions.

Michael van Notten's work adds to a growing literature on polycentric, decentralized, or non-monopolistic systems of law. While his incomplete draft material did not adequately reference his indebtedness to scholars in this field, the reader who is interested in investigating the subject will find an early but useful introduction and guide in Tom W. Bell (1991). Other writers include Randy E. Barnett (1998), Bruce L. Benson (1990, 1998), A.S. Diamond (1975), David D. Friedman (2000), and Bruno Leoni (1961). Van Notten is no less indebted to the great classical-liberal tradition of, among others, Frederick Bastiat, Milton Friedman, Friedrich Hayek, Spencer Heath, Ludwig von Mises, Leonard Read, Murray Rothbard, Adam Smith, Lysander Spooner, and Herbert Spencer.

A word should be said about the author's reliance on the concept of natural law and natural rights, since this view of the world is less fashionable in academia today than it once was (although that may be changing, see Barnett 1998, Tibor Machan 2001, Tara Smith 1995). Suffice it to say that there is nothing mystical about his use of the concept. He uses it, following the Belgian scholar Frank van Dun, to refer to underlying principles of successful human social organisation—"successful" here meaning organisation that can endure because it respects the integrity of the individuals ultimately comprising it. At one point, he simply characterises it as the timeless and universal principles that protect life, liberty, and property.

It will interest Somalia scholars to know that, besides the draft of this book, the author left material sufficient for a second that, as a companion volume, could be titled *The Politics of the Somali*. That material addresses the prospect of a voluntary confederation of independent clans that would constitute a viable and distinctly African alternative to the European model of government.

FEATURES OF THE LAW

The kind of law system described in this book, once the norm for human society, is rare today. A striking feature is that it is compensatory rather than punitive. Law-breakers, instead of being imprisoned or otherwise punished, are required to compensate their victims. Any fines that are to be paid go to the victim rather than to the government, and they seldom exceed the compensation due. As Anthony de Jasay (1997:240,fn.6) comments, "customary law is overwhelmingly restitution-based, while legal systems where justice is provided by the state tend to veer towards retribution."

Viewed in global perspective, Somali law stands with the Latin and Medieval laws and the English common law against the statutory law that only became prevalent in continental Europe with the rise of the modern nation state. Somali law requires no legislature because it is not *made*. Somali traditional judges never think of their activity as "law-making," and the assertion that anyone could *make* the law would strike them as weird, if not obscene. What Bruno Leoni (1991:81, 83) says about Roman law holds for Somali:

> A large part of the Roman rules of law was not due to
> any legislative process whatever ... private Roman law
> was something to be described or to be discovered,
> not something to be enacted.

Another feature of Somali law that is characteristic of many systems of customary law but sounds odd to the European ear is that every Somali is insured by near kin against his or her liabilities under the law. Consequently a victim seldom fails to receive compensation, even if his or her rights were violated by children or by adults who are penniless, mentally ill, or who have fled abroad.

Because Somali law, being based upon custom, has no need of legislation or legislators, it is free of political influences. That independence makes for better law. The author maintains that crime is lower where customary law is followed than would be the case under legislated law. He suggests that much of Somalia today comes close to what might be called the "natural order of human society"—the hypothetical pattern of human association absent social distortions by political governments. Even so, he points out areas in the law that are in need of change. But these do not require legislation. He explains how many desirable changes, such as ending restrictions on the sale of land and enhancing the status of women, are implicit in economic development.

This book argues that the Somalis' traditional system of law and politics is capable of maintaining a peaceful society and guiding them to prosperity. In the absence of legislation at home and interventions from abroad (which fuel clan conflict by keeping alive the expectation of a central government with its awesome powers that each clan, in self defence, must attempt to control), natural adjustments can be expected that will enable Somalis to maintain internal peace and participate fully in the global economy. Not only is there no need to set up a democracy, the author shows why any attempt to do so must inevitably produce chaos.

Among the controversial propositions in this book are these:

1. The concepts of property, freedom of contract, and justice were discovered and first developed not by the technologically advanced societies but by tribal societies.
2. Crime can be defined in terms of property rights.
3. Governments can neither add to nor subtract from the principle just stated, since property rights do not demand that criminals be punished but only that they compensate their victims.

4. Property rights are better protected by private agencies such as insurance companies than by a central government.
5. Every person should be insured for his liabilities under the law.
6. Law consists solely of principles and rules relating to property rights.
7. Custom provides a better basis for law than legislation.
8. Customary law generally shows a high regard for property rights.
9. Where the two conflict, Somalis usually prefer their customary law to Koranic law.
10. Political democracy is incompatible with property rights. The political system that is compatible with property rights is called "kritarchy."
11. Many Somalis prefer kritarchy to democracy.
12. Democracy is incompatible with a close-knit clan society.

A NOTE ON THE EDITING OF THIS BOOK

A major problem in editing this book was the fact that Chapter 8, "Economics," was unwritten. It had only a brief start and the cryptic note, "Further information to be drawn from the books of George Ayittey. Start with describing the economic miracles of Bossaso ... Idem Merka." On reflection, however, it seemed that Bossaso and its implications for the future of Somalia did not fit the book's order of presentation of traditional Somali law and politics. This lack of logical fit may have accounted in part for the chapter remaining unwritten. Accordingly, with critical input from George A. N. Ayittey, I prepared a brief text for Chapter 8 relating to traditional economics and then dealt with the question of economic development, including an account of the "miracle" of Bossaso, in two chapters added at the end.

Among the lesser problems was the fact that the author had indicated by asterisks, throughout the manuscript, references he intended to make, but the references were not found. Also, throughout the manuscript and especially in Chapter 5, "Rules of Conduct," the author left notations about questions of fact and information he had yet to gather. For the reader to whom these might suggest interesting avenues for further research, they are available on request.

I had assisted Michael van Notten in editing several published articles. It was an honour to be named in his will as the principal editor of this work. John Mukum Mbaku, Mauro Tosco, and Frank van Dun became major editors with me by virtue of volunteering many long hours of work. Mauro Tosco painstakingly checked Somali terms for accuracy and spelling; Frank van Dun contributed substantially to the organisation of Appendix C and helped to clarify the author's references to natural law; and John Mukum Mbaku suggested that I retrieve material I had written and placed in the Appendix, where he felt it would be ignored by students, and place it instead at the end of the book under a new section, "Part III—Economic Development." Since several people joined in the editing, the occasional editorial footnotes are identified by initials.

Michael Van Notten was competent in eight languages, including two Somali dialects. But English not being native to him, he always encouraged a free hand in editing to make his thought more idiomatic. I have taken the liberty, therefore, as if he were at my shoulder, of editing the draft material freely, while taking care not to change his meaning. In the section on sale of land in Chapter 11, I expanded the discussion in ways I believe are consistent with his thought. The term "freeport-clan" is mine. Most of my contribution, however, aside from Chapters 8, 14, and 15, and Appendix C, had to do with smoothness of expression and transition.

Many people contributed in many different ways to the completion of this work, proof of the saying that the gods provide thread for the web begun. I am grateful for their assistance. Dr. Mohamed Buwe Osman, a noted artist originally from Merka in southern Somalia and now practicing medicine in Fayetteville, North Carolina, generously volunteered his art for the jacket, adding warmth and colour and perhaps a measure of geographic balance to a text that mainly reflects the central and northern region of Somalia. Michael van Notten's daughters, Marina, Henriette, Isabelle, and Ariane worked diligently to locate and send from Holland the draft materials for this book while Isabelle tracked the process of the book and made important editorial suggestions. Larry Zempel, of Cartifact, Los Angeles, responded valiantly at the last minute to produce a frontispiece map. Roy Halliday contributed hours of meticulous proofreading and made suggestions in the section on natural rights. The author's friend, Bob Haywood, also proofread the entire manuscript and made welcome suggestions, as did Jon Abbink, George A.N. Ayittey, Stefan Blankertz, Faisal Ahmed Hassan, Emalie MacCallum, John Mukum Mbaku, Mauro Tosco, Frank van Dun, Kevin S. van Horn, Isabelle van Notten, and Carl Watner. The greater contribution of Faisal Ahmed Hassan still waits. He has volunteered to translate this book into his native Somali.

Spencer Heath MacCallum

Part I

THE LAW

Chapter 1
Introduction

This book tells the story of a nation organised on the basis of folk law, or custom. This is unusual, since most nations in the world today are based on statutory law, or legislation. Statutory law is designed by politicians, whereas customary law consists of the rules that judges discern in the customary behaviour of people.

For most of its existence, humankind lived by customary law. But in very recent centuries statutory law, consisting mainly of regulation imposed by domestic or foreign rulers, has become the norm. This happened in Somalia as it did elsewhere. In 1991, however, the Somalis returned to their customary law. The Somali nation is the first in modern history to do that.

Somalis are strongly attached to their customary law, and they cherish the judges who adjudicate and enforce it. Foreigners may regard this as stubborn chauvinism, but Somalis believe they have good reasons. In this book I shall analyse their reasons, first describing their law as it functions today and then evaluating it to see why it is that, despite a number of evident weaknesses, Somalis value it so highly. I shall then speculate on how the Somali nation might develop and the effects that could have on other African nations. Finally, I shall evaluate United Nations policy with respect to Somalia.

The media often suggest that the political turmoil in Somalia is symptomatic of problems afflicting the entire African continent. They are right. The problems are largely a legacy of the colonial era and are much the same everywhere. Before Africa was colonised, nearly all African societies were based on customary law. Foreigners were welcome to visit or settle provided they respected their law. However, the European colonisers had other ideas. They set out to dominate the local populations. They did so by applying brute force to impose their colonial rule and its legal system. When the colonial era came to an end, the colonial administrators hastily trained a few indigenous politicians in the art of governing and set up each new nation with its own government. They modelled these governments on political democracy, despite the fact that such a political and legal system does not suit Africa. They did so because political democracy is premised on statutory law, which suited their own near-term interests.

The indigenous politicians soon flooded their countries with statutory laws, enacting these primarily to extort money from the population. Predictably, the inhabitants rebelled. Some rebelled in order to do some legal extorting themselves, but others only wanted to defend themselves from such extortion and preserve their own freedom. Indeed, not all of the political unrest in Africa has been due to the avarice of individuals wanting a larger slice of the central government's revenues. Some rebels have been motivated by a desire to preserve their customary laws and institutions.

How Europe Abandoned Customary Law

It was not long ago that something similar happened in the Western world. As recently as the eighteenth century, the bulk of law in Europe and North America was still based on custom. The massive shift to statutory law first occurred in Napoleonic France following the 1789 Revolution. Politicians of other nations soon followed the French example.

At first, the attempt was to codify the customary law and make it conform to general principles of law and justice. It was thought that by weeding out the anomalies, injustices, and other instances of corruption that had accumulated over time in the customary law, codification would prepare the way for a true "rule of law." All too often, the corruption of the customary law had provided a pretext for rulers to substitute their own legal order for the customary order. A purified customary law would destroy that pretext. It would make it possible to limit the role of the state to the formal administration of justice, the substance of which would be found in customary law. This idea provided the core of the programme for constitutional government that many thinkers had begun to advocate in the seventeenth and eighteenth centuries as an antidote against the arbitrariness of absolutist royal rule. But the programme contained a fatal flaw.

In the era of royal absolutism, a doctrine of "legislative sovereignty" had arisen and come to be accepted by most people. That doctrine implied that a group of rulers, calling themselves legislators, could make and impose any rule or regulation they wanted. The only proviso was that in so doing, they should act legally, in accordance with procedures they or their predecessors had prescribed. Although the programme for constitutional government called for a drastic revision of the doctrine of legislative sovereignty, it nevertheless, despite the absolutist connotation, assumed that doctrine as a premise.

In the constitutional programme, legislative sovereignty was to be restricted in two ways. First, legislative power was to be transferred from an unaccountable king to representatives of the people, who could be removed from office in periodic elections. Second, that legislative authority was to be limited in its scope to the formal organisation and operation of the state apparatus itself. While the people themselves would be subject only to the "rule of law," meaning the customary law, state and other political officials would be constrained, in addition, by "legal rules" imposed by the people. In short, the principle of legality would apply only to officials. It would not apply to ordinary individuals except on those rare occasions when they chose to act in an official capacity, as voters in a general election or as members of juries. In their daily life and work, they would be expected to conform to the general requirements of law, which meant in particular having respect for other persons and their property, good faith in contractual relations, and personal responsibility and liability for their own acts.

All of this was essential if the programme for the constitutional state was to work. The purpose was not to create yet another institution of the rule of some over others, but to create an institution that would guarantee people their freedom while keeping the organisations of political power on a short leash. To ensure that political power would not be used to benefit some at the expense of others, but only to administer justice and maintain the order of law, required a strict separation of society and state.

Unfortunately, the representatives of the people soon extended their legislative power to cover not officials alone, but also private individuals and their families, associations, and organisations. They thought nothing of interfering with the requirements of natural and customary law, which they regarded as no more than another set of legal rules.

Thus began a process of weaning the population from a concern for natural law and justice and habituating it to accept the arbitrary commands of the rulers, all under the pretext that they, as elected officials, merely executed the desires of the people.

People began to feel increasing need to form associations (political parties and pressure groups) to secure legal powers, privileges and immunities, and material benefits for themselves, and to impose the costs of these advantages on others in the form of taxes and regulations. Increasingly, they came to realise that political power and influence often provided an easier path to their goals than the lawful instruments of work, saving, investing, and forming voluntary associations.

Thus, the separation of society and state gave way on the one hand to an extensive politicisation of social life, and on the other to an equally extensive socialisation of politics. No longer was the state seen to have its raison d'être in the administration of justice. Instead, it now came to be seen as a tool that could serve any group or organisation for whatever purpose that group or organisation could place on the political agenda.

At the root of this development was the assumption that the authority to codify implied authority to modify the natural and customary law. This had sparked a lively debate in the early nineteenth century between supporters and adversaries of the customary law. Prominent in the debate were the German professors Friedrich Karl von Savigny and Georg Wilhelm Friedrich Hegel.[1] Savigny held that customary law is the only true law, and he feared that with codification it would stultify and die. Hegel, on the other hand, thought codification was necessary; he thought the customary law should be systematised, strengthened, and written down in a legal code. But both opposed the idea of modifying it.[2]

For Europe, this spirited defence of the customary law came too late. The cult of national legislative sovereignty had emboldened its politicians to discard the long tradition of customary law. In a short time, almost all law on the European continent became statutory. Politicians came to be seen as the sole originators of the law. The result was that people became less free and less well off than they would have been had the system of customary law continued; for Europe's customary laws during previous centuries had more or less closely approximated natural law. Natural law implies a respect for property rights and for freedom of contract, whereas statutory law mostly infringes those rights and that freedom.

In Africa, customary law is still very much alive. People tend to follow it. They abhor the statutory laws made by politicians and only obey them when forced. Much of the political turmoil in Africa is caused by the fact that Africans find statutory laws oppressive; abolishing statutory laws, many believe, would end much of that political turmoil.

When the Italian, British, and French colonisers withdrew from the Horn of Africa in the 1960s and '70s, Somalis should have made their customary law the supreme law of the land as it had been from time immemorial before the colonial period. The traditional law system was still operational, the reason being that the colonial governments had abolished it only in their own dealings with the local population. Relations among their subjects being of little concern to them, they had left the settlement of violent conflict such as murder, rape, and robbery largely to the Somalis. But on departing, the colonisers pushed the Somalis into establishing legal and political structures like those of Italy, England and France, insensitive to the fact that these structures, now almost wholly imbued with statutory law after the victory of the doctrine of legislative sovereignty, reflected a culture totally unlike that of the Africans. The result was that the Somalis found themselves at the mercy of a government soon to become an enemy of the common people and a destroyer of the economy.

The government of the Republic of Somalia began in 1960 as a democracy. Nine years later, it became a dictatorship. When in 1978 the Republic lost its war with Ethiopia, Somalis realised that both democracy and dictatorship had totally failed them. Many wished for an opportunity to return to their traditional form of governance. That opportunity came in 1991 when, on the ouster of dictator Siad Barre, no consensus emerged for appointing a new head of the Republic. In that stalemate the government disintegrated, and its erstwhile citizens returned to their traditional system of law and politics.

The transition was not easy and is still far from complete, for the demise of the central government did little to end the ravaging of Somali society and culture that it had set in motion, especially in the area around Mogadishu, the former capitol. The reason is that the expectation, actively promoted by the United Nations, that a central government would be re-established in the near future led clan militias and remnants of the former government into armed conflict, often in disregard of customary law and their elders. Each group manoeuvred to be in the most favourable position to capture the formidable array of powers of the future government. Because any clan that controlled the government could be expected to use it in the interest of its own members at the expense of all others, each felt compelled in self-defence to enter the fray. In this situation, order could only resume when the expectation of a central government receded. But the United Nations has spent billions keeping that expectation alive.

WHAT IS OVERLOOKED ABOUT SOMALIA

Many commentators describe Somalia today as lawless and chaotic. But that description makes no sense. Most Somalis abide by their customary law and respect the verdicts of their courts of justice. Disorder prevails only in those few areas where politicians of the defunct Somali Republic, frequently called "warlords," still try to impose their will.

What commentators miss is that traditional Somali society is organised more or less like the Internet. Like that communications system, the Somali way of maintaining law and order has no head or tail. Its system of governance has no executive and no legislature. It functions without a minister of justice or a supreme court, and yet it provides for rule making and adjudication. Many outsiders fail to understand how this works. Because they see no one making and enforcing laws, they think there are no laws. Consequently they propose that the Somalis establish a democracy. They overlook the fact that democracy is incompatible with the egalitarian character of Somali society. Somalis strongly oppose being divided into two political groups, those that rule and those that are ruled. And that is precisely what democracy does.

A complicating factor in understanding Somali society is that, during the past 30 years, a million or more Somalis have emigrated to Europe and North America. From there, they have become a highly vocal political lobby in their country of origin. These Somalis are enjoying every advantage of the clan system while being spared most of its disadvantages. The advantages they enjoy are mutual support and comradeship. The main disadvantage they are spared is the clans' destructive involvement in politics. While these Somalis of the diaspora see that the clan structure has become a system pitting all clans and even all sub-clans against one another, they generally fail to detect the cause. They don't see that the clan system only became such a monster with the introduction of democracy. They also overlook the fact that the essence of Somali society consists not in the clans, but in the customary law. Finally, they don't understand that the "West" owes its wealth not to democracy, but rather to the protection of property rights, and that democracy is undermining and destroying those rights.

Because of these weaknesses in their political analysis, Westernised Somalis see no solution for the difficulties of the clan system but to abolish the entire traditional political and legal structure of Somali society. So they propose introducing one or another form of democracy, without realising that in doing so they are unwittingly compounding the problem.

Of the many books that have been written about the Somalis, those of I.M. Lewis excel in their scholarly approach. Almost everything he has found corresponds with what I have discovered myself. Like Lewis, I found that the Somali nation consists of many independent families, each with its own government. The average family consists of from 600 to 6,000 people. Officials of these "family governments" perform their duties on a part-time basis and are remunerated by those who require their services—their clients. These family governments form more or less temporary alliances with other family governments, depending on the policy they happen to pursue. The Somali system of governance, therefore, is best described as a network of independent organisations, each exercising its authority over a particular extended family irrespective of where its members reside. This is indeed unusual. Most governments in the world consist of a single organisation exercising authority over all the people within a given territory, irrespective of their relationship to each other.

Given this character of the Somali political system, and the attachment that the Somalis have to it, Lewis correctly concludes that all efforts to establish a Western type of democracy in Somalia will be doomed to fail.

It is at this point that I wish to enter the public discussion on Somalia. Most observers of the Somali political scene suggest that the Somalis need to improve their structure of law and politics. But that is more easily said than done. Which laws and which institutions should be changed, and how should the people effect such change? In this book, I shall endeavour to give some answers to those questions

Notes

1. Savigny, *Vom Beruf unsrer Zeit für Gesetzgebung und Rechtswissenschaft* (1815). G.W.F Hegel, *Grundlinien der Philosophie des Rechts; Naturrecht und Staatswissenschaft im Grundrisse* (1821).

2. "No greater insult could be offered to a civilised people or to its lawyers than to deny them ability to codify their law; for such ability cannot be that of constructing a legal system with a novel content, but only that of apprehending, i.e. grasping in thought, the content of existing laws in its determinate universality and then applying them to particular cases." (Hegel, *Grundlinien der Philosophie des Rechts*, quoted from the translation by T.M. Knox, *Hegels's Philosophy of Right*, Oxford, Oxford University Press, 1952, paperback issue 1967, p.136).

Chapter 2
Methodology and Terminology

METHODOLOGY

To discover the characteristics of a system of law, a researcher can basically use either of two methods, the ideological or the descriptive. In the first, the researcher asks practitioners of a law system what rules they have, how they follow and apply them, and why they do so. In the second, he observes and analyses the behaviour of the people living within the system and induces from that behaviour the rules that seem to prevail. He often limits his investigation to data contained in reports by indigenous lawyers of particular disputes, grievances, or troubles and how these were resolved. Each of these methods has its weaknesses.

Many people tend to idealise their society. They form an image of ideal people and ideal rules. However, idealised rules are more often observed in the breach than in compliance. Moreover, the aspects of their social life that people like to report may not give a full picture of that life. They may not like to report certain rules because their motives and reasons for following them hardly fit the ideals that would justify doing so. For example, rules that effectively give official sanction to slavery or discrimination against and maltreatment of women are less likely to be reported as being part of "the law" than, say, rules that provide for and enforce honest dealings with and respect for one's equals. Consequently the ideological method rarely provides a realistic insight into the law system being studied.

The second method, the descriptive, also has its shortcomings.

The behaviour the researcher happens to observe may not be that which usually prevails. Moreover, the fact that people behave *as if* they were following a particular rule does not prove that they behave in that way *because* of that rule. Finally, a weakness of looking only at actual dispute resolutions is that the focus is on conflict situations rather than on behaviour of people living in harmony with one another. It is harmony, rather than conflict, that generates the best law.

The present study does not pretend to be exhaustive. It aims to give an overview of the law system prevailing in the region called Awdal in the northwest part of what is now called Somaliland, and from this overview to make cautious generalisations for all of Somalia. Given this particular format and purpose, I will not discard either of the above-mentioned methods of research.

Before proceeding further, it must be stressed that Somali customary law (*Soomaali Xeer*), is tied to localities as defined in the old concept of *Carro reer hebel*, meaning the land of a specific clan. "Carro" means land, or territory, or country of—as, for example, *Carro Samaron* or *Gudabiirsi, Carro Dolbahante, Carro Isse, Carro Warsangeli, Carro Ogaadeen.* None of these localities correlates with modern geopolitical terms like "Somaliland."[3] Each has its own customary law, or xeer, yet running through all is a common, multi-stranded thread. Even so, the case law given in Appendix A should only be seen as illustrations and not as conclusive evidence of the law that I have found. Hopefully this book will encourage other researchers to study Somali law more thoroughly and thereby confirm or disprove my tentative conclusions.

Terminology: "Law"

Having stated the format of this study and the method of research, let us now turn to terminology. To begin with, the term "law" has four different meanings. It denotes:

1. Rules legislated by politicians, known as statutory law
2. Rules that emerge spontaneously, known as customary law
3. Rules agreed to by contract, known as contractual law
4. The natural order of human beings, known as natural law

Nowadays, people tend to think of law primarily as a set of general commands or legal rules issued by or in the name of a sovereign political authority. However, that is true only of statutory law, which applies to every person in the realm under the control of that authority. Statutory laws typically express the view of the rulers on how people in the realm should conduct themselves—what they may and may not do.

Customary laws, on the other hand, are neither commands nor legislated rules, although they may come to resemble them when applied and enforced at the discretion of a particular ruler or official. They typically are *conventions* that have emerged and are respected spontaneously, without formal agreement, among people who have found them to be useful and otherwise agreeable to themselves and those with whom they have regular dealings.

A contract likewise creates a set of binding rules, but it applies only to those who have specifically agreed to it. It does not entitle any party to it to infringe the rights of others who have not consented to its provisions. If it is a convention, it is not one that emerged spontaneously but rather one that the parties explicitly designed to suit their particular purposes.

Natural law is a different notion altogether. It is not a command, custom, or contract, but an objectively determinable order of existence that people must respect if they are to live together in peace.

This quadruple meaning of the term "law" is a source of much confusion, particularly among people who think that all law comes from governments. Such people tend to call a nation without statutes a lawless society, implying that crime must be rampant. In reality, such a nation may have customary and contractual laws that are fully compatible with natural law, in which case it will be a perfectly peaceful, orderly society.

Natural Law. To understand natural law, one has to ask what people should do in order to live and work in peace. The answer is that they must (1) avoid physical damage to one another's person, work, and property, (2) honour their contracts with one another, and (3) compensate those whom they have harmed by infringing their person or property. When people conduct themselves in this manner, we say that there is peace, that natural rights are respected, that respect for natural law prevails.

Contrary to what many think, even lawyers, the etymological root of "law" is not the Latin word *lex*, which means a choice or decision made by a ruler or public authority. *Lex* is related to the verb *legere*, meaning to choose, in particular to choose or conscript men to do military service. Thus we can readily understand that legal rules (Latin *leges*) connote commands given by a public authority. The etymology of the word "law," however, takes us in a different direction. It derives not from the Latin *lex,* but from the Germanic *lag,* meaning order. "Natural *law,* " therefore, means "natural *order.*" It is the natural order or constitution of the human world.

The constitution of the human world is given in the fact of the existence of many separate individuals, each capable of feeling, thought, speech, and action, independently of every other. Consequently, the order of the human world is described fully by a report of the objective boundaries that separate one person from another and his words, works, and actions from those of other persons. When people respect that order and the boundaries that define it, they act justly—justice being nothing else than the will to respect the order of the human world and to recognise in word and action what belongs to another.

When people act justly, they refrain from treating another person as something other than a person or as some person other than he is, and from treating what belongs to one person as if it belonged to another. They minimise and may even eliminate confusion about who said, did, or produced what. This in turn makes it possible to attribute responsibility, praise and blame, merit and demerit, to whom it is due. In short, it does not fudge the data that are essential to the working of our "moral compass." Thus when people behave justly, they do not threaten one another's life, freedom, or property, but act towards one another in peaceful, friendly ways.

If "law" (*lag*) means order, its opposite means disorder. Indeed, the old-English *orlaeg* meant the ultimate disintegration of order. The word survives even today in the Dutch language, where *oorlog* means war—and the etymology of "war" points to a condition of confusion and trouble.

So, in its original meaning, "law" denotes a condition of order, and "natural law" a condition of order defined in terms of the objective constitution of the human world. Respect for that order leads to peace and friendly relations among individuals, while failure to respect it leads to disorder, trouble, war, and enmity. In that sense, law is not a command, a rule, a norm, or other directive statement, but a condition of life that people generally value.When referring to the natural law, therefore, there is no need, for the plural "laws" unless one wants to identify particular patterns or aspects of order in the human world.

The meaning of "law" changed when people began to use the word to denote rules enacted by governments and parliaments. It was then that "laws" came to mean commands.

Customary Law. Customary laws are enforceable rules that emerge spontaneously as people go about their daily business and try to solve the problems that occasionally arise in it without upsetting the patterns of cooperation on which they so heavily depend. 'Customary law' does not mean that all customs are recognised as laws. When someone deviates from common usage and a conflict results, a court of law may hold that that person, in breaking a well-established custom, misconducted himself. When a large number of verdicts consistently uphold a particular custom, that custom becomes a law.

In societies lacking a central government and, in particular, in societies based on kinship, customary laws are likely to be the only general rules that will be enforced. In such societies, customary laws are enforced in ways that differ considerably from the kind of enforcement commonly found in societies in which a central government has monopolised the adjudication and enforcement of rules of conduct. For example, no official or court will take the initiative to investigate or judge an act where no one claims to have been victimised by it. Moreover, as a rule, courts are made up of judges from the group or clan of the victim as well as that of the malefactor. Once a customary court has rendered a verdict of guilt, it is up to the victim to decide whether he wants the verdict to be enforced. In the affirmative, the judges may order his kinsmen to assist the victim in collecting his due or authorise the victim to execute the verdict at his own expense. In short, the enforcement of the customary law typically is left to the interested parties themselves—to the victim and his kin and those kinsmen or other associates of the malefactor responsible for him under the customary law. Not only in its genesis but also in its application and enforcement, the customary law is truly a "people's law."

In societies dominated by the State, the expression "customary law" refers only to the genesis of certain enforceable rules. The application and enforcement typically are monopolised by the State or one of its subdivisions.

STATUTORY LAW

Statutory laws are rules of conduct designed, legislated, promulgated, and enforced on the authority of rulers or politicians. Usually they are designed by government employees, legislated by a parliament, promulgated by a government official such as a king or a minister, and enforced by a police force controlled by that official. The police typically have a legal monopoly over the use of the weapons required for redressing injustices. The people have little to say in all of this. In a modern democracy, for example, they are asked every four years or so to cast their vote for a politician of their choice, after which they must accept any laws imposed upon them. In short, statutory law is typically "politicians' law."

Statutory laws can be oppressive to the point of creating a sort of permanent war between the government and its people, and customary laws can be barbaric. Rules that are oppressive or barbaric are surely incompatible with natural law and therefore do not really deserve to be called laws. Indeed, it would be best to use the terms "law" and "laws" in the original Germanic sense, to refer to timeless and universal principles that protect life, liberty, and property. In order to avoid confusion, I will spell the word "law" in that context as "Law"—capitalised. The plural, "laws," I will mainly use to denote the rules that can be derived from the principles of Law. As for the rules enacted by governments, I will call them not laws but legislated rules, or legislation, or statutes.

This brings us to the title of this book, *The Law of the Somalis*, which suggests that a nation has the power to determine the content of the Law. In reality, the Law is coeval with human nature and therefore independent of any declaration concerning it. It would exist even if all the people in the world said it did not. People, including the judges among us, can do no more than discover and recognise the Law. Therefore, a more accurate title for this book would be *The Law According to the Somalis.*

Terminology: "Rights"

In this study I often speak of "rights." Again taking a clue from etymology, we can say that a person's right (from the Latin verb *regere*, to rule, to control, to govern) is whatever is under his control or rule. Consequently, a person's natural right, in the strict sense, is that which according to nature belongs under his control or rule. In this interpretation, the terms "natural rights" and "natural property" are synonymous. They are the rights that inure to every person because they are inherent in human nature. Natural properties are rights that are *proper* to human beings. A person's *natural* right or *natural* property encompasses his mind, his body, and his faculties or powers of control over them, which constitute his organic freedom of action. It is necessarily limited by the natural property of another person.

I will use the general term "right" to denote not only a person's natural rights but also those things that a person lawfully has brought under his control—that is, without violation of the natural and the already lawfully established rights of others. Because all of those rights are consistent with the natural law, there is no harm in calling lawfully established rights "natural rights in a wider sense."

It follows that rights, properly understood, never conflict. If a presumed right conflicts with another, then one or the other is not a right. This is evident for natural rights in the strict sense because of the objective fact of the separateness of human persons. It is also true for lawfully established rights because it is always possible (though not always easy) to determine objectively how a person established control over external resources.

Respect for his natural rights by other persons ensures that a person can live and act freely among others. Respect for rights ensures, therefore, that people have the freedom to acquire, use, and transfer resources as they see fit, provided they respect the same freedom in all others. Implicit in this concept is that no one needs the permission of another to exercise a right, and one is entitled to defend himself against any who interfere with such exercise.

When I speak of rights, therefore, I refer to natural rights in the broader sense, which includes the rights a person has established lawfully, with due respect to the natural law and the other persons that constitute it. In a still broader sense of the term, natural rights include the right to do some thing or other that is a lawful use of one's rights.

Lawyers also speak of rights established by contract. This may be a misleading expression because a contract does not really *establish* control but merely transfers it from one person to another. Obviously, a contract is lawful if it involves no violation of any lawfully established right of a third party. When a government creates (grants) "rights" for (to) some or all of its subjects, we would do better to speak of "legal rights" (or political privileges). Although possible in theory, it is highly unlikely in practice that such rights will be lawful and therefore consistent with natural rights.

Terminology: "State", "Nation"

Another word wanting clarification is "State." I will use it to denote a government that monopolises the use of retaliatory force, i.e., the force that is used to redress injustices and to remedy violations of property rights. Such a monopoly exists whenever police use force to stop others from offering police services. Indeed, a state is primarily a police monopoly. A euphemism for such a monopoly is "central government." As the term is used, a central government is always a police force that has contrived a monopoly for itself and imposes specific rules of conduct on the population.

I shall use the terms "stateless nation" and "stateless country" to denote a population in which there is no monopoly of the use of retaliatory force. One reason to avoid such monopoly is that competition is important to prevent policemen from misusing their force. A stateless nation need not be lawless or chaotic. It may have just laws and be orderly. Such a nation may have many independent police forces, each ready to correct those among their competitors who have misused their powers. I use the word "nation" in the sense of a group of people living together on the basis of a set of mutually agreeable principles but having no formal agreement with one another and not necessarily knowing one another personally. In this sense, the word "nation" is less ambiguous than the word "society," which is as likely to evoke the image of a rather formal organisation as it is that of regular, peaceful intercourse. In any case, "Somali society" suggests more than does "Somali nation."

SOMALI TERMS

In every community where rules emerge for settling conflicts, the rules at first are indistinguishable from the culture, the proverbs, the lifestyle, and the customs of the people. Gradually, people separate out these concepts. That is happening in Somalia. Some Somalis use the word *xeer* for the entire hodgepodge of culture, proverbs, lifestyle, custom, and customary law. Other Somalis, however, distinguish between these concepts. For culture they use *hiddiyo dhaqan*, for custom they use *caado*, and the word *xeer* they reserve exclusively for what English-speaking people call customary law.

Despite such exclusivity, the term "xeer" can have different meanings. It can mean, for instance, "law in general," "law of a particular clan," or "procedural law." This will be discussed further in Chapter 4. I shall use the term primarily to denote the Somali customary law and in particular those Somali principles and rules that protect life, liberty and property.

My use of a number of other Somali terms also deserves comment. I shall translate the Somali word *xolo* (pl. *xolooyin*) as "clan," following the usage set by I.M. Lewis. He eschews the term "tribe" because, for him, it implies a close-knit community within fixed geographical boundaries under centralised political institutions. The Somali nation, on the other hand, is a loose-knit community composed of thousands of small groups linked by family ties and contract rather than residence. The legal and political institutions of these families are informal and independent, not subject to any central command.

A clan is an agglomerate of many groups of people, the smallest being the *reer*, which is best translated as "camp" or "hamlet." The *reer* consists usually of half-a-dozen households or nuclear families and has no jural or political life of its own. The same is true of the larger group called *degmo*, or village. Next comes the *juffo*, or *jiffo*, which has both a geographical and a juridical meaning. It usually includes all the descendants of the same great-grandfather and their spouses and children. As a juridical unit, it guarantees the security of its members and the payment of their debts arising out of minor violations of the law. In addition, the members of a juffo usually help when a young man wishes to marry and his father cannot pay the *yarad*, the customary bridewealth, to the family of the bride.

Several juffos descending from the same ancestor form a *jilib*, which is best translated as the blood-price-paying group. The smallest independent unit in the Somali system of law and politics, this group rarely consists of less than 300 or more than 3,000 males, including boys. Several jilibs belonging to the same clan can form a "super jilib," and several of these can team up and form a "super-super jilib," and so on until one reaches the level at which they become a clan. The Somalis have no separate names for these intermediate levels between jilib and clan. Some writers distinguish them as sub-clans and primary and secondary lineage groups, but these have no specific meaning in Somali law or politics.

Several clans descended from the same ancestor will be referred to as a "clan-family." The Somalis use the word *xolo* also for them. Best known are the Daarood, Hawiye, Dir (including Isaaq), and Digil-Mirifle, each of which has more than two million members.

The term "Somalia" was the name of the twin-country that was formed in 1960 by merging the former British and Italian Somalilands. It was given a central government whose constitution called for uniting all five Somali territories, including those in Kenya, Ethiopia, and Djibouti. That central government disintegrated and disappeared in 1991 and was replaced by a large number of independent political entities. This change did not put an end to the Somali nation but only made it stateless, restoring it in that respect to the situation in precolonial times. Most Somalis now use the term "Somalia" in a non-political way to denote all the territories inhabited by the Somali-speaking people. I shall do the same.

Soomaalinimo usually means Somali unity and sometimes solidarity. The question arises whether it has a meaning in law. It would be useful indeed to give it such a meaning. The unity of the Somalis goes well beyond having common physical features and a common language, lifestyle, religion, and history. In particular, the Somalis enjoy a common set of legal principles. It is quite likely that the Somali nation became numerous and relatively prosperous due to these shared principles. Soomalinimo, therefore, as a law concept, might best be understood as a common respect for the Somali principles of law, particularly those that recognise each person's right to his own life, liberty, and property. At the political level, Soomalinimo could be understood as respect for traditional political principles, for instance the idea that politicians should exercise no legislative or executive powers.

A Somali judge (*oday;* pl. *odayaal*) has only one thing in common with the judges employed by the member states of the United Nations, and that is that his vocation is to settle conflicts. He differs from those state judges in everything else— in the way he is trained, selected, appointed, organised, and paid. He has different powers, and he applies an altogether different type of law. In Europe, one would call such specialists "arbiters," except that arbiters apply only the rules in their area of specialty. Somali judges, on the other hand, all apply exclusively the Somali customary law. Hence my preference to translate *oday* as "judge."

Similarly, I shall speak of Somali "policemen," despite the fact that there is neither a standing police force in Somalia nor a standing army. Exceptions to this rule are the militias of the "war lords," but these are in fact holdovers from the defunct Republic of Somalia who operate outside the customary law system and even in violation of it. When a customary court of law calls for enforcement of a verdict, it enlists all able-bodied clansmen (*waranle,* literally "spearman") to act as part-time policemen. They are instructed to use force against the condemned party, but the law sets the limits within which that force may be exercised. Clansmen who refuse to answer such a call will be fined.

The spelling of Somali names and certain key words is problematic, since the Somalis tolerate a great deal of variation, especially when writing in a foreign language. For example, many Somalis, and not only the expatriates, adapt their spelling of Somali words and even their name to the orthographic norms of, for example, English or French. Moreover, although for all practical purposes Somali has been a written language only since 1972, when the official National Orthography was adopted, older transcriptions turn up in the literature. One may find, for example, *Mohamed, Muhammad,* and *Mahamed* for what would be written in Somali *Maxamed.*

For the interested reader, Appendix D gives a key to Somali pronunciation. A crucial point on which Somali spelling may seem odd to the foreign reader is in its use of the signs "c" and "x." Both denote typical pharyngeal sounds (also called guttural sounds, i.e., "made in the throat") that occur also in Arabic in the common names Ali (often spelled with an initial apostrophe, 'Ali) and Hasan. In Somali these are spelled *Cali* and *Xasan.* Throughout this book, I shall stick to the Somali spelling, from time to time adding in parentheses a simplified spelling.

Notes

3. The idea that the territorial borders of the former colonial 'states' represent anything meaningful or desirable causes many problems. For the most part, they were created by Europeans for the benefit of European politics or diplomacy. Yet despite the fact that many of these lines are truly arbitrary and divide the traditional lands of various clans and tribes, most African governments and international groups like the Organisation for African Unity insist that such borders be upheld, even where, as in the case of Somalia, there is no longer a government to defend them.

Chapter 3
The Somali Mind Set

Somalia accommodates a range of lifestyles and livelihoods. Maria H. Brons (2001:73-113) gives an excellent overview of the variants within Somali culture, which include small enclaves of fishermen, a small but growing bourgeoisie in the towns and, until the collapse of the central government in 1991, an ever-growing multitude of public servants. In addition, a substantial minority of agriculturists combining agriculture and cattle (rather than camel) herding are concentrated in the relatively fertile areas of southern Somalia between the Jubba and Shabelle Rivers (in Somali *Jubba* and *Webi Shabeelle*, the latter meaning "Rivers of the Leopards"). These southern agriculturists speak their own dialect, often scarcely comprehensible to other Somalis, and have their own traditions and organisation. Massimo Colucci (1924) has produced an important work in Italian on their customary law. Nevertheless, like the camel herders in the extreme northwest that are the chief concern of this book, the majority of Somalis are nomadic pastoralists.

From his seventh to his twentieth year, almost every nomad Somali boy of the northwest treks with his brothers and cousins through the largely barren Somali land to herd his father's camels. Herding is usually carried on far from the hamlet, where the boy's parents remain behind to care for the family's other livestock consisting of sheep, goats, and cows. The camel herds will stay away for six months or so, moving from place to place in search of grass and water. It is a hard life for the herdsmen, who sleep in the open and feed themselves mostly on camel milk and meat. They will often walk more than a thousand kilometres on such a journey. The average herd has from 80 to 100 camels, the semi-arid land being unable to support larger numbers. Such a herd will be made up of several smaller ones, each belonging to a different owner. The herdsmen of a given owner look primarily after his camels, but the milk and the meat of the entire herd are shared by all.

By combining their herds into a team, the herdsmen obtain several benefits. They gain companionship and can somewhat specialise their labour. It also gives them numbers enough to defend themselves and their animals against hostility. The team need not stay together during the whole trek. If particular herdsmen disagree with the way the team is nomadising, they won't hesitate to team up with other herdsmen. But never will they team up with herdsmen of another clan. A multi-clan herd would not be able to defend itself should an armed conflict erupt with a single-clan herd, because it would be unable to make a tight common front.

When a Somali man deals with politics and law, he uses the same organisational formula as when herding his father's camels. He operates in a small group of cousins who make up his jilib and adroitly concludes alliances with other similar groups. That is how he brings about law and order. The jilib protects the rights of its members and engages in social and political activities as the need arises.

One finds these continuously shifting alliances between politically independent families in at least a dozen other African nations, such as the Gikuyu and the Igbo, but nowhere do they bring together so many people as in Somalia, where several clusters of clans sometimes unite more than a million people.

The Somali nomads observe many customs over such widely diverse areas as economic survival, family life, security, social conduct, and religion. Non-observance leads to social ostracism and sometimes also to condemnation by courts of law. I will briefly discuss each of these categories.

ECONOMIC SURVIVAL

While Somalis of the northwest mostly raise camels, goats and sheep, those who have become skilled in collecting and storing water also keep cows. In some places they have also learned to grow sorghum and maize, following the example set by the Oromos, their neighbours to the west and south.

In their quest for a livelihood, Somalis practice a rigorous division of labour. Men care for the bulk of the family's livestock and crops, maintain the water wells, settle conflicts, defend their family and belongings against enemies, and participate in the meetings of their community. Women build the family's habitat, cook its dinners, fetch its water and wood, look after its domestic animals, milk its livestock (with the exception of camels—a man's job), churn its milk into butter, fashion and wash its clothes, raise its children, trade its excess produce on the market, and weave its grasses into mats and other utensils. Children from the age of five watch over the very young domestic animals. Boys seven and older assist in herding camels.

Among the men, there is the classic division between men who can fight (*waranle*) and men of the spirit (*wadaad*). The implication is that, apart from a few religious dignitaries, every Somali should be ready to defend his tribe against armed attack. A second sharp division is that between pastoralists and artisans. The former, called *gob*, traditionally herd livestock; the latter, called *midgaan, tumaal* or *yibir*, engage in leatherwork, woodwork, pottery, hairdressing, metal work, male circumcision, and the blessing of newborn babies. Pastoralists and artisans do not intermarry.

Of late, many members of herding families have become medical doctors, merchants, accountants, lawyers, engineers, farmers, teachers, and civil servants. In a way, they have become artisans. Yet the social separation between the two groups remains, even in places where artisans have become wealthier than pastoralists.

In southern Somalia, most people are farmers and speak a distinct dialect. Their physical features often resemble those of the Bantu-speaking groups of Kenya, Uganda, and Tanzania. Probably many of these were not Somalis originally but, over time, assumed the Somali language and lifestyle. Also in the south are Somalis with Arab and Portuguese features, the one group engaged mainly in trade and the other in fisheries.

In addition to these divisions of labour, reminiscent of the mediaeval guilds in Europe, there are several kinds of cooperative labour. One of these is the custom of joining one's neighbour to plough his fields (*guus*). It is not uncommon to see one field being ploughed simultaneously by a dozen ploughs. *Guus* also serves for the construction and maintenance of communal wells, schools, clinics, roads, or the fencing of some communal land. Another common form of cooperation comes into action when a family decides to move with all its livestock and other belongings to another place (*reer gura*).

Other sharing customs related to economic survival are the obligation to lodge travellers (*marti*), to offer nomadising herds access to communally held watering and grazing areas, and to share an abundant harvest with less fortunate neighbouring families (*deeq*, literally "generosity," "gift").

FAMILY LIFE

The smallest social unit in Somalia is the minimal extended family, consisting of a married couple and most of their children and grandchildren. Sometimes it includes some or all of their great grandchildren as well. These people divide the various tasks of daily life such as providing water, food, clothing and shelter, educating children, settling conflicts, engaging in commerce, and manufacturing utensils. Men tend to marry in their twenties, girls shortly after reaching puberty. When a man's oldest children have reached adulthood, he may take on a second wife and father a second set of children. The more male children a man has, the more secure his livelihood during old age, and the better defended his family wealth. Husbands are expected to provide equally for their wives, whose number rarely exceeds four.

Given the sharp division of labour in the household, husband and wife tend to respect each other's activities, one rarely interfering in the other's work. This causes husbands and wives to respect each other's person. It cannot really be said that, within the limited context of the nuclear family, either spouse dominates the other. If any dominate, it is the parents who dominate their children. Children are brought up to look after their parents' well being until the day the parent dies.

A mother takes charge of her children until they reach the age of five or six, then transfers the task of educating her sons to her husband, who trains them in herding livestock and cultivating land.

At birth, a boy is given a young animal, *wax loo xuddun hiray* (literally, "that attached to one's umbilical cord"). The offspring of that young camel also belong to him. Thus it is that when a boy reaches adulthood, he has acquired both the skills and the animals needed to provide for his own livelihood, as well of that of his parents if need be.

For economic survival and to protect their property rights, such extended families ally themselves with other families descended from the same ancestor. These alliances are known as *juffo, jilib*, and *xolo*, as the size increases. The juffo usually includes one's parents, uncles, brothers, and first cousins. A jilib consists of several juffos and averages from a few hundred to several thousand people. It is by no means a stable unit but often splits or merges with other jilibs of the same clan. Indeed, where a larger group is called for, jilibs will team up as often and as much as the situation requires. *Xolo* denotes clan, an agglomeration of several jilibs. It can even mean a cluster of clans.

Somalis have brought the cult of the family to such a point that they all claim descent from a common ancestor, Samaale. An exception is made for the farmers who live between the Jubba and Shabelle rivers, whose common ancestor is said to be Sab. When the Somalis adopted the Moslem religion, they felt the need to express their religious unity in similar family terms. Hence they acknowledge Akiil Abuu Taalib, an uncle of the Prophet, as their Moslem ancestor.

SECURITY

During their trek in search of grazing lands and watering places, Somali herdsmen often find themselves wanting to herd their animals in the same place. Frequent conflicts would arise if measures were not taken to avoid them. The Somalis therefore have adopted a rule common to many societies, generally known as "first come, first served." It means that when a herdsman arrives at an unoccupied pasture or watering place, he is entitled to take complete possession of it until such time as he moves on. Other herdsmen cannot simultaneously share that natural resource unless invited by the person who arrived first. If they try to force their way in, the first herdsman can be expected to defend himself. We have already seen that he does so by teaming up with other camel owners. Theoretically, such teams could use their fighting strength for aggression as well as for defence. However, Somalis stress only defence. If fighting erupts, the purpose is not to destroy the attackers, but to stop their aggression. The defenders seek to create a balance of power that is conducive to settling the conflict by mediators and arbitrators rather than by force. This practise has given rise to the development of institutions resembling law and law courts. The conflicting parties each choose their judges from their own clan. These judges tend to be impartial and are careful only to apply rules generally respected by the clan.

Evidently this was how a system of law and order developed that was completely in harmony with the basic structure of Somali society. The Somali habit of living in small, independent groups and concluding temporary alliances with similar groups remained unchanged. As each clan perceived a need for communicating and conducting business with neighbouring clans, it developed rules for that purpose. The Somalis thus hit upon a formula for law and order that is quite different from that of most present-day nations. Whereas nations elsewhere in the world tend to maintain a single organisation that makes laws and provides judges and policemen, the Somalis leave the performance of these typically governmental services to their many independent families.

When Somalis speak of their property (*hanti*, literally "wealth," or *xoolo*, "cattle"), they usually mean livestock, huts, household utensils, and weapons. The cultivators among them also own parcels of land (*beer*), ploughs, seeds (*shinni*), and their harvests (*beer go'in*). The Somalis also set great store on preserving their dignity and the integrity of their body, which for women includes their beauty. They value communal property (*wax la gudbay*), particularly pastures (*daaqsin*) and wells (*ceelo*), which are controlled, if not actually owned, by several families. Lastly there is the forest, which belongs to the entire clan. The acquisition, use, and disposal of these valuable things are subject to a great many customs, among which are laws prohibiting homicide, assault, abduction, robbery, burglary, theft, arson, extortion, fraud, etc.

Social Conduct

Social conduct among the Somalis is also subject to innumerable rules, much more so than is commonly the case in Europe or America.

Until recently, Somali society was rather closed and static. For every type of activity there were standard rules of conduct, in particular how to dress, how to greet and talk with one another, how to cook, how to build one's house, how to guard one's livestock, how to plant grains, how to select a spouse, how to educate one's children, how to bury one's dead, how to engage in trade, how to conduct war, how to make peace, how to celebrate a successful harvest, and how to elect a new head of the clan. For example, married women always cover their hair whereas nubile girls wear theirs loose. Boys cut their hair very short until the age of puberty. A man must never be in the same hut with a nubile girl. Obviously this last rule aims at protecting young women against the advances of passionate men, but an unmarried woman who has failed to find a husband can find it useful. She can force a man to marry her simply by going inside his house. His only way out of such a situation is to marry her or pay her family the bride price.

Most Somalis consider these rules a part of their customary law. However, most of these rules do not protect their freedom and are hard to justify in terms of natural law. In that sense, they are not strictly rules of law but elements of culture and folklore. At best, such rules facilitate social intercourse. At worst, they obstruct it and infringe upon the natural rights of people.

RELIGION

Religion among Somalis invariably means Islam, of the Sunni kind. Insofar as Somalis apply Islamic law, they follow the Shafi'ite school. They adopted this religion gradually, of their own volition; it was never imposed. Their faith, therefore, tends to be wrought with ancestral beliefs and relics of their previous religion, which centred on the worship of Waaq (literally, "Sky"), a god still popular among the tribes of the neighbouring Oromos. Somalis, for example, continue to honour an ancestor or a famous Sheikh by organising a *siara* to thank him for guiding them through a difficult period in their life or to commemorate his teachings. For this festive gathering they will sacrifice a camel or a smaller animal from their livestock, dedicating it to the person's memory. The camel, cow, sheep, or goat that was slaughtered is then cooked and the meat shared by everyone, including the destitute.

These five spheres of activity—economics, family, defence, society, and religion—clearly show that there are customary rules for virtually every kind of conduct, including settling disputes. Whatever criticism one might level at Somali society, it would surely not be the lack of rules. On the whole, the Somalis are highly rule-conscious and law-abiding and thoroughly grasp the concepts of private property (*hanti, xoolo*) and freedom (*xorriyad, xornimo, gobannimo*).[4]

Until 1972, the Somalis had no universal alphabet. Since lack of a written language necessarily limits access to a great deal of abstract thought, one might suppose that an unlettered people would have little interest in abstractions but would limit their discussion to people and events and issues closely related to family, village, and job. Thus it is sometimes argued that concepts such as property, freedom, and law are not likely to arise in an oral society. Yet I have heard many an unlettered clansman argue with fervour the institutions of private property, freedom of movement, free trade, and birthrights. The fact that the Somali language has a separate word for each of these evidences interest in such matters.

Prior to 1972 there were no texts in the Somali language except for a very few written in an alphabet developed by some of the Samaron clan, or in the Osmania alphabet devised by a Majarteen in the 1920s. Yet many Somalis, depending on what schools they had attended, could write in Arabic, English, French, Italian or Amharic.

In seeking to capture the essence of the Somali character, it has struck many observers that the Somalis have no mystic bent. In their religion they look on their god more as a friend to whom one turns for advice than an almighty being who lords it over everyone and everything. Nor have they much interest in magic, witchcraft, or sorcery. When they try to scare their children, for instance, they don't tell them that the devil or some evil spirits will come and get them. Rather, they may say, "the white-skinned men are coming."

These features and customs discussed above, as well as many others not mentioned here, have left a firm imprint on the Somalis and their society. The first characteristic noticed by every observer is that most Somalis are imbued with a healthy dose of self-esteem.

The first European to note this may have been the British traveller Richard Burton, who in 1856 called the Somalis "a fierce and turbulent race of Republicans." A century later, I.M. Lewis (1956:1) observed:

> The Somali have no indigenous centralized government. And this lack of formal government and of instituted authority is strongly reflected in their extreme independence and individualism. Few writers have failed to notice the formidable pride of the Somali nomad, his extraordinary sense of superiority as an individual and his firm conviction that he is the sole master of his actions.

Somalis are indeed outspoken in their opinions and fear no one. In their individual life as well as collectively as a nation, they tend to be extremely independent.[5] Yet every person has a fixed place in Somali society, determined mostly by accident of birth into a close-knit family and by the need for economic survival in a semi-arid natural environment. Thus Somali society shows a remarkable blend of independence and order, of freedom and discipline.

Somalis believe their form of society is superior to that of most other nations. Unimpressed by foreign political systems, they hold to the institutions and rules of law they have developed themselves. They make a persuasive argument for this, which is mainly that the basic rules of their society tend to be non-oppressive. If a leader of any group of Somalis tried to lord it over his fellows, he would soon find himself alone. The others would simply pack up their belongings and start a new group elsewhere. There is little that attaches a Somali nomad to a particular piece of land and much that makes him want to preserve his independence.

Because of the tendency of Somali fathers to rule as potentates over their children, it has been argued that the Somali nation is bound to become a dictatorship. That argument, however, does not explain why all of these fathers would freely accept domination by a super-father. Rarely, in fact, does any nation freely choose to be ruled by a dictator. Would-be dictators tend to impose themselves, and generally their first step in doing so is to establish a standing police force or army. This is precisely why the Somali customary law opposes this way of organising, for either individual or collective security.

Notes

4. The term *xorriyad* is actually Arabic and is much used in the sense of "political freedom," whereas *gobannimo* is an abstract noun derived from *gob*, meaning literally "nobles, aristocracy." This brings to mind the French political philosopher Bertrand de Jouvenel who in his treatise, *On Power*, wrote a chapter, "Liberty's Aristocratic Roots." For the adjective *xor*, "free," a new Somali abstract, *xornimo*, "freedom," has also been formed. –Editor MT

5. Every Somali considers himself to be at least the equal of any other. This aspect of the culture is appealing and shows up in many traditions. For example, Somalis do not rise to speak. There are two reasons for this. First, when Somalis meet they confer as equals; no man among them puts himself above the others. There is no raised platform or dais or podium in their meeting halls. Each makes room for himself and his neighbors on the floor or on the ground around a tree. Second, there is a related tradition that a Somali who speaks while standing might not mean what he says. If he expects to be taken at his word, he takes the time to sit down. –Editor JD

Chapter 4
The Somali System of Law

This study is limited to the customary laws of the people of Awdal, the most northwestern part of the former Republic of Somalia. Awdal is inhabited by people mainly of the Samaron clan. From the law of this region, conclusions will be drawn about the law of the entire Somali nation, encompassing more than sixty clans. What might appear to be a daunting undertaking is really quite feasible, since the many differences that exist among the rules of the various clans relate chiefly to matters outside the scope of this study. We are primarily interested in the rules protecting life, liberty, and property, and here the differences are minimal.

TYPES OF LAW

When Somalis speak of their law, they use the word *xeer* (not to be confused with *xer*, the name of a chain of Muslim settlements). The Somalis distinguish between two different types of law: general law, which they call *xeer guud*, and special law, *xeer tolnimo* (literally, "paternal kin law"). The former laws have nation-wide applicability, whereas the latter are those adopted by a particular jilib or set of jilibs. Such special law arises, for instance, when the members of a jilib want to establish rules concerning joint payment of the blood price or to establish particular fines for particular types of wrongdoings. These special rules are established by contract. When Somalis say to each other *xeer baa innaga dhexeeya*, which literally means, "there are laws between us, laws bind us," it denotes special rules (*xeer tolnimo*). The general laws need no contract in order to become applicable.

Somalis hold that their laws apply to every person born as a Somali. They realise that neighbouring nations, such as the Oromo and Afar, live under different laws. The question therefore arises as to what rules apply when a Somali meets a person from a neighbouring nation. Is there something like international law? There is, indeed. The basic principle is that law applies to people not because they happen to live in a particular territory, but because they belong to a particular clan. Thus, each person must abide by the laws of his own nation. When these laws contradict each other on a given point, a compromise must be found.

THE SYSTEM

The Somali law system consists of these building blocks, which I shall discuss in order:

1. Six major principles
2. Rules of conduct in society
3. Organisations that adjudicate and enforce the rules
4. Procedural rules
5. Rules of insurance
6. Verdicts of the law courts
7. Doctrines developed by learned men.

1. Six Major Principles (*dulaxaan* or *gudaxaan*)

- The law is separate from politics and religion.
- The law has a built-in method for its development.
- There is a plurality of jurisdictions and norms.
- Government personnel must abide by the law.
- The law originates in the reason and conscience of the community.
- Judges are specialists, each with his own method of analysing the Law.

We can generalise about each of these principles:

Separate from Politics and Religion. Somali politicians and religious dignitaries have no role in the formation of the law. Nor have they any say in establishing courts of law. As a rule, a judge (*oday,* or "*elder*"), jurist (*xeerbegti*), investigator (*guurti*), attorney (*garjaxaan*), witness (*markhaati*), or policeman (*waranle,* literally "spearman") cannot also be a dignitary of a political or religious organisation. Indeed, the Somali law is in principle completely separate from politics and religion. Somali folk wisdom has this to say about the difference between religion and law: *Diinta waa la baddali karaa, xeerka la ma baddali karo* (One can change one's religion; one cannot change the law). A second maxim is, "Between religion and tradition, choose tradition."

The rule that religious officials play no role in the settling of disputes before a court of law has two notable exceptions. One is that matters relating to marriage and inheritance usually are brought before a judge who applies Koranic rather than Somali customary law. The other is that when a judge wants to know the precise extent to which an assault victim has been injured, he will ask a religious leader to investigate the matter and testify accordingly. But he will reserve to himself the decision as to who was at fault and what compensation should be paid. Religious dignitaries tend to respect this rather sharp distinction between law and religion. Thus when asked to say a few words at the opening of a court session, they will speak only about the need to settle the dispute in order to preserve the unity of the clan. They will not comment on the conduct that led the conflicting parties to submit their case to the court.

Built-in Method for Developing the Law. Somali judges will never say that the law is silent or unclear on a given kind of conduct. Somalis look at their law system as a set of principles and rules applicable to any type of conflict. They recognise that people constantly innovate and that precise rules do not exist for human action that has not yet been conceived of. That is why Somali customary law consists of broad principles. It ensures that judges will always be able to assess whether a given conduct is or is not lawful. This enables the law to develop in step with the ever-increasing complexity of the nation.

Somalis hold that the law must originate with the people rather than with judges or politicians. Accordingly, judges may not apply their own standards of conduct, but only those that are held by the population. This rule ensures that the law will develop in concert with the values held by the nation.

Plurality of Jurisdictions and Norms. Rules are generated everywhere in Somali society. Each household has its own rules, and conflicts arising under those rules are usually settled by the head of the household. Likewise, religious, political, business, charitable, artistic, and recreational associations in Somalia have their rules about becoming a member and abiding by the association's rules. Usually there is a procedure for settling disputes that fall under those rules. In theory, there is no limit to the scope of an association's rules. It is free to stipulate that members who violate one another's fundamental rights will be judged by the association's own court. Examples of this are found in the religious communities of the Qaadiriya Sufi Order. But most Somalis prefer that serious wrongdoings be judged by their traditional judges under the law of their ancestors, the xeer. That is the body of law applicable to people who have no contractual relation to each other.

Of the many rules that emerge in a nation, some are eventually recognised as laws. These are rules governing weighty matters like murder, rape, and robbery. Such rules tend to be timeless and universal in nature, based on objective criteria and applicable irrespective of one's culture, opinions, achievements, family, or physical features. In Somalia there are many courts of law, each independent of the others, that recognise and adjudicate these laws. Courts of the same clan tend to have a unified jurisprudence. That doesn't mean that verdicts in a given clan never conflict. It means that when courts have differing opinions on what the law is, it will not be long before such differences disappear and a uniform interpretation emerges. On the national level, however, where there are dozens of independent clans, it takes much longer, if it ever happens at all, for a particular view of the law to be accepted by all.

This plurality of norms and jurisdictions does not bother the Somalis. Just as a living language is continuously enriched by new words and new grammar, the Somali customary law is always developing. Innovations may start in one clan and gradually spread to other clans. That is how the general law (*xeer guddoon*) takes form.

In addition to this multitude of sources of law and jurisdictions, the Somalis generally agree that matters concerning marriage, divorce, and inheritance should be decided by the religious judges (*qaaddi* or *qaalli*), who apply Koranic law. Interestingly, however, these same dignitaries often apply Somali rather than Koranic law. In matters of inheritance, for instance, they do not allow the women to inherit land or camels from their fathers, as the Koran would have it. Neither does it disturb a Somali customary court of law when a plaintiff or defendant invokes the Islamic law, Sharia (Somali *shariico*), as a justification for his or her complaint or defence. The court's point of departure in these situations is that the customary law takes priority over the religious law. But if a particular religious rule would settle the conflict in a way more in line with the customary usage of the community, the courts will not be averse to incorporating that rule into the customary law.

Further evidence of the Somalis' tolerant view is the fact that people are free to settle their cases outside of the customary law. The need for this occurs, for instance, when the family of a murdered person refuses to accept the customary 100 camels but is willing to settle for, say, 130 camels. Such a deal (*xeer jajab*) is not prohibited, but it cannot create a precedent under the customary law.

Government Personnel Must Abide by the Law. The powers of judges are generally the same as those of any clansman. For instance, they have no power to summon someone before their court. The Somalis go even a step further. A judge who violates the law suffers heavier penalties and fines than would normally be imposed. This practice is widespread among traditional African societies. The daily conduct of a judge is supposed to be exemplary. Nothing less is expected from him than a deep and unfailing respect for the law. The same applies to all political and religious dignitaries.

Origin of the Law. Somalis do not consider that their judges are endowed with superior intellect and wisdom. It is not up to a judge to offer new rules of conduct for his community, or standards he thinks would be better for everybody. His only task is to settle conflicts by applying the basic rules that people in the community already generally observe. Somalis hold that the law originates in the interactions of people. It is the product of the reason and the conscience of the community. They hold that the law is neither of a religious nor of a political nature. The ultimate standard of what constitutes customary law is the prevailing norm of the community members.

People discuss at length the verdicts rendered by their customary courts. If there is a consensus that the court has deviated from the norms that prevail in their community, they will mention this to the judges who rendered the verdict. If the judges disagree, they will lose the confidence of the community and likely not be asked to settle further disputes.

As for the origin of the Somali law system as a whole, nothing is really known about it. Enrico Cerulli published the first study of Somali customary laws in 1919,[6] and a dozen authors since have written about them. None of them offers evidence that the Somali law system originated outside of Somalia or was greatly influenced by any foreign law system. It has little in common with that of the neighbouring Oromo and Afar nations and even less with that of the Amharas and Arabs. Moreover, Somali legal terminology is practically devoid of loan words from foreign languages. We can therefore safely conclude that the Somali law system is truly indigenous.

Judges are Specialists. Somali judges receive no special education or training in the law. They educate and train themselves. Yet they are specialists; none but these judges will be asked to settle disputes according to the Somali law. Somalis definitely do not judge their accused in peoples' courts or in political courts. To become a judge, a Somali must first become the head of his extended family, and indeed family heads are chosen for their wisdom and knowledge of the law. There are no rules as such for educating and training judges. They learn by attending the sessions of the courts and listening to the comments of the villagers when verdicts are being discussed.

A Somali judge is free to develop his own principles of law

and his own doctrines. The test of whether such principles and
doctrines are acceptable to the community comes as soon as he
has given his verdict on a conflict. If a verdict deviates from
what the community finds reasonable and just, there is little
chance that its author will be asked again to sit as a judge.

2. Rules of Conduct

Because Somali law consists largely of rules that protect people's life,
liberty, and property, it prohibits conduct like murder, assault,
rape, robbery, arson, theft, extortion, and fraud. It stipulates
sanctions for violations of the law and authorises the use of force
in the event the wrongdoer refuses to honour his obligations to
his victim. Details on rules of conduct will be found in Chapter
5.

3. Law Courts and Police

When a conflict occurs, the families of the conflicting parties urge
their judges to form a law court. If the judges agree to settle the
conflict, they invite both parties to state their case, then hear witnesses
and render a verdict. Should enforcement be necessary, a police force
forms at the request of the court. All able-bodied villagers can be
recruited for this duty. Somalia has no permanent courts of law or
standing police forces. Further details on the courts and police will be
found in Chapter 6.

4. Procedural Rules

The basic rule of procedure is that every person is considered innocent
until such time as proof has been submitted to the impartial court of
law that will judge him and he has been given an opportunity to
refute the charges against him. This rule presupposes, however, that a
court of law has accepted jurisdiction over the case. If a court was
not constituted in time, or fails to render a verdict, the victim and his
family are free to enforce restitution or compensation themselves. If
excessive force is used, however, or more compensation is collected
than was due, the initial perpetrator will be entitled to compensation
at the expense of the initial victim. More details on procedure will be
found in Chapter 6.

5. Insurance

Every Somali is insured against liabilities that he might incur under the customary law. Surety is provided by his extended family, which guarantees payment of any compensation the court might require of him. Somalis are not free to decide whether or not to insure themselves; the law obliges them. For this purpose a jilib, which includes all the living descendants of a given paternal great-grand father or further removed ancestor, constitutes a surety group. The literal meaning of "jilib" is "knee," implying that this group of guarantors is a part of a larger body, the clan. Just as, within the clan, a jilib guarantees payment of a judgment owed by any of its members, so does the clan guarantee such payments vis-à-vis other clans.

A family is free to terminate its insurance of a member who repeatedly violates the law. In such a case, the family will publicly declare that it absolves itself from its obligation to pay for that particular person's future liabilities. When this happens, the person becomes an outlaw and must leave the jilib of which he was a member. Usually this means that he must leave his clan, as well, and settle elsewhere, outside the clan's territory.

6. Verdict (*gar*)

A verdict is the decision of a court regarding the substance of the law and how it applies in a particular case. Viewed in this way, it might easily be assumed that the sum of all verdicts amounts to a statement of what the law is all about. Yet the Somalis do not look at their nation's jurisprudence as a source of law. Rather, they hold that the law is to be found in the customs of the clan. A court is of course free to educate itself by looking at the jurisprudence of other courts, but ultimately judges must discover the law within the reason and conscience of the community where the dispute occurred and not in the verdicts of other courts.

7. Legal Doctrines

Everywhere we find people engaged in the study and perfection of the law. Such people frequently offer suggestions to correct perceived errors or fill in perceived lacunae, and the courts often follow their suggestions. In Somalia, however, the courts are not free to innovate.

They can only apply rules that people are effectively abiding by and that have thus become customary.

RE-EDUCATION OF CRIMINALS

A person who violates someone's rights and is unable to pay the compensation himself notifies his family, who then pays on his behalf. From an emotional point of view, this notification is a painful procedure, since no family member will miss the opportunity to tell the wrongdoer how vicious or stupid he was. Also, they will ask assurances that he will be more careful in the future. Indeed, all those who must pay for the wrongdoings of a family member will thereafter keep an eye on him and try to intervene before he incurs another liability. They will no longer, for example, allow him to keep or bear a weapon. While on other continents the re-education of criminals is typically a task of the government, in Somalia it is the responsibility of the family.

DO THESE RULES AND PRINCIPLES FORM A SYSTEM OF LAW?

Having described the main principles and rules that form the basic structure of Somali society, we will now test whether together they form a system of law. To this end, we will apply two tests. One was developed by the American jurist Lon Fuller (1964) in order to ascertain whether a rule deserves to be called a law. He postulated that such a rule must be known by the people, understandable, non-contradictory, stable, and applied as known, and it must prescribe conduct that is within the power of people to follow.

The other test was developed by the Belgian legal philosopher Frank van Dun (1983). He postulated that rules form a law system only when, taken together, they assure the protection of peoples' life, liberty, and property. In the Fuller test, one of the most exacting requirements is that one rule must not contradict another. If, for instance, a rule restricts a freedom that is guaranteed by another rule, one or the other cannot be a part of the Law. In the Van Dun test, a rule of law must refer to objective criteria such as the discreteness of human beings and their capacity for independent thought and action.

Without going into further details here, I will only report that most Somali judges I talked with were aware of these requirements.

In their opinion, Somali customary laws by and large meet the standards just described. This coincides with my own finding, although I am well aware that there are shortcomings. Nevertheless, I conclude that the customary rules of the Somalis do by and large protect life, liberty, and property, and that therefore they do constitute a system of law. I shall evaluate this system and analyse its strengths and weaknesses in Chapters 10 and 11.

Morality, Contract, Law, Legislation, Politics

Before describing in any detail the rules the Somalis have developed for their basic conduct in society, I should discuss the relationship between morality, contract, law, and legislation. Not only will that help us understand the various rules of conduct, it will help us distinguish the system of law from other sets of rules in society.

Personal Rules and Morality. Every human being lives with rules, not all of which are imposed by others. Every individual must make some rules of his own to give coherence to his life and projects. He needs to decide what to do with his life, which goals to pursue and which standards to apply to his own actions. With these rules, he sets his standards, for example, for eating, sleeping, hygiene, earning his livelihood, and organising his social and recreational activities. Such rules remind a person that "this is good for me, that is bad for me." Some of them most people follow, such as "wearing warm clothes when it's cold outside," or "achieving one's happiness by pursuing one's own goals with one's own means." Other rules, such as those that prescribe a particular diet or physical exercise, may have value for only one person in the entire world.

Rules of morality are an important subcategory of these rules. For a rule to qualify as moral, it must be compatible with respect for natural law. However, a person usually has many alternative courses of action that are all equally lawful, yet have widely different positive and negative effects on himself and others. A morality is a set of rules that prescribe to what extent and under what circumstances one should take into account the interests of others when making a decision. Here, too, we find some moral rules that many people follow and others that only a few follow.

Because by definition all moralities are lawful, human beings are free to follow any particular moral rule or not. The same is true for rules of strictly personal conduct. No one has the right to force warm clothes on any adult person. That does not mean that all moralities and all manners of personal conduct are equally sound. It does mean that one is free to disregard sound morals or to adopt an unhealthy lifestyle, provided one does so at his own risk.

Contracts. Another kind of rule one makes for oneself is contractual. Sometimes only two parties are involved, as when buying, selling, hiring, renting, or marrying. At other times, a multitude of parties may be involved, as when joining a football club, a religious association, or a business corporation. In that case, we enter into a "web of contracts." Such contracts may contain many regulations, including those relative to joining and quitting the association.

Any Somali is free to conclude contracts (*heshiis*) with persons of his choice and to establish mutually agreeable rules relative to one another's services or belongings. Contracts enable people to cooperate and undertake long-term projects together. They generally deal with activities like sell/buy, rent/hire, usufruct, loan/borrow, employment, marriage, peace/truce, and judicial procedure.

When people have freely and voluntarily entered into a contract, they are bound by it. They are no longer free to disobey its rules. For instance, if someone buys a television set and takes it home while promising to pay the next day, he is bound to that promise. If he refuses to pay, then the seller has the right to use force. After all, the seller only agreed to transfer title to the buyer on the condition that the price would be paid. However, if the contract was about rendering a personal service, for example in the context of employment or membership in a club, then the contracting parties are at all times free to break that contract, but they must pay the severance fee, if such a fee was agreed upon.

Law. Everyone comes into contact with people with whom he will never make a contract. These are the passers-by and the strangers whom one encounters by chance. They often have traditions alien to one's own. We may have no thought of associating with these people or of being bound to them by contracts or regulations. For this reason, we need to rely on rules that ensure our safety during these uncertain encounters.

The chances that such rules will be obeyed increases accordingly as they refer to objective criteria applicable to all human beings irrespective of their particular culture, achievements, opinions, family, or physical characteristics. The concept of property rights meets this requirement, and principles and rules derived from it are collectively known as "the Law." The chief principle is that each person should refrain from physically aggressing against the life, liberty, or property of another—or, to put it differently, every person has the right to his own life, liberty, and property.

The beauty of the Law is that its principles obtain regardless of what people say or do about them. In that respect, these principles are like the laws of physics and genetics, which existed long before scientists recognised them. Philosophers of law long searched for proof that the right to one's own life, liberty, and property is universally valid. They succeeded in their quest only upon discovering that one logically cannot argue that such a right does not exist without supposing it to be respectable.[7]

Why should you respect my natural rights? To answer this, try arguing that you need *not* respect my natural rights. You will find that the argument cannot be supported in a discussion without contradiction. For unless you do respect my natural rights and refrain from violence and threats against me, the fact that you win the argument against me is no indication of its logical force. If you want to prove your thesis to me by rational means, you must recognise that you ought to respect my natural rights. Otherwise you get caught in a contradiction. Of course, if you do not want to prove your thesis by rational means, you can easily avoid that contradiction, but then you had better stay out of a philosophical argument about it. This holds not only for you and me, but for any pair of persons. The obligation to respect natural rights can be defended rationally—

and in that sense exists—even where no contract exists between oneself and those people whose rights one must respect.

The same holds true for the question as to why one *ought* to respect natural rights. This answer as well can be found by arguing its opposite, that one need *not* respect the natural rights of other persons. That argument can't be supported in a discussion without contradiction. Therefore, this obligation exists even where no contract exists between oneself and those people whose rights one must respect.

When we use the word "Law," we refer to the orderly way in which people respect one another as human beings, that is, that they are prepared to reason with one another and to carry out the commitments they make. It is also the orderly way in which people respect their obligation not to initiate physical aggression against one another. From this basic obligation, a second universally applicable rule derives. That is, that every person aggressed against has the right to defend himself. It should be noted, however, that no one has an obligation to defend himself. Should a poor and hungry boy steal an apple from an orchard, for example, the owner, rather than demand punishment and compensation might feel sorry for him and offer him an entire meal and even a job.

The types of rules we have discussed thus far—morality, contract, and the Law—are needed to organise one's life, both one's individual life and one's life as a part of any collective one might choose to participate in. Be it family, job, leisure and recreation, or social and artistic life, every human activity can be undertaken in the context of these three types of rules.[8]

Legislation. If every human activity can be organised within the framework of morality, contract, and the Law, then where does legislation fit in? What purpose is served by the rules politicians legislate and call "laws" and impose upon others? There are only two ostensible motives for politicians to legislate rules. Either they want to impose a specific morality on others or, in the name of justice or efficiency, they want to substitute for the thousands of independent contracts that regulate particular aspects of people's lives a single, codified set of regulations. Both motives have their problems.

One cannot make people virtuous by imposing a morality on them. Imposing a morality simply reduces a person to the level of a will-less person, a moron, a slave. Virtue is a matter of free choice; a person becomes virtuous by choosing the good when confronted with a choice between good and evil. Using political means to impose a morality is wrong from the standpoint of both morality and Law. Some have given a name to the act of imposing a morality. They call it fundamentalism.

Politicians who substitute legislated rules for the regulations people voluntarily establish by contract obviously want to change peoples' behaviour. But whatever the behaviour to be changed, whether economic, recreational, educational, social, religious, artistic, charitable, or other, the immediate question is whether it would improve the quality of those people's lives. Supposedly someone has calculated that without legislation, everyone would be four to seven times wealthier than they are now. This is not surprising. Politicians who legislate 'laws' pretend that they know better than individual people what is good for them. But they are not and cannot be privy to the knowledge required for the regulations they want to establish. Not only is that knowledge always changing, it is dispersed and known only to the people themselves. It is continually being bundled by the market mechanism and manifested in the form of prices. The only way such knowledge can be effectively used is by people freely making contracts in open markets. In that way, resources are allocated in concert with people's preferences. Legislation, on the other hand, reflects the preferences of the legislators and not of the people themselves, which is why rules created by legislation inevitably misallocate resources.

Regulation by politicians is problematic for still another reason. It infringes upon the freedom of people to organise themselves as they see fit. Some have given a name to the act of substituting imposed regulation for voluntary. They call it fascism. And the combination of fundamentalism with fascism is known as totalitarianism.

We have seen that the Law is a set of principles enabling each person to walk among other people without fear for his life, liberty, and property. These principles are inherent in human nature. Politicians who think they must make rules forbidding crime don't know that such rules exist already, and that their existence dates from long before the first politician appeared on the human scene. Nor must they legislate rules for adjudicating and enforcing the Law.

Indeed, many Somalis might say that the only purpose and effect of legislation is to make people victims of the politicians. Because they were gravely victimised by their politicians during the period 1960-1990, Somalis have a good understanding of the effects of legislation. At present there are almost no legislated rules in Somalia. There are none at all at the national level and only some in those few parts of the country where the local or regional government has a fascist or fundamentalist bent.

Politics. Somalis define politics as the management of the affairs of the clan. *It has nothing to do with the making of laws.* The Somali political system is completely separate from the nation's law system; its politicians have no power to enact statutory laws, and they can make no decisions that would run counter to the customary law. I shall discuss this more in Chapter 9. Let us now turn to a more detailed discussion of Somali rules of conduct, specifically those that directly protect everyone's right to life, liberty, and property.

Notes

6. Cerulli authored numerous books and articles on Somalia. See, for example, his *Somalia: Scritti vari editi et inediti* (3 volumes), Instituto Poligrafico dello Stato, 1957-64. However, some pertinent texts on the customary law of the Marrehan Somali as well as that of the northern Somali (Mijirtein) are not included in that volume. –Editor FvD

7. Further explanation of this can be found in Van Dun (1983).

8. Let us consider an activity that might be thought to be an exception because it is ordinarily undertaken by a government. Suppose we want to build a road from town A to town B. Several questions arise. Who will build the road, who will use it, and who will police it? One answer is that anyone interested in building a road is free to

do so, provided he buy, lease, or otherwise obtain permission to use the right-of-way on which the road will be built. If a particular landowner is not interested in making his land available, the road can be constructed around him or along an entirely different route. Eminent domain is not necessary. [The El Paso Natural Gas Company, in Texas, built a network of natural gas lines across the United States without recourse to eminent domain. They avoided the holdout problem by mapping in each case three alternative routes, any one of which would do, and then letting it be known that they would deal with the first group of owners who successfully assembled the necessary right-of-way options. The owners themselves then took on the job of assembly as neighbour pressured neighbour, and the strategy always worked. –Editor SM]

Chapter 5
Rules of Conduct

OVERVIEW

Somali customary law prohibits conduct like homicide, assault, torture, battery, rape, accidental wounding, kidnapping, abduction, robbery, burglary, theft, arson, extortion, and fraud. Also prohibited is tort, the unintentional causing of damage to another person's property. That means that Somalis recognise in principle every person's right to his life, liberty, and property.

The law further stipulates that any person who violates this right of another must restore his victim to the situation he was in before his right was violated. If restitution is not possible, compensation must be paid. Payment is assured because the extended family of every Somali constitutes a surety group that guarantees payment for his liabilities under the law.

Fines are due when rights have been violated intentionally. The amount of the fine is usually the same as that of the compensation. Thus, if someone accidentally kills someone's cow, he will be asked to replace it with another of like value. If, however, the killing was intentional, he must give two such cows in return. In this way, the victim is compensated for all the costs and trouble accompanying his loss.

Force may be used against wrongdoers who refuse to pay the compensation that the court has adjudicated to their victim. Enforcement is carried out either by the family of the victim or by all able-bodied men in the area where the verdict is to be executed. In the latter case the court issues an order to the people who must execute the verdict.[9]

Only the victim or his family can start a procedure before a court of law, not his clan or a third party. If the victim is a man, complaints can be brought by the father, brothers, or uncles of the victim. In the case of women, complaints can be brought by both her husband's family and her own.

EQUALITY BEFORE THE LAW

Seven classes of people are subject to a special legal status:

1. Foreigners are denied a legal personality of their own. They are treated as guests (*marti*) of the clan among whom they live and therefore need a patron (*abbaan*) to act as their guardian. A patron's jilib pays compensation when his client (ward) violates someone's rights, and it initiates proceedings when his client (ward) has been aggressed against. Such aggression is considered an affront to the honour of the patron's jilib and therefore compensation (*xaal*) is due. Foreigners as such cannot own or rent land. The status of guest was conceived primarily to accommodate transient Arab and Indian traders and to allow foreign merchants to open a shop in the territory of a clan.

2. The former bondmen, or serfs, of the Somalis, the *Midgaan, Tumaal* and *Yibir*, once had no legal personality of their own. Traditionally they were attached to a particular Somali clan or jilib, which would represent them in any conflicts in which they were involved. At present, many of these former bondmen have formed their own jilibs, so that they can take part in Somali society with full responsibility for their own conduct. They are not allowed, however, to own land or camels.

3. Some well-known clans like the Akisho and the Madigaan live scattered among the other clans and therefore find it difficult to form effective jilibs. They have solved that problem by associating, on an individual or collective basis, with a well-established jilib of their host clan, despite the fact that they have no blood relationship with it.

4. Some Somalis may belong to the clan in whose territory
    they are staying but do not have enough brothers and cousins
    to form an effective jilib. These will often form a jilib with
    fellow-clansmen who are in a similar position. Because such
    jilib*s* consist of people having only distant ancestors in
    common and lacking a territory of their own, they usually
    seek to obtain a long-term lease of parcels of land from their
    landed fellow clansmen.
5. Some Somalis leave the protection of their own clan and
    receive protection (*magan*) from another. This happens, for
    instance, when a person has committed a murder and fled.
    Such a person cannot own land or camels while living among
    his protectors.
6. A Somali living not with his own clan but with his wife's
    clan is called *inan layaal*. His presence is tolerated as long as
    he remains insured by his own jilib and does not bring his
    own camels with him. The host clan will not allow him to
    own land in the territory of his wife's clan, and his children
    will belong to his own clan, not to his wife's clan.
7. A clan's political, jural, and religious dignitaries are also
    subject to a special regime. Because the law expects
    exemplary conduct from them, they must pay higher fines
    and penalties than other people.

PROPERTY RIGHTS

Rights in One's Body. Somali law prohibits murder,
manslaughter, torture, assault, and the unintentional wounding
of other people, but there are a few exceptions. Killing in
wartime, for example, and wounding children in the practise of
the cultural custom of female genital mutilation (e.g.
clitoridectomy) are not thought of as violations of the law.

Rights in One's Freedom. Somali law recognises that people
have a certain measure of freedom inherent in their nature as
human beings. The Somalis call this *xor u dhalasho* (free by birth)
or *xeer u dhalasho* (law by birth). It includes freedom of speech,
contract, movement, and trade. In addition, people have the
freedom to appropriate unclaimed objects. However, Somali

law sets some limits to these freedoms, limits that go beyond the principle that holds that one's freedom ends where the same freedom of all others begins. Thus, one's freedom of speech does not include the freedom to insult or defame others. Freedom of contract is restricted by the rule that a woman cannot be married to more than one man, nor can a man be married to more than four wives. The principle of free trade does protect a person against taxation and other forms of regulation and extortion, but trade in alcohol is prohibited, probably because of its incompatibility with Koranic law. As for conscription, one must perform military duty as well as civil duties such as repairing a communal well or enforcing a verdict if requested by a court of law. Lastly, the freedom to appropriate objects not claimed by others, such as air, or fish in the open seas, does not always include land. Most clans, for instance, are reluctant to recognise property rights in grazing lands.

Rights in One's Belongings. Somali law recognises property rights in movables such as livestock, shelter, clothing, food, household utensils, and weapons. In particular, the law recognises the right to acquire, use, and dispose of these objects as one likes, provided one respects the property rights of others.

Different rules apply with respect to land. One must distinguish between grazing land, agricultural land, wells, trees, and settlements.

Grazing Land. Traditionally, Somalis are reluctant to recognise property rights in grazing land (*daaqsin*), which includes forests. They tend to think of such land as belonging to all Somalis. What they do recognise is the right of possession. Whoever arrives at a particular pasture or watering place first with his herd will enjoy the exclusive use of that resource until he vacates it. When, in a given area, the grazing and water get scarce, clans tend to consider the entire area the property of the clan. That means that herdsmen of other clans must ask permission to enter that area with their herds. It is considered to be immoral, however, and sometimes even an act of war, to refuse such permission in time of drought, especially if the survival of another clan's livestock is at stake.

Clans that have become partly or wholly sedentary tend to recognise the right of individuals to acquire and use small parcels of grazing land on an exclusive basis. But alienation of such parcels is subject to the following restrictions. One cannot sell, bequeath, or give land to anyone not a member of one's clan. Renting or loaning land to outsiders, on the other hand, is allowed, but only to people having a special tie with one's own clan such as a man being married to one of its women (*inanlayaal*), or being accepted as its protégé (*magan*). Such rental and loan contracts automatically terminate when the woman in question dies or the original beneficiary or his offspring lose their special protégé status.

The reason clans refuse to let outsiders own parcels of land within the clan's boundaries is that landowners have certain obligations to the clan, in particular to help defend the clan's territory against bandits and raids from neighbouring clans. They are also supposed to join in work on the communal lands and wells, practice charity, engage in *guus*, assist in providing justice, etc. There are no guarantees that outsiders will participate in this. A still greater problem is the custom that the male offspring of such *inanlayaals* and *magans* cannot become a member of the host clan. A clan that admitted outsiders as landowners would have to tolerate an ever growing enclave of foreigners in its midst, and if these belonged to a neighbouring clan with which it was at war, it could no longer defend itself.

Agricultural Land. Somalis who practise agriculture recognise the right of individual clansmen to acquire and use particular parcels of land, but not to dispose of them as they like. The disposition of agricultural land is subject to the same restrictions as grazing land with respect to selling, renting, etc.

In addition to these near-property rights in land, Somalis recognise communal property. In fact, many swaths of land are owned by particular jilibs or even by an entire clan. Such land can be subdivided and allotted to individual owners only with the consent of all male clansmen.

A well-known temporary restriction on land-ownership is that of *usufruct*, the right to enjoy the use or fruit of something owned by another. Widows usually acquire the usufruct of the land that was held by their husband. A widow is entitled to use the land as she sees fit or to share in its yield. She is not entitled to alienate it, because ownership of the land devolves on her husband's children.

Water Ponds and Wells. The law recognises private property as well as communal property rights in water ponds and wells, particularly of people who have expended physical effort in their construction, improvement, and maintenance. The custom is that owners shall not deny passing nomads access to their water ponds and wells, but they are entitled, if they choose, to collect a water fee from them.

Settlements. A notable exception to the rule that land can only be owned by a clan or its individual members is land that has been granted to religious communities. There are several of these, for example the communities known as Xer or Gaadsan, belonging to the Muslim order of Gadaraawi. They acquired their land as grants from clans in the area. Ownership in this land automatically reverts to the previous owners if the community closes down. In fact, it closely resembles the perpetual leasehold, a leasehold that terminates only when aggressive acts are undertaken.

RULES OF CONDUCT

Somalis distinguish five basic types of violation of rights:

1. Homicide, particularly murder and manslaughter
2. Wounding, particularly assault, battery, rape, enslavement, abduction, and kidnapping
3. Damage to property, particularly arson, robbery, burglary, theft,
   extortion, fraud, embezzlement, and mere negligence
4. Defamation, which typically includes insulting words, spreading false information, adultery, marrying a girl

betrothed to another, and causing damage to a person's guest
5. Breach of contract

Homicide *(dil).* The basic sanction for homicide is that for a
life taken a life must be given. But this rule must not be taken
literally. It suggests, rather, that there must be a proper
relationship between the compensation that is due and the
aggression that has been committed. Though it does sometimes
happen that a murderer is condemned to death and executed,
more often the bereaved family will agree to be compensated.
In principle, the law makes no difference between premeditated
murder, murder, and unintentional killing. In all three cases the
same compensation, called blood price *(mag)*, is due to be paid
within a year's time. For the death of a man, this price is usually
100 camels, for a woman half of that number, and for a baby
one third.

There are, however, several variations on this rule. If the
perpetrator and the victim are of different clans and the killing
was intentional, the family of the victim may ask for the death
of the murderer. If the murderer has escaped, the family of the
victim is entitled to put to death two people of the murderer's
clan, preferably people of equal status as the victim. This may
strike one as a disproportionate and unjust sanction, but it must
be remarked that this rule is rarely enforced because the family
of the murderer, under the threat of losing two of its members,
usually cooperates in capturing him before he flees. Even then,
the principle of "a life for a life" is not always applied. If the two
clans have a good relationship, one now at risk because of the
murder, the clan leaders of the victimised person will often ask
the bereaved family to soften its demands.

In some situations, however, the courts will decide that the
criminal must be executed even if the family of the victim is
willing to accept the blood price. Also, it can happen that the
court will require that the blood price be paid within 48 hours,
rather than in the usual period of one year. Lastly, the family of
the victim is free to ask for more than 100 camels, and the family
of the murderer may pay the extra number, but such a private

arrangement, called *xeer jajab* (literally, "broken law"), cannot constitute a precedent in law.

No compensation is due for killing during time of war. Although the rule is that the lives of women and children (*maati*, literally "dependents") should be spared, there is no sanction if they are killed.

One may wonder to whom compensation must be paid if someone kills his brother. Obviously, it would be nonsensical to force the members of the murderer's family to pay the blood price to themselves. The law stipulates that in that case the nearest kin of the criminal must pay 100 camels to the victim's farthest kin.

The law does not call for imprisoning a murderer. Somalis do not believe that any good can come from humiliating and punishing a criminal, and the task of re-educating lawbreakers is left to their families and jilibs. Criminal law does not exist in Somalia. The focus of the law is on restitution and compensation.

Wounding *(qoon)*. Anyone who harms the body of another is obliged to pay compensation. The list following at the end of this chapter shows that women sometimes receive higher compensation than men. For example, damage done to the face of an unmarried young woman calls for a greater compensation than damage to the face of an unmarried young man. If the young woman's face is harmed to the point of spoiling her chances of marriage, the full blood price is due. Beauty is not the sole criterion for women, however. The law recognises also their domestic function. Somali women are supposed to engage in all sorts of handcraft, particularly turning grass into ropes, mats and baskets, and for this they use their teeth, particularly the canines, or "hook" teeth. Therefore, when a woman loses a canine tooth through the fault of another person, she gets a greater compensation than when this happens to a man.

If the damage done to someone's body is such that the victim requires health care, the perpetrator is obliged to provide this care and, if necessary, lodge and feed his victim until he has recovered his health. If the victim dies during the time of his lodging, his host must pay the blood price to his family.

A rapist is usually condemned to marry the woman he raped, in which case no compensation is due, only the bride price. The same is true if a woman is abducted. Women have the right to refuse to marry their rapist or abductor, but usually the victim is pressured by her family to consent to the marriage.

It should be noted that parents have the right to choose wives for their sons and husbands for their daughters. They usually exercise this right in order to acquire wealth for their family in the form of land, cattle, or other property. Girls can be married off as soon as they have reached puberty, boys when they are twenty. Likewise, the parents have the right to decide whether the genitals of their sons and daughters will be subjected to circumcision, excision, or clitoridectomy. This usually happens when they are seven or eight years old. Somali law does not prohibit these customs, although increasingly women's organisations oppose them.

Damage to Property. A person must give back the object he alienated, whether he did it intentionally, by negligence, or by mistake. When restitution is impossible, compensation must be paid. The basic rule is that damaged or alienated objects must be replaced by similar ones. Thus, it is important to know whether a stolen camel was a he or a she, young or old, pregnant, with milk, a transport camel, etc. Likewise, for a stolen tree, the judges would want to know whether it was a fruit tree, gum tree, fuel wood tree, shade tree, grazing tree, boundary tree, cemetery tree, etc. For each type, the law fixes a particular compensation. Instead of having the alienated objects replaced or receiving a certain number of camels as compensation, the victim may agree to accept their equivalent in money. For this, the current market price of the standard camel will be taken.

Damage may also be caused by someone's failure to abide by a particular customary law. There is, for example, a rule about how to prevent a conflict when two herds converge simultaneously on the same public watering place. Because herds cannot be watered simultaneously, one must be given priority. The law rules in favour of the smaller herd. The logic of this rule is that if an animal should die of thirst during the waiting time, the owner of the smaller herd would suffer a comparatively greater loss than the owner of the larger herd.

Insults and Defamation *(cay) (dhaliil).* Honour is a big issue among Somalis. When a family member has been victimised, the honour of the entire family is at stake. The blemish on that honour disappears only when the victim's rights have been restored or compensated and due fines paid. Somalis also have a strong dislike for being treated for less than they think they are, hence the concept of "harm to one's individual dignity." Compensation that must be paid for this is called *haal*. Thus when a man is struck on the face in public by another, the victim can claim five camels. Similarly, when a young man insults a young woman, he will likely be condemned to pay five camels. If she is unmarried and the insult risks destroying her chances for marriage, the compensation may be as high as the blood price. When an elderly man tells a young man that he is out of his mind and compares him with an animal held in low esteem, such as a donkey, it is not considered an insult. But when a young man calls an elderly man a donkey, it is. A man's failure to marry the woman to whom he was betrothed also calls for compensation. When a man marries a woman already betrothed to another man, he must pay compensation to the family of the other man. When a woman commits adultery, her husband can claim compensation from the man who committed it.

The prohibition against insult is somewhat mitigated by the fact that often the offender is only condemned conditionally. In such cases the compensation is due only if the perpetrator repeats his insult after the verdict has been rendered. Usually the person who made the insult can prevent the insulted person from seeking a court condemnation by apologising. The best apology is for him to go to the insulted person, accompanied by his oday, or extended-family head, frequently translated as "elder," and offer a small gift while the oday places his turban (*cimaamad*) on the head of the insulted person. Such a gesture effaces the insult.

Breach of Contract. Somali law requires that a person abide by any contract (*heshiis*) he has voluntarily and freely concluded. Here we must distinguish between two different types of contracts, those by which one irrevocably transfers a property title and those by which one promises to render particular services. In the case of a sales contract, for example, whoever breaks it must restitute or compensate the other party. Thus, someone who sold a camel but did not receive the sales price has the right to retrieve his camel or to exact the sales price by force. A contract to render particular services, on the other hand, can always be unilaterally terminated, but if a cancellation penalty has been agreed upon, it must be paid. Take employment, for example. Pastoralists sometimes enlist the assistance of a herdsman when they have no sons capable of looking after their herds. They may employ a herdsman for a year, during which time they will lodge and feed him. In exchange, he will look after part or all of his host's herd. At the end of the contract, the owner is obliged to give the herdsman an animal as a reward. If the pastoralist fails to pay the herdsman his due, the court will condemn him to do so. But if the herdsman terminates the contract prematurely, he forfeits his reward.

A contract (*heshiis*) is binding when it has been confirmed by certain rituals that mark the conscious will of both parties to bind themselves to each other. It is customary, for example, that they shake hands and cover these hands with the blanket that they usually carry over one shoulder. The term "*heshiis*" implies that the contract is definite and cannot be changed. In the case of the sale of a camel, for instance, the parties cannot unilaterally change the price after a heshiis has been concluded as evidenced by their putting their hands under the same blanket. Likewise in a contract to supply a service at a given date, neither the service nor the date can be changed unilaterally. Breach of such contracts obligates the breaker to compensate the other party for his loss. If he is unable to do so, his jilib will have to pay.

Contracts about marriage, children, divorce, death, or inheritance are usually concluded with the help of a religious official, or *sheekh*. If there is a dispute over its implementation, the parties will request the same sheekh to settle the dispute. A problem may arise if the sheekh applies Islamic law and one of the parties prefers ancestral law. There are many differences between these two bodies of law, and usually the sheekh applies a mix of the two.

When a man and a woman marry, it is agreed that the husband will provide household money (*masruuf*) and that the wife will manage the house (*aqal*). Failure of either to do so is recognised as a ground for divorce.

The marriage contract is usually negotiated between the respective parents. The family of the boy starts by offering a small gift (*gunti,* literally "a man's body cloth") to the family of the girl. Thereupon, the parents of the future bride offer a small gift, usually half the value of the gift received, to the family of the future bridegroom. These gifts need not be returned if the marriage doesn't take place. Thereafter, the parents from both sides discuss what each family will contribute to the household of the new couple. The family of the future bridegroom is expected to make a gift of livestock (*yarad*), and the family of the future bride is expected to provide the house (*aqal*) and its decorations and utensils. If the couple divorces, she can take the livestock that was contributed.

Divorce is possible under Somali law, which allows a man to have four spouses, provided he treats them equally. A woman is denied this right. The law accepts non-payment of the masruuf as grounds for divorce. The divorce is final when one spouse says three times, "I divorce you."

When a husband dies, his widows are usually offered an opportunity to marry one of his brothers. If they refuse, they lose their claim for a masruuf from the late husband's family. When a husband dies, his widows will be asked whether they are pregnant. If they are, they must stay with the clan of their late husband until the child is two years old, after which the child will remain with his father's family until adulthood. Widows are entitled to draw benefits from the herds and the land of their late husbands until their own death, after which these properties will be divided among their children. When a married woman dies, the widower is usually offered an opportunity to marry one of her sisters, but neither party will be required to do so. When a girl who is betrothed to a man dies before she is married to him, one of her sisters is usually given in marriage to that man.

Should a man die intestate, custom stipulates that his sons and unmarried daughters inherit equally. Women lose their right to inherit from their parents on the day they marry. The law requires this in order to keep the assets of the various clans separate.

A person can make a will and thus void the rule that his children should inherit equally. If his land is too small to divide, he usually bequeaths it to his eldest son, leaving nothing to the others.

Notes

9. In so doing, the court is not necessarily carrying out the wishes of the family who bring the complaint. A court convenes only if the victim or his family call it into existence, hence all its acts derive from their willingness to have it meet. But since it may rule in a manner they find less than optimal, it does not need any further sanction from them. Indeed, the court may impose its ruling over their objection (see pages 53, 60). –Editor JD

Chapter 6
Rendering Justice

We have seen that Somali law requires that every person refrain from violating the life, liberty, and property of others. But what must a person do who has nevertheless violated someone else's rights? The answer is that he must stop any ongoing violation, return any alienated goods or compensate their value, pay any costs incurred by the victim, and pay the victim a fine if the violation was intentional.

These activities are usually called "rendering justice" to a person. The ancient Romans called it *suum cuique tribuere*, or "giving each his own." The term "justice" is derived from the Latin word "ius," which in turn comes from the verb *iurare*, "to swear." It means the order of human affairs that arises out of the commitments people make to each other in solemn speech. Violators have a choice. They can voluntarily render justice to their victim or wait until their victim forces them to do so. Should the victim decide to use force, he had better first ask an impartial person to establish to what extent his right was violated and who exactly was the perpetrator. Otherwise he risks the possibility that the violator will defend himself and that, instead of justice, more damage will be done. Once the identity of the violator and the nature of his obligation to justice have been established by a court, the violator again can either honour the verdict or let himself be forced to do so. If he chooses the latter, the victim has the option of either applying the force himself or letting others, as policemen, apply it on his behalf.

It thus becomes clear that "rendering justice" may require the intervention of three "institutions"—courts of justice, police, and a set of procedures. These three institutions must guarantee the rights of both the accused and the accusing person during the process of rendering justice.

COURTS OF JUSTICE

Forming a Court. The most visible institution of Somali customary law is the court of justice (*guuddi*), formed by the judges of two conflicting parties.

At birth, every Somali becomes a member of his father's extended family, consisting of all the male descendants of the same great-grandfather and their spouses and children. Two or more such families normally form a jilib. Although the head of an extended family has no special powers, he is responsible for seeing that justice is accorded the family members. He undertakes this task with no means other than his knowledge of human affairs and his wisdom. His appointment to head of the extended family, called "elder" (*oday*), is an elaborate affair. Candidates for this position are generally known long in advance of a vacancy and are closely observed by the clan. When the time comes to appoint a new head, the various clan elders meet during several weeks or months and discuss every detail of the lives of the candidates. The discussion lasts until a consensus forms.

The head of an extended family automatically has jurisdiction over all of the family members. If one of them violates the rights of someone outside the family, he must seek out the head of the family of the victim and form a court of law with him. If these two judges cannot agree on a verdict, they must appoint a judge from a neighbouring family and let him make the final decision. Thus the head of a family automatically becomes one of the judges of the law court that will be formed when a member becomes involved in a conflict. If someone on becoming an adult wants a different person to be his judge, he has the option of leaving his own extended family and forming a new one, or else teaming up with another. Alternatively, he can try to convince all the members of his family that its head should be replaced. Indeed, a head of a family is constantly under pressure to maintain his position. If he is not performing properly, he runs the risk of being put aside. This may happen immediately after he has made a great mistake, or gradually. In the latter case it sometimes happens that a family has several heads at the same time.

Should the judge of a wrongdoer refuse to assume jurisdiction over the conflict, i.e. refuse to form a law court with the judge of the victim, a problem arises. This happens occasionally when the conflicting parties belong to different clans. In that case, the family of the victim is allowed self-help. It is entitled to use force to redress the injustice that was done to it. It need not do so immediately, and indeed it sometimes happens that years go by before an opportunity for self-help arises.

Customarily, it is not the conflicting parties themselves who ask their judges to assume jurisdiction and form a court, but their respective families. Indeed, justice is a family matter rather than one between individuals. This is understandable because the families of the litigants have a stake in the settlement of the conflict. The families guarantee that the compensation and fines awarded by the court will be paid.

Powers of the Court. Judges must base their verdicts on the facts as presented and may not judge an individual on his opinions, achievements, associations, or physical characteristics. Verdicts need not be in writing. In fact, they are almost always oral. A court has the power to order the able-bodied men in the community to assist the victim and his family to enforce a verdict. If, however, the court is a multi-clan court judging an inter-clan conflict, it has no power to enforce its verdict. The task of enforcing then devolves on the clan of the victim, at its discretion. Judges often demand beforehand to know whether the litigants will respect the verdict. If the answer is negative, they may refuse to judge the case. If the answer is positive, the litigants may be requested to sign a statement to that effect.

Appeal. Both parties have the right to appeal a verdict. They can ask a different set of judges to hear the case. A court of appeal must have a larger number of judges than the court whose verdict is being appealed, and the judges must be drawn from a wider group of families or clans. The Somalis have no standing courts of appeal. If the other party refuses to go along with the idea of an appeal, then the aggrieved family is entitled to self-help. To this end, it can gather a party of able-bodied men, or ask the court to do so, and obtain its compensation by force. If the other party is willing to cooperate with the appeal, however, it must—just as must its opponent—appoint its own judges to the court of appeal. If the verdict in appeal confirms the verdict in first instance, it will be the final verdict. In some clans, a verdict is final only when two verdicts have been rendered in the same sense. As many as 12 appeals are permitted in other clans. Among the Isse, the number is eleven.

The bench. When the dispute is between members of the same clan and jilib, the court usually consists of only the two judges of the disputing parties. When the dispute is between members of different jilibs of the same clan, there tend to be more judges. When the dispute is between members of two different clans, the numbers tend to increase again.

Procedure. Once a court forms and accepts jurisdiction over a case, it appoints a recorder (*doodqaad*), who will repeat loudly during the hearing each important point made by the speakers. The court then announces when and where it will hear the case. There will be no exchange of written documents prior to the hearing. Nor will a transcript of the proceedings and verdict be made. The hearing often starts with a homily by a religious dignitary to admonish everyone to give his best efforts to see that justice is done. Then the court invites the plaintiff to state his case. The plaintiff has the right to appoint a representative to make the presentation on his behalf. During this presentation, the plaintiff will be given the opportunity to confer with his family to make sure that he has not forgotten anything. When the plaintiff has finished, the court asks him to summarise his case and state his demands. Finally the court asks the defendant to present his defence and any counter claims. The court then adjourns to deliberate whether witnesses should be heard.

In a somewhat different scenario, the judges sit together and the judge of the defendant says, "I have heard the accusation. Let me take this up with the accused person." After doing so, he may say, "My clan will pay the requested compensation." In this case the accused person never appears before the court, and no stigma sticks to him except that his clansmen will protect him from revenge and will keep him away from weapons. Note that here the judge of the accused becomes his representative!

A disputed fact is admitted as evidence only when at least three witnesses have testified to its truth. The parties can also call in experts and character witnesses, and written evidence is also admitted. If the victim has died or has been wounded, the court will instruct a religious dignitary to assess how the victim died or was wounded. These dignitaries assess injuries usually by applying the standards enumerated in the commentary of the twelfth-century Muslim scholar, al-Nawawii's Minhaaj at-Talibiin (Lewis 1956:150).

When the plaintiff has thus elaborated his case with witnesses and evidence, the defendant is given a chance to refute the plaintiff's charges, arguments, and evidence. It is not customary to cross-examine witnesses.

Then the court adjourns again to evaluate the evidence. If less than three witnesses support a fact, or if the witnesses contradict each other, the court will proceed to oath taking, a procedure called *lugqabta*. There are several types of oaths. The simplest starts by the oath-giver saying, "I swear by my virility." Alternatively, he can say, "I swear by Allah (the Qur'an)." A stronger oath is the so-called triple oath (*Wallaahi iyo Billaahi iyo Tallaahi*), in which he swears the same oath three times. A stronger oath yet is the one that is repeated fifty times. Also, there is the so-called divorce oath, in which the oath-giver swears by his marriage(s). If it is later found out that he lied, his marriage(s) becomes null and void.

It should be noted that even if the plaintiff fails to convince the court of his case, the court nevertheless will not usually rule in favour of the defendant before the defendant has taken an oath of innocence. In some clans the litigants are entitled to one appeal only, in others up to eleven or twelve.

POLICE FORCE

Although rarely needed in Somalia, since wrongdoers are usually apprehended by their own family members and verdicts are usually voluntarily complied with, police force is occasionally required to stop a continuing violation of the law, to collect penalties, or to execute a verdict. The victim or his family can exercise the necessary force on its own initiative, or it can request a court of justice to assemble a team to do so. The court will then call upon a number of able-bodied men of a given village or neighbourhood. Those who refuse to be enlisted in such a temporary police force may be considered associates of the wrongdoer and become liable to pay compensation to the victim's family. Custom dictates what type of force may be used and for what precise purpose. It is commonly understood that no more force should be used than is customarily thought to be necessary to execute the verdict. This may include destroying some of the wrongdoer's harvest.

Small families tend to ally themselves with other small families or to team up with an existing larger family. There are two reasons for this. One is the obligation of its members to be insured against any liability they might incur under the law. The larger the family, the less each has to pay in the event one of them is convicted of a crime. The other reason is that enforcement is the responsibility of the family of the victim. The larger the family, the more able-bodied men there will be, and the easier the enforcement.

Verdicts are enforced as follows. The court that rendered the verdict admonishes the defendant to comply within a specific time. If the condemned person fails to comply, the court imposes a penalty (*yake*), of which there are several kinds. The least onerous is the payment of a certain quantity of honey. Next comes the tying of the condemned person to a tree covered with black ants, which will bite and cause considerable agony. The court will order the able-bodied young men of the village to do this. The man who has been tied to a tree must stay until he complies. In addition, the villagers may be ordered to slaughter one of the man's sheep or oxen and feast on it in front of him. When the feast is over, the villagers will be ordered to slaughter another of his sheep or oxen, and so on. No cases are known in which the village refused to execute a verdict in the above way, or where the defendant did not ultimately agree to comply.

COMPENSATION/PENALTIES

Penalties usually consist of loss of animals. On learning that a person refuses to honour a verdict in which he is condemned to pay compensation or a fine, a court may decide to impose a penalty for each day he continues to refuse. The most common penalty is to slaughter and eat one of the wrongdoer's animals, such as a sheep or a goat, while he remains hungry. Or if the wrongdoer is a woman, the penalty may consist of burning before her eyes grass mats she has woven.

Under Somali law, compensation and fines are always computed in terms of camels (*geel*), just as anciently the monetary unit of the Romans was a cow (in fact, the Latin word for money is *pecunia*, from *pecus*, cow). Not just any camel will do. It must be a healthy she-camel aged three to six years. The court usually appoints a board of elders (*bash gudi*) to assess the livestock offered in payment. By mutual agreement, the parties may decide that the compensation will be paid in cows, sheep, or goats, or in money. The law fixes the rate for this substitution. Thus, a camel has the same value as 3 cows or 10 goats or sheep. The monetary value of a 3-year-old she-camel is its current market value, which tends to fluctuate between one and two hundred U.S. dollars.

Compensations and fines are not due to the victim, but to his family, just as they are not paid exclusively by the criminal or tort-feasor himself, but in part by his entire family.

The compensations and fines enumerated below are generally considered to be a maximum. The family of the victim is free to accept less. A crime between members of two different clans usually draws the maximum compensation/fine. If the clans are friendly with each other, the receiving clan may decide to return from 10 to 40 percent of the compensation/fine to the paying tribe as a goodwill gesture.

The general principle in the case of murder is that he who takes a life loses a life—his own. However, the family of the deceased may decide to accept the *mag*, which is 100 camels for a man and 50 for a woman. If the murder has been particularly violent, the murderer must be put to death, even if the family of the victim would prefer the mak. If the murderer flees abroad, then a person of equal status among the family of the murderer must be put to death. The latter rule ensures that the family of the murderer will cooperate in his arrest. The murder of a baby draws a compensation of 30 camels for a boy and 15 for a girl. A baby becomes a person when it can run.

When a man is killed unintentionally, his family receives 60-70 camels. The norm for a woman is 30-35 camels, for a baby boy 30, and for a baby girl 15. If a sailor who serves on board a ship drowns while on duty, the ship owner must pay 100 camels. If he was off duty, 50 camels. If it was clearly the sailor's own fault, nothing is due.

The norms of compensation for rape vary depending on who is raped and who did the raping. The highest number of camels is due for the rape of a girl who is both a minor and a virgin. The lowest number is due for a widow.

The norms of compensation for inflicting permanent bodily damage are as follows, doubling if intentional:

Loss of an eye	50 camels, two eyes 100 camels
Loss of the nose	50 camels
Loss of an ear	36 camels, two ears 72 camels
Loss of the tongue	50 camels
Loss of a tooth	Up to 35 camels depending which tooth
Loss of an arm	Right arm 40 camels, left arm 30 camels
Loss of a finger	Up to 5 camels, depending how much of it
Loss of a thumb	10 camels
Loss of a leg	40 camels
Loss of a toe	5 camels

If a man seriously wounds another, his family must take the one he wounded into their home and look after him until he is healed. If he dies during his treatment, 100 camels are due. For a woman, the norm is 50. If serious permanent damage was done, the man's family will receive up to 200 camels, a woman's family up to 100 camels. A thief who steals an animal must return two similar ones. A thief who cuts someone's gum tree must pay 10-20 camels. Theft of a car that cannot be returned because it was lost calls for payment of a new car to replace it.

A person who accidentally damages another's property must compensate him or her. If the driver of a car runs his car accidentally into an animal on the road, he must replace that animal or pay its value. Roads are not the exclusive domains of cars; drivers must respect all other users, including stray animals, which deserve the same protection as stray children.

Chapter 7
Contacts with Foreign Law

Somalis have been exposed to several foreign legal systems, which have left their imprint on the practitioners of the customary law. The Moslem legal system, the Sharia, was the first of which we have any knowledge, followed by the colonial systems of Italy, France, England, and Ethiopia. The United Nations then served as trustee over Italian Somaliland. Finally there came the legal system of the Somali Democratic Republic (1960-1991).

The Somalis reacted differently to these legal systems. Whereas they adopted some of the Muslim rules, they flatly opposed the colonial laws whenever they could. They even corrupted the laws of their own Republic—simply by staying faithful to their own culture. According to Somali culture, a clansman cannot approach a person of another clan for the first time without both of their elders being present. If they encounter each other without these elders, they are said to "confront" (*hor imaad*) one another, a military term that denotes enmity. A policeman of one clan is not free, therefore, to arrest people belonging to another clan without both parties being accompanied by their elder. By contrast, a policeman of the Republic might have thought that he represented the laws of the entire nation, but the population did not perceive him in that light. Nor could a prosecutor of the Republic summon a trespasser before one of the Republic's law courts. A Somali has the right to be judged by a court consisting of his elder and that of his opponent. His clan would never honour a verdict rendered by a court that was constituted differently.

A similar problem arose when the Republic of Somalia began

to grant permits and licenses to its citizens. A Somali civil servant was not seen as a servant of the nation, but as a member of his clan who happened to "own a chair" (*kursi buu haystaa*) in the organisation of the Republic. Generally speaking, the Somalis considered government policy and instructions irrelevant; a civil servant was expected to exploit his office as much as he could and to distribute the proceeds among his clansmen. Therefore, they found it normal that civil servants should charge fees not for their services, but for not using their powers— their nuisance powers. This fee, elsewhere known as a bribe, the Somalis called "that which makes work light" (*hawl fudeydin*). The only way to avoid paying this price was to make the services of the central government a matter of clan policy. That meant bringing together one's own oday with that of the office holder. When the elders of both parties agreed that the permit or favour should be granted, the office holder had to obey and forego his bribe.

The rule that the elders of both parties must be present at a first encounter makes good sense. It facilitates the settlement of any conflict that might later arise. This custom of not directly addressing a person from another clan has its counterpart on the intra-clan level. If a clansman should want, for example, to buy, sell, hire, or rent something, he will rarely, if ever, deal with a person of another jilib directly. If he thinks he can conclude a contract with such a person, he will ask an intermediary to contact that person and negotiate on his behalf. Such a person will be someone of his own jilib who already knows the person of the other jilib.

One might think this rule unsuited to a modern nation because of its rather time-consuming nature. But similar customs exist everywhere in the global market economy, where before entering into a business relationship people exchange credit and identity cards, testimonials and references, inspect one another's bank accounts, and agree on what court of arbitration will settle their conflicts, if any. It is not likely, therefore, that Somalis will be willing to change this custom. At best, they will adapt it to the requirements of a modern society. It is so ingrained in the Somali lifestyle that it is most unlikely that it could be eliminated by any constitution or propaganda that portrayed the central government as an organisation acting in the interest of the entire nation. The Somalis will always want to have their relationship with any government ruled by their customary law, and not by laws emanating from that government.

With the demise of the Somali central government in 1991, the customary law became Somalia's supreme law. That does not mean, however, that the Somalis went back to an antique law system. As noted earlier, their customary laws and institutions are always developing. One of these developments is that during the time of the Republic the jilibs, which previously had been primarily judicial and social units, became suppliers of politicians and administrators for the political institutions of the Republic and later also for the political committees established by the United Nations.

In Ethiopia's Somali Region, most customary judges have established a working relationship with the military and civil servants of the government of Ethiopia, both on the central and the regional level. For example, shortly after it toppled the regime of dictator Mengistu Hailemariam, the EPRDF militia invaded Ethiopia's Somali Region. In the beginning, Ethiopian soldiers randomly killed a few Somalis. The Somali judges thereupon ruled that for every Somali life taken, two Ethiopian soldiers should be killed. After a few applications of this ruling, the Ethiopian military commander accepted it—and the number of random killings by his soldiers fell off dramatically.

After a federal government was established in Ethiopia, its police force in the Somali Region occasionally was asked to arrest certain individuals who had already been judged by a customary court of law. The people making the request were sometimes plaintiffs or defendants who hoped to get a better deal from the federal government than they had from their customary court. To counter such moves, the customary judges introduced a new policy. On rendering a verdict, they would inform the police and the courts of the federal and regional governments. Also, they began requesting the litigants in advance to agree in writing that they would honour the verdict. The result was that the police no longer listened to such malcontents.

When a customary court condemned a perpetrator to death, the normal procedure was to ask for volunteers to enforce the verdict from among the young men in the village where he had been condemned. This was always a messy affair. It has now come about that the customary court asks the federal police or military to execute its sentence. If the response is positive, the court hands over its proven criminal to the federal executioners and requests that the body be returned to them.

Another noteworthy rule developed when the border police and its soldiers began seizing cars of passers-by to use in the pursuit of persons suspected of smuggling. The elders then ruled that a Somali who allowed his car to be seized by such policemen and soldiers would be considered an accessory to any mischief the latter engaged in. It should be clearly understood that the customary law, which protects freedom of movement and free trade, does not prohibit smuggling. During the early 1990s, it happened that the border controllers offered to pay the blood price when they killed someone crossing the border at night. At first, that was accepted. But after several years, when the practise of killing nightly border crossers continued, the border police and its soldiers were told that those guilty of such killing would become outlaws, meaning that any Somali would have the right to kill them with impunity.

The relationship between the Somali customary law and the Ethiopian legal system is a curious one. In practise, these two systems coexist. In theory, according to Articles 34.5 and 70 of the Constitution of December 8, 1994, the Ethiopian law acknowledges the existence of customary laws in its realm. But it limits their scope of application to matters of marriage and divorce. Since no laws have been enacted thus far to establish a working relationship between the customary courts and those of the Republic of Ethiopia, the Articles remain dead letters. As a curiosity, it may be worth noting that the Somalis inserted these articles into the constitution by way of a last minute amendment.

Under British rule in the northwest part of what is now called Somaliland, it became customary to register property titles to land as well as any contracts establishing law between two jilibs. But efforts of the colonial powers failed to make collaborators of the chiefs of jilibs and clans. Even today, a *caaqil* takes orders from no one, nor does he have authority over anyone. Those who call themselves village chiefs have only an administrative function. It is their job on occasion to talk to visiting officials of state agencies, but they have no power to make any decision on behalf of their jilib.

Chapter 8
Economics[10]

For quite some time after the business firm gained prominence in England and America following the industrial revolution, the family continued there as the chief production unit in agriculture, manufacturing, and trade. This was apparent only a hundred years ago in the names of many companies—"Smith Bros.," "Anders & Sons," etc. Gradually, however, the firm displaced the family. The firm represented an advance in efficiency in doing business because it consisted of individuals related contractually rather than by kinship status. It could be more rational and goal-oriented, hence more competitive than the family, which necessarily had a mixed agenda of social and business obligations. The family cannot as easily recruit specialised talent, for example, but must accommodate Aunt Sadie and old Uncle John. Thus in many countries of the world, the autonomous individual has become the basic productive unit and seeks his best advantage by associating with other individuals as he sees fit. He retains his society of familiars, his source of psychological fulfilment, yet interacts freely in the impersonal world of business, the global economy. He lives in two worlds.

In Somalia, the basic economic unit as well as the basic social unit continues to be the family, in this case the extended family. This entails for the individual social obligations that to a Westerner seem onerous. But they are understandable in their context. George B.N. Ayittey (2003) observes from his broader African perspective that most families have a "welfare fund" into which all individual members are required to contribute. Individuals needing money to start a business can borrow from this fund and are expected to pay it back. If the business fails, the individual can fall back on the extended family for sustenance. And if he is under threat, the extended family comes to his defence. Thus, the extended family serves as a "safety net," provides "venture capital," protection, insurance, etc. for individual members. Obviously, for these services, an individual member is required to make a contribution to the upkeep of the extended family.

An individual unwilling to do so is always free to leave and set up on his own somewhere else. But he cannot stay in the extended family, enjoy all the protection it offers, and refuse to make a contribution. If he doesn't do so voluntarily, family members are entitled to go to court and compel him. What an individual "loses," however, the family gains. Recall again that the family is the basic economic and social unit; the individual is secondary. Thus, although social obligations may limit an individual's capacity to accumulate capital in his own right, it is the ability of the family to accumulate capital that is important. As between families, however, no Somali law mandates that one family must share its wealth with another.

However understandable in context, this limitation on the ability of individuals as such to freely save and invest inhibits wealth production. A further inhibiting factor is a limitation on individual ownership of land. An individual cannot sell or rent land to non-clan members. Consequently, the value of land cannot be optimised. How these inhibitions are likely to be resolved over time is discussed in Chapter 11.

Despite such inhibitions on land use and capital accumulation, Somalis nevertheless do capitalise and pursue business ventures and have done so since time immemorial. They have a holy respect for private property, particularly livestock, crops, habitats, handicrafts, and weapons. The elders are not considered owners of the clan's communal territories, but only their custodians; they are obliged to allot land to members of the community when requested, and to grant private grazing rights, all of which rights can be sold, gifted, or bequeathed within the clan. The elders are also obliged to respect the principles of freedom of contract and voluntary exchange. Free enterprise and free trade are highly regarded. A Somali does not need permission from his oday, or extended-family head, to engage in any economic activity, be it livestocking, agriculture, fishing, forestry, mining, commerce, or industry.

Indeed, Somalis have a known history of trade and commerce dating back thousands of years to the Egyptian Pharaohs (Bruce Bower 2005).

Among institutions of pre-colonial Africa that promoted peaceful trade throughout the continent, Ayittey (2003:335) cites the custom of forming a bond of friendship with prominent individuals along a route or at a destination. He quotes Lewis (1962) on this custom among the Somalis:

> To reach the coast in safety a caravan had to have protection on its journey among many different and often hostile clans. This was achieved by an institutionalised form of safe-conduct. The leader of the caravan .. entered into a relationship of protection with those amongst whom he passed on his way to the coast.. Attacks on a protected caravan are attacks on the patron [*abbaan*] and his lineage whose honour and 'name' ... can only be upheld by prompt retaliatory action.

Throughout the continent, therefore, trade is an indigenous African institution. Observing that basic beliefs and political, legal, and economic institutions are everywhere "strikingly and structurally the same," Ayittey (1991:xliv) notes (370) that

> Markets and trade were free and open ... Prices .. were, in general, determined by market forces—supply and demand. These principles were understood by the natives, and they bargained over prices ... At most markets, systems were in place to settle trade disputes.
>
> Though some powerful merchants tried to control markets and fix prices, open competition was the rule. Nor could such competition be eliminated. There were numerous suppliers, middlemen, brokers, trade routes as well as substitutes.

Somalis strongly embrace competition today (Davidson 2003):

> Open competition in telecommunications has resulted in exceptional service. While it takes weeks to get on a waiting list for a telephone in some African capital cities, in Hargeisa or Mogadishu phone service is hooked up the same day it is ordered. Cellular phones are turned on when purchased. Thanks to all the competition, Somalis pay the lowest international long distance rates in Africa. As many as ten phone companies compete for landline service in Greater Somalia.

Thus is Somali culture, like that of traditional Africa as a whole, compatible with the classical-liberal view of a just society. At least in principle, anyone respecting the property rights of others enjoys full freedom under the customary law to engage in any economic pursuit of his choice.

Notes

10. Michael van Notten made only a brief start for this chapter with the cryptic note, "Further information to be drawn from the books of George Ayittey Ph.D. Start with describing the economic miracles of Bossaso ... Idem Merka." On reflection, however, it becomes clear that the story of Bossaso and its implications for the future of Somalia does not fit the book's order of presentation of traditional Somali law and politics. This lack of logical fit may account in part for the chapter having remained unwritten. Accordingly, with critical input from George A. N. Ayittey, and drawing largely from the author's notes from elsewhere, I offer this brief account of traditional economics and deal with the economic "miracle" of Bossaso and its implications in a new Chapter 14, "Prospects." Readers interested in contemporary Somali economics should consult, among others, Maria H. Brons (2001) and Peter D. Little (2003). –Editor SM

Chapter 9
Politics

*The Somali population ... accommodates itself rather
willingly to ... the absence of a state of which it has, anyhow, never
felt the need nor understood its usefulness.*

—Christian Bader, 1999

SYMBOLIC HEAD

Most clans formerly had a single individual who symbolised
the peace and prosperity of its members and also fulfilled
the functions of archivist and occasional ambassador. He was
appointed for life. When the clan engaged in rituals, he was the
master-of-ceremonies and central figure. When he fulfilled an
official function, he would be surrounded, supported, and
assisted by four elders chosen for the occasion from among the
members of the Assembly. In northwest Somalia he was called
ugaas, and in other areas *boqor, waber, gob, mudan, garad,* or
sultan. The use of *sultan* for the head of a clan or sub-clan is
now more widely used than any of the other titles.

The selection and inauguration of such a figurehead is an elaborate
event that may take a full year. He is usually chosen from the family
of his predecessor, but he is not necessarily the eldest son. He can be
an adult, an adolescent, or even a child. Usually he comes from a
sub-group that is neither small nor large. Account is taken of the
degree of respect his father and both grandfathers earned among
their fellow clansmen.

At his inauguration, an ugaas receives a gift, perhaps a

hundred head of cattle, from the groups that make up his clan. All the clansmen acknowledge in this way that he has become their ugaas. The gift also frees him from necessity so that he can give full attention to his function and not be tempted to mix clan duties with efforts for personal gain.

Somalis are not accustomed to using secular titles. The title of *ugaas* and its synonyms are among the few that occur. Another, *oday,* may be translated as "elder" or perhaps "alderman," although married women also use it loosely with reference to their husband. It does not imply any powers, but simply means that someone is respected because of his wisdom and his skill in settling conflicts. The title of *gudoomiya* is given to the chairman of a meeting, but only while the meeting lasts. Finally, a title that may carry some implication of hierarchy is *Caaqil.* It is sometimes used for the head of a jilib, but since the time when the Egyptians and British appointed *Caaqils* in their quest for malleable local dignitaries, it has rarely been used. In 1960, when Italian and British Somaliland became independent, several titles were created for the officials of the first central government. These titles were not always flattering. The president of the Somali Republic, for instance, was called *madaxweyne,* which literally means "big head." Although an official title, it conveyed to many the idea of a person imbued with his own importance.

The Samaron stopped having a figurehead for their clan after Sultan Omar Buhl died in 1954. The Ciise (Isse) similarly failed to elect a successor when their last ugaas died in 1999, and likewise for the Isaaq.

THE ASSEMBLY (*Guurti*)

Somalis have a deep respect for the political independence of their clans. No clansman will accept being ruled by a member of another clan, any more than by someone of his own clan. All clans adhere to one political philosophy, and that philosophy aims at preventing any form of dictatorship. This nation-wide attitude towards government probably has its roots in the great respect that the Somalis have for every individual's life, liberty, and property. Theirs is a well thought out freedom philosophy.

This shared philosophy results in all Somali clans having more or less the same political system, which works as follows. The supreme political institution is the Assembly (*Guurti*), composed of the heads of the most important families. This Assembly decides on war and peace, but has no power to conscript or employ soldiers. Neither is the Assembly entitled to legislate, or to render or overturn judgments. The job of settling conflicts, whether between members of the same or of different clans, is left to the clan courts of law. Even so, the Assembly is the watchdog over the customary law. It can recommend, for example, that fines be increased if particular laws are not being upheld. The Assembly is presided over by a chairman (*guddoomiye*), assisted by four advisors and an executive committee (*fulinta guddida*).

Decision-making in the Assembly involves no casting of votes. Rather, the Assembly members keep on talking until a consensus is reached. That is why the meetings can last a long time, sometimes several months. The reason why the Assembly operates by consensus is easy to understand: it prevents the Assembly from taking decisions that would infringe on anyone's freedom and property rights.

In peacetime, the Assembly has no police or military force at its disposal to enforce its decisions. That ensures that it cannot make decisions that go against the interests of the community. If it were to make such decisions, they would be ignored. It does happen, of course, that the Assembly will decide on a particular course of action with some people still opposing. In such cases, dissenters are not required to participate in the action, and in the extreme they are always free to quit the clan if they choose.

In wartime, a clan tends to appoint as commander someone with military skills (*oday abbaduu*). Such a person has limited powers. He cannot negotiate with other clans on economic matters, for example. If he did so anyhow and reached an agreement, it would be null and void. Only a peacetime leader can do that.

The Assembly usually deals with the following kinds of matters.

- Alliances and contracts (*xeerar*, plural of *xeer*) with other clans

- War and peace with other clans
- Conflicts between the clan's sub-clans
- Coping with drought and other natural disasters
- Dealing with foreign governmental and non-governmental organisations
- Managing communal lands and watering places
- Searching for and moving to new grazing areas
- Constructing schools, clinics, roads, mosques, etc.
- Fundraising for charitable causes
- Electing and inaugurating a new ugaas
- Deciding on ceremonies honouring the clan's founder, etc.

Bearing in mind that all units of Somali society are independent of one another, it goes without saying that each clan has its own system of law and politics. However, all follow more or less the same structure. Among them is a certain specialisation of function. Smaller political units deal only with matters of their own people and receive no instructions or commands from the larger. There is no hierarchy among the units. Even so, a person aspiring to membership in a larger assembly must first serve in a smaller one. In theory, an assembly is open to all adult males, with the exception usually of those belonging to the *midgaan,* or the artisan class. In practice, however, only those clansmen participate who are respected for their opinion and represent a number of households, families, and jilibs.

POLITICAL PRINCIPLES

It has been said that the Somali nation is organised as a confederation of sovereign families. Such a term suggests the existence of an organisation exercising a guiding or co-ordinating function throughout the nation. But there is no such organisation, nor is there an association of clan chiefs or even an annual meeting of such dignitaries. The "cement" holding the bricks of which the Somali nation is built is not some sort of central command of its political and judicial organisations, but rather a set of shared principles.

Segmental Opposition. The most important organisational principle of a Somali clan, an amalgam of families related by lineal descent and lacking a common command structure, is called "segmental opposition." This means that whenever there is a conflict between two individuals, their families will move in and establish an armed stalemate. They do this to make clear to the disputants that they must stop using force and let their dispute be settled according to the prevailing customary rules under the guidance of mediators, arbiters, or courts of law.

Each party to the dispute seeks aid from members of his family. But his kinsmen are only willing to come to his aid when asked to *defend* him. If asked to help attack someone, they refuse, since almost all families in the clan have kin ties with one another and consequently might find themselves attacking someone of their own family. Those coming to the rescue of their quarrelsome clansmen enlist further aid if needed until they form groups of equal strength, bringing about a stalemate. The stalemate can only be broken by a mediator, who usually has family ties to both parties. He may be a common cousin or someone chosen by a common cousin. Such a mediator can only settle the dispute on the basis of rights common to all clansmen. If he were to apply arbitrary standards that did not apply equally to everyone, he would be criticised and considered unfit to handle future conflicts.

In this behaviour of the clan, several fundamental principles stand out:

- Kinship pushes groups within the clan to use their power only for defensive purposes.
- Conflicts can be "frozen" by forming segmental groups of equal strength that bring about a stalemate between the conflicting parties.
- Expert mediators then emerge to settle quarrels and conflicts peaceably.
- Mediators settle conflicts by reference to property rights.
- Mediators do not use police to enforce their verdicts.

The German anthropologist Stefan Blankertz thus summarises in a parallel manner the logic of segmental opposition in clan societies:[11]

The first and most important principle of segmental opposition is that in every conflict, segments of equal strength oppose each other. It is impossible for one segment to conquer or dominate another, because the victimized segment gets help from the next relatives as long as the segment is indeed victimized.

The second principle of segmental opposition is prevention of conquest and power seeking. Because every one is related to every one else in some way, it is possible to get support in the case of defence, but not in the case of attack. If someone were to help another victimise a third person, he would be helping to victimise a relative—which is unthinkable in clan ethics.

This brings us to the third principle of segmental opposition and the probable origin of the juridical system. Segmental opposition is a system of balanced power that results in a standoff, in which no individual and no party can be the victor. It has need, therefore, of a peaceful procedure to bring quarrels to an end. This creates a strong incentive to call for a specialist in mediation—in early times called a "judge."

But how can a Wise Woman or Man restore quarrelling people to friendship? Who determines what is right and what is wrong? Judges have no legislation to fall back upon and no police at their command. All they have is their understanding, reason, and intelligence—wisdom, if you prefer the term. Accordingly, the fourth principle of segmental opposition calls for an accepted theory of justice on the basis of which the Wise Person can solve the problems he is consulted about.

There is such a theory. It is a widely accepted, general theory of justice that is best described by the words "property," "contract," and "consent." To understand why property, contract, and consent are the only possible standard by which judges in tribal anarchy can solve problems, let us take a closer look of the nature of quarrelling.

Imagine someone taking a cow that another person considered his. The first says, "I took your cow because I wanted it." The second says, "It is my cow." So they ask the Wise Person who is right and who is wrong. If the Wise Person says the first is right, then, of course, the second can take back the cow, because it would be considered the right of anyone to take what he likes. Therefore such a decision would not end the quarrel; it would be the starting point of endless fighting. The only way to end the quarrel would be to say that no one may take another's property without his or her consent. Only then could both parties keep what was his or hers.

The task of the judge is to establish whether the cow taken is indeed the property of the second person. That means that the judge has to find out whether that person took possession of that cow when no one else owned it, or whether he raised it, inherited it, bought it from someone, or received it as a gift.

This brings us to the fifth principle of segmental opposition. In a state of anarchy, the only reasonable way of thinking of a right is that it must be capable of being universalised—which means that whatever holds for one person must hold for everyone else as well. Clan societies discovered this natural law or natural rights theory through reasoning from experience.

These principles of political structure of centreless, segmental societies are:

1) *Balancing the use of power.* Segments of equal power oppose each other. This is the principle of "segmental opposition."

2) *Limiting the use of power to defence.* Helping someone victimize a third person would mean helping him to victimize one's own relative.

3) *Calling upon judges.* The balance and limitation of power is a strong incentive for settling quarrels peacefully by experts in mediation.

4) *Limiting the power of judges.* Judges have neither statutory law nor police power available to them, but only the power of their word to convince the quarrelling parties.

5) *Respecting property rights.* Judging can only solve quarrels by referring to the universal equality of rights. Because there can be no valid rights at all without property rights, this means agreeing to property rights as the foundation of justice.

These principles tend to emerge spontaneously in any community of people lacking a common command structure. The primordial order of human society is thus one without a central government. That does not mean, however, that such societies will remain forever peaceful. A society that sets up a standing army to defend itself against neighbouring clans will almost inevitably degrade into a command society. The reason is that such an army can use its powers in two ways: to defend its own community and also to attack and oppress it. If the soldiers of a standing army feel themselves closer to their commander than to their families, they will be tempted to choose his side when he sets out to become the ruler and oppressor of his community.

Somalis follow the principles of segmental opposition not only for settling intra-clan disputes, but for inter-clan disputes as well. They also encourage clan members to marry someone of a neighbouring clan. The men of a given clan can then ask their wives to convince their brothers of the need for a peaceful settlement of an inter-clan conflict.

Instead of a confederation, one might better describe the structure of Somali society as a network of constantly shifting political alliances between independent jilibs, sub-clans, and clans. Given the fact that all of these entities are founded on respect for natural law, one might call their society a near-kritarchy, a little used term that will be explained shortly.

No Rulership. Another principle of Somali politics, which also explains the absence of any standing military organisation, is that no one is conceded special powers over his fellow clansmen. This is doubly true in the case of anyone acting in a political or judicial role. Such a person is expected to be more law-abiding than Somalis who exercise no such functions.

It is thus a misnomer to call the Somali political system a democracy, as some writers have done, since, unlike a democracy, the Somali system establishes no political rulership. The political assemblies have neither the right to legislate nor the right to employ judges, policemen, soldiers, or other administrators to enforce the laws of their people. The assemblies do deliberate and make decisions, but never by voting, never by majority rule. A proposal will be discussed and modified until it is acceptable to everyone. In these discussions, each person has the right to voice his opinion. The final decision is never a mathematical computation of individual opinions but the result, rather, of well-argued discussion. The fact that participants tend to listen more carefully to successful herdsmen, farmers, or merchants than to those who eke out a meagre existence does not mean that "the rich" will always prevail over "the poor"; for as long as there are some who oppose a particular decision, it will not be taken. Those who remain opposed will not be asked to submit to or contribute to the project, and there is no power to stop a clansman from leaving his jilib and forming a new one. In fact, it continually happens that jilibs break up into several parts, each becoming an independent new jilib. All of this is radically different from democratic majority rule.

Africa's political history shows that African tribes are not incapable of conceiving and organising a political system like a monarchy or a democracy. At least half a dozen have established a monopoly of force and organised the lives of their subjects in the smallest detail. But none of these states survived. In the end they succumbed, after depleting the human and natural resources of their subjects. As elsewhere in the world, such dictatorships do not last.

Many Somali clans have stories about how, once upon a time, the elders gave their dignitaries legislative and executive powers, but how those powers were abused and shortly thereafter abolished. One such story is this:

> Once upon a time, the clan convened an assembly and decided to appoint a king. The king's first royal decree was to inform the clan that for breakfast, lunch, and supper he wanted only to eat the marrow of the bones of young goats. For each meal, he decreed that ten goats should be slaughtered for him. He believed this would secure his eternal youth and felt sure the clan would recognise that to be in its best interest. After feeding their king in this way for several days, the clansmen began to worry. It was not that they

feared their king would suffer indigestion. No—they feared because their herds were rapidly dwindling in size. So they convened another assembly and decided to collectively murder their king. And so they did, with the resolve never to appoint another.

Whether or not these stories represent history or legend is irrelevant. What matters is that all of the clans are fully conscious of the danger of a government becoming the nation's master instead of its servant. Their present political system reflects that concern. It is a political system without political rule—a *kritarchy*.

It was a long time before anyone coined a name for the type of political system that the Somalis practice. The term "kritarchy" was first used to describe the political system of the early Hebrews, who also lived without a central government. Their kritarchy came to an end when they adopted monarchy at the close of the second millennium BC, but it revived when they went into the Diaspora. What all kritarchies or near-kritarchies have in common is that their judges apply a customary law. Because customary law approximates natural law, the term denotes a political system that is in accord with natural law. Kritarchy is described in more detail in Appendix B.

Knowing their deeply engrained anti-statist attitude, one might wonder how it happened that in 1960 the Somalis were persuaded to accept the rule of a central government. The fact is that they were never given the opportunity to express an opinion. Politicians hand-picked by the colonial powers made the decision. For these politicians, the question was never *how* the nation should be governed, but *who* should govern it. It would have been an exercise in futility in any case to organise a referendum giving the population a choice between democracy and kritarchy. The reason is that the United Nations member-states habitually promise substantial funding to any group of politicians who give the appearance of being able to establish a democracy. Nor would the average Somali have believed, when democracy was introduced in 1960, that one of their indigenous politicians would ultimately establish a murderous dictatorship in their country. Now, forty years later and after bitter experience, most

Somalis seem to remember the collective political wisdom of their ancestors distilled in Lord Acton's dictum, "All power tends to corrupt, and absolute power corrupts absolutely."

POLITICS VERSUS LAW

The differences between Somali law and politics can be seen in the following box diagram:

	SHAPE	TASK	AUTHORITY
SOMALI LAW SYSTEM	Multitude/network of ad hoc institutions run by part-time officials	Limited to rendering justice i.e. protecting life, liberty and property as defined by customary law + social security	Over one's family/ jilib irrespective of territory
SOMALI POLITICAL SYSTEM	Multitude of ad hoc councils.	Limited to list in this chapter.	None except in time of war.

The law system and the political system of the Somalis are both based on the principle that the best way to prevent abuse of retaliatory force is to let it be exercised by a multitude of independent entities that can hold one another in check. The European path of monopolizing that force under the supervision of a popularly elected parliament has proved only to increase its abuse.

The genius of the Somalis was that they turned a legal and political system that suited them primarily for reasons of organisational and economic expediency into one that assured them protection of their individual freedom.

This came about when some Somali clans began to take up agricultural practices even while continuing to herd camels and other livestock. These clans became semi nomadic, beginning their trek after the harvest was in. They maintained the political structure of nomads, living in small groups and concluding temporary alliances when larger groups were needed to implement desired policies. Thus it made no difference whether Somalis were family-based or locally based. They maintained the same structure, relying only on part-time officials.

The underlying principle was that groups should remain small and without a chief. Large is more than unwieldy; it is unresponsive to individual preferences. Small, on the other hand, needs no governmental structure, no hierarchy. Small is beautiful and also practical.

Notes

11. Adapted from "Has the Nation Always been with Us? How Tribal Anarchy Works," a talk given at the Conference of the International Society For Individual Liberty, London, Ontario, Canada, July 2000.

Part II

Evaluation

Chapter 10
Strengths and Weaknesses
of the Law

The Somali customary law contains both strengths and weaknesses. Many of these have been noted one place or another in our discussion. This chapter will draw these together and briefly comment on each, followed by some general remarks. The next chapter will consider ways of remedying the weaknesses.

The strengths of the Somali law are that it

1. Is immune to political manipulation
2. Prevents political rule
3. Is close to natural law
4. Develops in harmony with the values commonly held in the nation
5. Is usually applied promptly
6. Is effective in preventing crime
7. Can be maintained at a very low cost, without taxation
8. Is highly respected by the Somalis
9. Has resisted many efforts to abolish it
10. Emphasises restitution or compensation rather than punishment
11. Interferes little with the market mechanism

The weaknesses are that it

1. Impairs individuals' capacity to save and invest money
2. Prohibits the sale of land to persons outside the clan
3. Inadequately protects the rights of women
4. Requires that victims share their compensation with their families
5. Fails to deal effectively with fraud
6. Neglects victims who do not invoke the law instantly
7. Forbids insult and defamation
8. Lacks extradition arrangements with foreign governments
9. Makes clansmen somewhat a prisoner of their clan
10. Offers little protection to individual foreigners
11. Lacks provision for compiling and publishing judicial verdicts

STRENGTHS
1. The law is Immune to Political Manipulation
The Somali law system is owned and controlled by—nobody. Every Somali is free to use it, whether as a provider or a seeker of justice, or as legal counsel, detective, witness, policeman, or insurer. No one has the power to establish the rules of this law system or to exclude anyone from it. Such freedom from manipulation by politicians and their pressure groups has enabled Somali law to reach a high level of sophistication.

This freedom from control is not a characteristic unique to the Somali legal system. We find it, for example, in some communications systems such as the Internet. Like Somali law, that system is owned and controlled by no one. Any supplier or seeker of information can make use of it. No person or organisation in particular sets the rules. Whoever comes up with the best rules gets the best customers. While the Internet was still owned by the United States government, few used it. But when the government relinquished control in 1983, millions began to use it, resulting in a tremendous upsurge in the economy.

Language is another communications system without an owner. Anyone is free to use it. No one in particular sets its rules. Anyone is free to coin new words, innovate grammar, and publish dictionaries.

For the prosperity and well being of any nation, its law system must not be allowed to fall into the hands of politicians, who are always tempted to replace true law by rules of their own making. Because a major objective of politicians is to generate easy revenue for themselves and the pressure groups they represent, the rules they make only pretend to protect the life, liberty, and property of the people.

2. The law Prevents Political Rule

Somalis clearly recognise the dangers of political power. Consequently, their customary law stipulates that

- There shall be no standing police force or army.
- Policemen shall not be paid a salary but shall work as volunteers.
- Policemen shall act only as instructed by judges.
- Judges shall not enjoy a monopoly.
- Laws shall not be made by some people and not others, but by the nation as a whole, through their gradual and voluntary acceptance as custom.
- Judges, politicians, and religious leaders shall suffer greater penalties than other people for committing a crime or a tort.
- Fines imposed on criminals shall be paid to the victims and their families, not to police or politicians.
- Every Somali shall be free to leave his judicial unit (jilib) to form his own or join another.

In every society lurks the danger of the police systematically misusing their force to extort money from the population. How this happens tends to follow a pattern. First, a group of police establish a monopoly, eliminating rival groups. Next they disarm the population, decreeing that people no longer have the right to defend themselves against aggression. The police will now exercise that right, and they must monopolise the use of force, they say, if they are to do a proper job. To provide money for the police, a parliament is created. To control the judges, the politicians monopolise the settlement of disputes, instructing the police to enforce only the judgments of courts they themselves set up. By this monopoly, they can influence the judges to apply a distorted view of natural rights. From then on, the politicians can make any laws, including tax laws, without having to fear that the judges will render them null and void.

An example of such a scenario is that surrounding the Universal Declaration of Human Rights. This document uses the language of natural rights to promote, under the name of "human rights," a wholly different concept. These so-called "rights" allow democratic parliaments to provide any "service" they want and to cover their costs by taxation. With such a huge mission and such unlimited powers, it does not take politicians long to bring a nation under their rule. Rather than rendering services and covering their cost through taxation, they use those services as a pretext for levying taxes. Ultimately, they levy any amount of taxes, collect any variety of fees, and create any number of privileges. Indeed, the United Nations concept of human rights is extremely useful to democratic politicians bent on generating revenue for themselves and the pressure groups who help them stay in power.

The temptation to misuse their power is something that all policemen and all politicians in the world have in common. Civilised nations have laws, therefore, that keep such people from establishing monopoly positions. The Somali nation is one such civilised nation. Its laws further stipulate that only the customary judges can decide what constitutes a crime; defining crimes is too sensitive a matter to leave to policemen or politicians. Also, Somali law holds that compensation shall be limited to the value of that which has been destroyed, and that fines must be paid to the victim rather than to the authorities. Last but not least, Somali law separates law from politics and denies politicians any power to enforce their decisions. The practical result of these customary laws is that traditional Somali politicians are not of a predatory type. There is no monetary gain in traditional Somali politics. The only opportunity it offers people is an opportunity to show their wisdom.

The question whether or not policemen should enjoy a

monopoly was known to the ancient Romans, who asked themselves: *Quis custodiet ipsos custodes?* (Who would police these policemen?) The correct answer is, of course, "other policemen;" for when policemen are denied a monopoly, there will be independent police. No policeman will dare misuse his weapons, for if he does, his company will lose both customers and money. It will lose customers to other police forces and money to its victims, who will find law courts willing and able to condemn such misuse and award them compensation and fines accordingly.

3. Somali Customary Law is Close to Natural Law
Somali laws are largely compatible with natural rights and obligations, the rules of conduct inherent in human nature. Only within the last few decades, after a long period of neglect by Western lawyers, have the origin, nature, function, and contents of these rights begun to be properly defined. The close resemblance of the Somali customary law to natural rights and obligations is a strength, since natural rights are based on facts of nature. As such they are objective, to be discovered, whereas statutory laws are contrived, subjective, and self-serving. Natural rights are particularly attractive to people who may have nothing more in common than their wish to live in the same country.

Unfortunately, Somali law deviates on certain points from the concept of natural rights. These deviations are the main reason why Somali women are subordinated to men and most Somalis are very poor. I will elaborate on this in the second part of this chapter.

4. The Law Develops with the People
Somali law has a built-in procedure for its own development. This procedure grows out of the judges' obligation to apply only rules that are actually being followed in practice by the people of their community. This ensures that the law will always be in harmony with values generally held by the community. Another factor aiding the continual growth of Somali law is that its judges are always exposed to competition. No sooner does a judge show signs of poor judgment than he is by-passed

by his clientele. Family members appoint others to be their judge, leave the family and join another, or start their own judiciary unit.

5. The Law Enables Prompt Rendering of Justice

Violent conflicts tend to be settled on the day they occur or the day the lawbreaker is arrested. The judges achieve speedy justice without sacrificing judicial procedure. They hear both parties as well as their witnesses and follow any other procedures required for rendering a valid judgment. This truly remarkable feature of Somali law comes about for the following reasons:

■ The victim and his family retain their right to enforce the law themselves, bypassing the courts of law if these are slow in assuming jurisdiction or rendering a verdict.

■ In the case of murder, the law stipulates that if the murderer is not apprehended quickly, the family of the victim is free to kill someone of equal stature in the murderer's family. Consequently, murderers are usually arrested by their own family.

■ Every Somali is obliged to retain a judge on a permanent basis, so that courts of law are always immediately available.

■ The courts, formed by judges retained by the litigants, usually agree quickly on a verdict because their failure to do so would oblige them to call in a third judge from a neighbouring family and accept his opinion as decisive— something considered shameful.

The atmosphere that reigns in a village where a crime has been committed is well worth describing. The victim or his nearest family loudly cries, "*gar iyo gardiye*" (literally "law," "judicial procedure"). It is a demand for justice to be done. That instantly mobilises the entire family of the victim. All the brothers, cousins, and uncles of the victim take up arms, search for the criminal, and think how they will enforce justice themselves if the criminal is not found. Likewise the family of the criminal take up their arms, search for their cousin who committed the crime, and think how to defend themselves against an attack from the victim's family. During the hours following, the suspense is almost unbearable. Everyone hopes that the judges will assume jurisdiction in time, even while preparing for the unhoped-for event that they will be too late.

Somali law is maintained not only by prompt litigation but also by the fact that the family of the perpetrator generally accepts the verdict of the court. Rarely do they appeal. Once the verdict has been accepted, the family of the victim can be at ease, because the perpetrator's family guarantee restitution, compensation, and payment of fines. Included under this guarantee are the misdeeds of impoverished clansmen, fools, and children. Thus, victims will always be compensated, even when the criminal flees his country.

The conflicting parties need not always convene a court of law to settle their differences. The rules on restitution, compensation, and fines are so clear and detailed that the parties can usually settle between themselves if they wish. When two parties agree not to involve their judges but to settle their own dispute, it is called *xeer jajab*.

6. The Law is Effective at Crime Prevention
Because every Somali must permanently retain a judge, judges always know their clients and are aware at an early stage if a conflict is shaping up. That gives them an opportunity to prevent a threatening conflict from becoming violent. Also, because they know their client, they often have opportunities to reconcile the conflicting parties after the law has been applied, thus reducing the likelihood of repetition or revenge.

7. The Law is Maintained at a Low Cost
The law is adjudicated by part-time judges who charge relatively small fees for their services, since they mainly earn their livelihood from a second occupation such as herdsman or merchant. Occasionally judges receive gifts from their clients. The same is true of policemen. This obviates the need for taxation and the consequent injustice and destruction of wealth associated with Western-style governments.

8. The Law Enjoys Great Respect

The Somalis see their law as part of their personal identity. As one Somali put it, "This law enables me to go through life as a civilised man." That hits the nail on the head; for the main reason why people need law is to subdue their primitive impulses for violence and vengeance. At about the age of seven, every Somali child is educated in the law. He learns by heart the different ways he can do wrong, the compensation each wrong requires, the name of his judge, and the members of his family who will have to pay compensation if he breaks the law. Throughout his life, a Somali is reminded of these teachings by proverbs and dictums that encourage respect for the law.

No single factor can explain the high regard Somalis have for their laws. Probably every Somali is aware of one or more of the many strengths of the law system and intuitively senses how well their laws have served them so far. Indeed, the Somali nation has become one of Africa's largest ethnic groups in part because its law does not attempt to regulate production or consumption, and in part because it enables neighbouring and conquered peoples to join them.

9. The Law is Resistant to Foreign Influences

When the colonial powers occupied Somalia, they declared Somali law inapplicable in their relations with Somalis and attempted to turn the clan elders into malleable servants of the colonial government. In 1960, they created the Republic of Somalia with a constitution that had no place for the customary laws and institutions. Following the collapse of the Republic in 1991, its former politicians and soldiers (now called Warlords and *Moriyaan*) tried to resurrect Western style government. The United Nations joined them in December of the following year, bringing in a vast military and political programme to establish democracy in Somalia. Concurrently, a group of religious leaders formed the Al-Ittihad, an organisation aimed at establishing a theocratic government based on Koranic law. Despite these four major efforts to abolish their customary laws and institutions, Somalis continue to honour their indigenous law and resist attempts to replace it with an alien one.

10. The Law Requires Compensation Rather than Punishment

Somali law is more concerned with the damage lawbreakers may have caused than with their re-education. Consequently, it focuses on restitution and compensation and does not call for imprisonment or the imposition of large fines. It does not seek to humiliate and punish criminals but leaves that to their families. This shows great wisdom. Jailing people and imposing heavy fines does nothing to negate the original violence but, on the contrary, adds to the total violence committed in the world. Moreover, punishment rarely deters crime; if it did, the world would be free of crime today. Worse still, prisons are schools where people can improve their criminal skills. Finally, building and operating prisons entails heavy costs which, when funded by taxes, brings about further violations of property rights. Indeed, imposing huge fines and imprisoning criminals may serve only to satisfy cravings for revenge, fill the public treasury, provide jobs for prison guards, and impress subjects with the power of the state.

11. The Law Interferes Little with the Free-Market Process

Under Somali law, a person is free to engage in any peaceful activity of his choice. None need apply for a licence or a permit to follow the profession of judge, policeman, soldier, herdsman, farmer, hunter, trader, doctor, dentist, veterinarian, accountant, lawyer, banker, insurer, pilot, sailor, fisherman, teacher, tailor, hairdresser, smith, etc. Nor do Somalis need a licence or permit to construct a house, mine gemstones, drill for petroleum, leave their country, employ foreigners, operate a telephone or aviation company, or establish any other type of business. Indeed, the customary law generally champions free trade. The few exceptions, such as trade in land and individual capital accumulation, will be considered below.

WEAKNESSES

1. The Law Impairs Saving and Investing by Individuals

Under Somali law, individuals as such are not really free to save money or to invest any savings they might have managed to keep despite the law. As soon as they have concluded a profitable deal, Somalis are expected to share their profit with their extended family. From what is left, family members in financial need will claim an additional share. If there is still money left after that, community projects such as the construction of a mosque or a school will claim a share. If after that there is still something left and its owner wants to lend it to someone, he is not permitted to charge interest. If the borrower is unable to repay the loan, the lender is expected to forego repayment. The rationale is that what he lent was "superfluous money." Usually, social pressure will be enough to dispossess someone of his money. People fear being called a *Hiblis*. But if that fails, sometimes parasites in the family will go to court over his refusal to honour their requests and will manage to get something.[12]

2. The Law Forbids Selling Land to Outsiders

There are two ways of maximizing the utility of one's land. One is to use it directly oneself. The other is to rent or sell it to someone who values it more highly. But most clans prohibit rental or sale to non-clan members, the reason being that outsiders may refuse to help the clan in times of natural or man-made calamity. For instance, a clansman who enjoys a bumper crop customarily donates part of his harvest to families of his clan who experienced less favourable climatic conditions. Will the outsider take part in this act of solidarity? Will he participate in joint ploughing campaigns (*guus*)? Will he fight with the clan or against it in time of war?

3. The Law Inadequately Protects Women's Rights

Somali customary law fails to forbid several types of violations of the rights of Somali women. At age seven, a girl's genitals may be mutilated. From 14 years onward, a Somali woman risks being married against her will. Her parents may force a husband on her, or a husband may force himself on her by abducting or violating her. When a husband has had enough of her, a woman must either occupy a separate habitat next to his and live on the meagre proceeds of some livestock, or she must return to her own family. Leaving one's husband is considered shameful, even when he takes on a new wife. In any event, a woman who decides to leave her husband will not be permitted to take her children with her. These "belong" to their father's clan, as the Somalis say.

When a woman marries, she loses her right to inherit from her parents, for on that day she stops being a member of the extended family into which she was born. Rare is the Somali woman who does not marry; being a spinster is considered shameful. The married couple almost always resides among the members of the husband's clan. If she divorces, however, the law stipulates that she must inherit equally with her brothers, except for her father's land and camels. These go to his sons only. If a woman is murdered, her family receives half the compensation it would have received had she been a man.

In many other respects, however, the rights of women are well protected. A husband who beats his wife, for example, must pay compensation. If a woman is mutilated in her face, the compensation is higher than for similar mutilations on a man's face and may even be as high as the blood price. And if someone smashes a woman's hook tooth, the compensation is twice as much as that for the hook tooth of a man.

These rules may suggest that the status of women under the law is clear. In reality, it is not. Judges of customary law courts, religious courts, and members of political assemblies are always men, which helps to explain why women are often deprived of their rights.

4. The Law Misdirects Compensation

When someone's rights have been violated and the violator is condemned to pay compensation and possibly also a fine, the payment must be distributed among all the members of the victim's extended family, or jilib. The law stipulates this for the obvious reason that it is an effective way to constitute a group of guarantors for each individual. Members of the group then have not only the occasional bad luck of having to give a camel, but also the occasional good luck of receiving one. Yet this rule violates the victim's right to personal redress, which is a natural right. Sometimes, not even the family receives compensation. That happens through social pressure when the clan's elders ask the family to pass up its demand for redress from a neighbouring clan in order to maintain good relations with that clan.

5. The Courts are Slow to Condemn Fraud

If someone tricks another out of his money, it is virtually impossible to obtain compensation. The court will likely rule that the money that was given was surplus money anyhow and that the victim should have been less credulous and more careful.

6. The Law Offers No Remedy when a Request for Justice is Delayed

Unless the victim seeks instant redress, judges hesitate to assume jurisdiction to settle a conflict.

7. The Law Holds that Insults Can be Unlawful

Under Somali law, compensation must be paid if someone insults or spreads false information about another or utters blasphemies. Under natural law, such a condemnation would surely infringe upon the culprit's right of free speech. The prohibition is somewhat mitigated by the fact that frequently the condemnation is only provisional; compensation only becomes due if the offender repeats his insult after the verdict has been rendered. Under natural law, every person who is the victim of insults or badmouthing has the right to provide the correct information about himself to the people who were misinformed. If he does so, the culprit will have paid dearly for his little pleasure, for he will no longer be taken seriously by anyone who heard of his verbal exploits. The prohibition against insulting a person, against spreading false information, and against uttering blasphemies raises the question of how to define these criminalised acts. There is no objective and verifiable standard. What is prohibited one year may be permitted the next. The reason the Law prohibits only *physical* aggression is because there are objective and verifiable standards for establishing such aggression.

8. The Law Does Not Provide for Extradition

No Somali clan has yet established a treaty with a foreign government relative to the extradition of criminals who have escaped Somali law by fleeing abroad. The Republic of Somaliland established such a treaty with the Republic of

Ethiopia a few years ago. It was applied once, when Somaliland extradited two men of the Ogaden clan to Ethiopia. The Ogaden still have not forgiven Somaliland this "treason" to the concept of *Soomalinimo*.

9. The Law Makes Clansmen Somewhat a Prisoner of Their Clan

The requirement that every person must retain a judge and be insured against future liabilities under the law can be an excellent way to create a law-abiding nation. Unfortunately, the Somalis customarily retain their judge and obtain insurance only within their own extended family. The family takes advantage of this by extracting all sorts of benefits from its more successful members. That custom prevents entrepreneurs from saving money and letting it grow. This makes them more or less a prisoner of their extended family. Another negative aspect of the extended family is that, in order to bring about or preserve internal cohesion, it may foment animosity against other families.

10. The Law Offers Little or No Protection for Foreigners

Under Somali law, foreigners are treated as outlaws unless they place themselves under the protection of a particular clansman and his jilib. For many foreigners, this is unacceptable. They expect the Somalis to look upon them as independent persons under the law. Hence the reluctance of foreigners to visit or do business in Somalia.

11. There is no Documentation Centre for Jurisprudence

As yet no organisation collects all major verdicts rendered under Somali law and makes them accessible to those who seek or dispense justice in Somalia. If such an organisation existed, the integration of all clan law into a single body of common law would proceed far more rapidly. Merger of the dozens of clan law systems would much enhance the possibilities for conducting business on a nationwide scale.

COMMENTS ON THE STRENGTHS AND WEAKNESSES OF SOMALI LAW

The strengths of the Somali law system enumerated above are the main reason for the Somalis being such an outspoken and proud people and, on the whole, law-abiding. Indeed, the Somali law system stands up well against the legal systems of other countries. People in other countries often do not realise the extent to which their laws attack human dignity and foster crime. It may be well, therefore, to briefly review those two weaknesses of most foreign legal systems.

Human dignity comes under attack whenever and wherever government violates natural rights with impunity. A typical government practise is to require permits to engage in activities that, according to natural law, every person should be free to engage in. By enforcing licensing laws, and especially when it does so selectively, government restricts people in the exercise of their natural rights, thereby degrading them to the level of slaves and animals—of beings lacking capacity for rational thought. Worse, it renders everyone in its territory subservient to its officials.

Crime is promoted every time a government establishes a monopoly, levies a tax, awards a subsidy, conscripts a soldier, or regulates production and consumption. People who refuse to comply with such laws are considered to have committed a "crime against the state." The government then is so busy prosecuting those who fail to comply that it has no time, money, or inclination left for prosecuting victims of common crimes such as murder, rape, and robbery. When it does, however, catch some murderers, rapists and robbers, it locks them up together so that they can learn from one another how to avoid getting caught the next time.

Another way in which the law systems of other countries promote crime is in not requiring, except in special cases such as driving a car, that anyone be insured against liabilities that might arise under the law. Consequently many people have nothing to lose by engaging in murder, rape, or robbery beyond the possibility of spending some jail time. These people would hesitate longer before engaging in such crimes under a law system that required full insurance coverage because, if caught violating someone's rights, they would face a hefty increase in their insurance premium. Another factor contributing to criminality is that most laws made by governments severely increase the cost of doing business. Government regulation of production and consumption so drastically increases the costs of production that it becomes difficult for many people to make their living in the market and they turn instead to crime.

But to return to the Somali system, the combination of laws affronting the dignity of women and impeding economic activity explain much of the nation's slow economic growth. Economic development hinges on the free interplay between technicians, investors, and entrepreneurs. Significant economic progress cannot be expected where individuals are not free to engage in any economic activity they want, to seek rewards for their services, and to save and invest their wealth. Until the Somalis can square their customary laws with these requirements for economic progress, the nation will be sorely hampered in its economic growth despite the dramatic strides made possible by the virtual absence of governmental restraints over the past fourteen years. Finding solutions for these stumbling blocks in Somali law will be the subject of the next chapter.

Note

12. Yet this does not altogether hobble enterprise. Ayittey (1991:30) observes, "It is true that [in most tribal systems] the rich were harassed by a large contingent of kinsmen. But they were also at liberty to manufacture as many excuses as they could. Most Africans today know of tight-fisted rich relatives." —Editor SM

Chapter 11
Directions for Growth
in the Law

The time has now come to explore ways in which some of the more important weaknesses of the customary law summarised in the previous chapter might be overcome through the continued growth and development of the law.[13]

The chief areas of opportunity for progress in the law are to

- Remove restrictions on the sale of land
- Offer choice in insurance
- Widen the possibilities for saving and investing
- More adequately protect the rights of women
- Facilitate cooperation with foreigners
- Establish a documentation centre for jurisprudence
- Facilitate cooperation between independent police

Progress in each of these areas would result in the customary law coming into closer harmony with the natural law. Before addressing each area, however, I want to offer some thoughts about timeliness, process, and possibilities for change in the Somali cultural context. There has never been a better time for strengthening the Somali customary law than now. This is because (1) there is no central government in Somalia and no national statutory law, (2) the population abhors the idea of re-establishing a central government, (3) many customary judges have done an admirable job of maintaining law and order during the past 14 years, and (4) public discussion of the traditional structure of Somali society is beginning to open up.

Until recently, there was no nationwide discussion of the customary law. Topics prevailing in the Somali mass media were steadfastly related to politics. Prior to 1991, politicians and intellectuals worried about the central government's powers and revenue, whereas after 1991 they discussed what kind of central government they should establish—whether unitary, federal, or confederal. The major bone of contention was always the number of seats in the envisioned parliament that should be allotted each clan. Only in 1998, after the Cairo Accords had fallen apart, did public discussion begin occasionally to address the traditional structure of the Somali nation. This trend towards traditionalism has continued despite the adoption, at a two-year-long conference that opened in 2002 in Kenya, of yet another resolution to form a central government.

Indeed, now is a golden opportunity to strengthen the customary law of the Somalis. But how shall this come about?

Under normal circumstances, customary law changes slowly. This is particularly true in Somalia, where the population is made up of many sovereign clans. Because the smallest change seems to require almost endless discussion at the village level, it can take a long while for a family or a village to adopt a new custom and for its judges to acknowledge it and declare it law. Then other families and villages adopt the custom, and it comes to be acknowledged by their judges. Gradually, the new custom spreads through the entire clan and becomes clan law. Then it begins spreading to other clans until all of them have adopted it and acknowledge it to be law.

But under exceptional circumstances, this procedure can happen much more quickly. This was shown when the Republic of Somalia disintegrated and large numbers of heavily armed soldiers turned to banditry. Very quickly, the population demanded of their judges that they increase the severity of the sanctions for murder. This successfully reduced the incidence of murder in many areas.

Today an exceptional circumstance is the fact that about a million Somalis are residing abroad. Most of these people emigrated because of the war with Ethiopia or because of the civil war that started shortly afterwards and, in some parts of Somalia, still goes on.

The greater part of them went to the Arab Peninsula, Europe, and North America. Many regularly send money to their family back home. Through this ongoing contact with their village of origin, they have spread knowledge of the new ways of life they have discovered abroad.

Besides these refugees, other Somalis have left their country because they found the customs in their home village suffocating. These emigrated to Ethiopia, Kenya, and Djibouti and beyond, some to adopt a different religion or to marry someone of another ethnicity, while others simply sought an education or a job that was not available in their clan's territory. All of these expatriate Somalis are sending powerful messages to their kin to tolerate different lifestyles and to make their laws more congenial for conducting business.

Somalia is no longer the closed society it was fifty years ago. There are many signs of change. Through newly acquired radios, televisions, telephones, and computers, Somalis are following world events on a daily basis. A continuous flow of new products and services from distant countries reach their markets. This hustle bustle in the market place calls for new customs and, eventually, new customary law. It is a natural avenue for growth in the law. How best can this be facilitated?

FREEPORTS

What is the most promising path for economic development in Somalia? No less astute an economist than Peter F. Drucker has stated that, "To create wealth, jobs and incomes in desperately poor countries, the freeport is the only program that works." Prime examples are Singapore, Hong Kong, Taiwan, Korea, Dubai, Mauritius, Puerto Rico, Northern Mexico, Ireland, and Curaçao. Freeports in these countries have attracted hundreds and even thousands of foreign industries.

Developing countries tend to become prosperous sooner if they can attract foreign enterprise. The most successful formula for this has been "production sharing," or cooperation between the labour force of a developing country and a well-established foreign manufacturer who has a worldwide market for its product. Manufacturers look for such cooperative arrangements in order to reduce production costs. The cooperation usually starts by the manufacturer moving one of his many factories to a low-cost country. If it is successful, more factories follow.

The World Trade Organisation (WTO) recently analysed production sharing in eight developing countries— Bangladesh, China, the Dominican Republic, El Salvador, Mexico, Morocco, the Philippines, and Tunisia. In five of these countries, exports grew three times faster than the world average. In four of them, production-sharing companies accounted for half of all exports.

A manufacturer seeking opportunities for production sharing must carefully analyse the customs, laws, and political risks of a developing country before investing money there. The easiest way to become familiar with all of these is to locate in a freeport, where laws and regulations are usually reduced to a minimum. Nineteen African countries have established freeports: Angola, Benin, Burundi, Djibouti, Egypt, Cote d'Ivoire, Kenya, Liberia, Libya, Madagascar, Madeira, Mauritius, Morocco, Mozambique, Nigeria, Senegal, Tanzania, Togo, and Zimbabwe.

Freeports come in many forms, but they all have in common that they are places not fully subject to the economic regulations of the host country. The goal of a freeport is to create a business environment that will prove equally attractive to foreign employers and to the local people whom those firms will hire. The special legal status of a freeport protects the firms from arbitrary behaviour by agencies of the host government. Richard Bolin, director of the World Economic Processing Zones Association (WEPZA), writes that freeports (he calls them "processing zones")

> form a buffer between the fiscal and regulatory drive of the sprawling bureaucracies on the one hand and the foreign business companies inside these processing zones on the other. Processing zones are a proven method to ease the pain of bureaucratic procedures and delays inflicted on manufacturers trying, in unfamiliar environments, to produce for the global market. Their success is usually a function of the degree of autonomy they enjoy.

While governments operate most freeports around the world, experience in Mexico shows that privately owned freeports provide by far the best service. Private investors put infrastructure in place and construct offices, factory buildings, and residences in advance of demand. Then they offer prospective tenant firms quality services—property maintenance, banking, financial, and legal services, insurance, telecommunications, transport to world markets, and managerial and technical training, to name a few. Freeports create jobs and train local people to fill those jobs. They earn substantial amounts of foreign currency and stimulate a wealth of technology transfers. Moreover, their operations tend to be stable. For Somalia, with its largely pastoral economy, an added virtue of the freeports is that they would concentrate economic development within defined areas, minimizing scattered development that might intrude upon or disrupt grazing lands.

Some small island-countries have adopted a laissez-faire policy over their entire territory. Examples are Anguilla, The Bahamas, British Virgin Islands, Cayman Islands, Turks and Caicos Islands, Isle of Man, and Macao. A few small European countries such as Monaco, Andorra, and Liechtenstein have done the same. What these prosperous mini-countries have in common is a near total absence of taxation and burdensome government regulation.

The freeport idea is as old as western civilisation. There is nothing new about it. The Romans established such a port on the Greek island of Delos during the second century BC, drawing traders from all over the ancient world who came there to do business without risk to life, liberty, or property. This made Delos, until its destruction by Pontic invaders in 88 BC, the most prosperous island in the Mediterranean seas.

Form a New Clan. We have seen how, in many respects, the traditional Somali system of law and politics brings about a business environment like that of a freeport. The exceptions, however, pose a significant problem, discouraging foreign investment and slowing economic development. Many Somalis think their country's main weakness is a lack of infrastructure. But freeports could and would supply that structure. What discourages foreign investors is what might be called the Somali *superstructure*, in particular what they perceive as defects in the Somali system of politics and law. A freeport could help solve this by designing within its perimeter not only suitable infrastructure, but a superstructure that would prove attractive to foreign investors.

A question immediately arises, however. The concept of a central government is familiar to investors and developers. Warranted or not, they are accustomed to look to a central government to guarantee security of tenure and to give some assurance of law and order. How could investors be attracted to commit resources for development in a purely customary-law setting? How could a freeport operate compatibly with traditional Somali law and politics?

I had no answer for this question when I raised it in a gathering of Somalis at which a number of elders were present. We were discussing the need for rapid change in a number of laws pertaining to the business environment. One of the elders sitting at the gathering suggested a specific procedure: "Gather with your business friends," he said in effect, "and form a new clan on Somali territory. It should be a clan embodying all of the strengths and none of the weaknesses you have detected in our clans. Be certain that its laws are compatible with our own law system so that we can settle any conflicts that might arise between the new and the existing clans. If the new clan prospers, the existing clans will not lose a moment in adopting its superior business environment as their own custom." Those present at the gathering discussed the proposition at length, and none found anything wrong with it. My friends even suggested a name for the new clan—"Soomaali 'Ad," which translates "the White Somalis."[14]

Here two distinct concepts merged—the foreign concept of a freeport and the Somali concept of creating a new clan. A freeport could be cast in a form resembling a Somali clan, or the new clan in a form resembling a freeport. It would come to the same thing.

Such a new clan could function in all respects as a freeport in the world's markets. It is easy to see how its business environment might quickly spread to the existing clans. The new clan at first would consist mainly of foreign entrepreneurs in need of local employees. Once employed, many Somalis would gain first hand knowledge of this new business environment. They in turn would prompt Somali entrepreneurs to move to the territory of the new clan, where they would be most welcome to start their own business. Such an exodus of productive Somalis to the new clan would induce the existing clans to quickly remedy the weaknesses in their own customary laws. Such remedy would be their only means of stopping the brain drain that would otherwise take place.

The chances of success for this kind of rapid improvement in the customary law would depend on a number of things. Would enough foreign businessmen be willing to come together to form such a new clan in Somalia? Would they find a clan willing to host them on its territory? Would the host clan respect its commitments to the new clan? Would Somali entrepreneurs come to settle among the foreigners? Would the traditional clans adopt the new business environment?

Compatible with Somali Law and Politics. A freeport committed to principles of natural law would meet both the needs of foreign entrepreneurs and the requirements of traditional Somali law and politics. A proposed legal structure that would seem to satisfy both sets of requirements is presented in Appendix C. It stipulates, among other things, that every resident and visitor must be either self-insured or insured with a commercial insurance company against liabilities he or she might incur under either freeport law or the law of the Somali host clan. It would thus provide a means of settling disputes that arose between members of the freeport and members of the host clan.

The land tenure of the freeport would fundamentally resemble customary Somali land law in following a land-lease policy rather than subdivision. Land leasing is commonly used for commercial, residential, and industrial estates in English speaking parts of the world and is the functional counterpart in a market economy of indigenous land tenures, where a reversionary interest remains with the clan.

The freeport's management structure, however, would differ from the clan model. Somali clan policy is decided by the members collectively. Formulation and implementation of freeport policy, on the other hand, would be the responsibility of the owners and operators of the freeport. Only in that way can a freeport be made attractive to foreign entrepreneurs. In its daily operation, however, the manager's role would greatly resemble that of the head of an extended Somali family. He would act as a peacemaker, leader, or facilitator as the occasion required, but never as a ruler. His role would be like that of the manager of a shopping mall in the United States (MacCallum 1971).

Because the members of a freeport so constituted, although not kinsmen, would be related in a network of contracts, they could function in all respects as a clan under Somali law. Day visitors, as opposed to those who contracted for space as renters or lessees, could become members for a day upon agreeing to observe the rules of the freeport during their stay, or they might occupy the status of a *marti*, or guest, the owner of the freeport being their *abbaan*.

Once the first freeport-clan was fully operational and seen to be successful, other clans might want to replicate it in their territory. Nothing promotes a healthy freeport like competition. Neighbouring clans would be free to adopt aspects of the business environment of the freeport-clan, developing variations on the theme to suit their local circumstances. Ultimately, all of Somalia might come to enjoy a business climate ideally suited to production sharing or other cooperation with foreign business enterprises.

Besides bringing about a prodigious boost to the local economy, freeports would give Somalia a ready bridge to the cultural and economic life of the world. The bridge, moreover, would carry traffic in both directions. Of the more than a million Somalis living abroad, many are reluctant to return to Somalia because of poor employment opportunities there. Freeports would offer these Somalis attractive job and investment possibilities.

Besides Somalia's thin employment opportunities, another reason for the reluctance of many to return home is a fear of getting caught up in clan politics, as well as the limitations that would be imposed on their lifestyle. Such fears would be groundless in freeports. First, freeports would be apolitical. Second, since those living and working there would be fully insured by commercial firms, it would be optional whether they wanted to keep, in addition, their membership in a jilib. Third, they would be drawn from virtually every Somali clan, and many would have had extensive experience living and working abroad. Under such conditions, an individual Somali's clan affiliation, while retaining its social and cultural advantages, would have no necessary political or legal consequence.

Objections. Some foreign commentators entertain doubts about the ability of Africans to cooperate with Europeans, given their different attitude towards law. They point out that for more than two millennia Europeans have been immersed in Western, abstract thought. By contrast, they say, Africans live in an oral society committed to tribalism, mysticism, and a concept of undifferentiated time.

Having lived among the Somalis in the Horn of Africa, I am well aware that most tend to be very much set in their lifestyle, a style that happens to be circumscribed by many customs. But I have also noticed their skill in adapting to change. This adaptability may well be rooted in their nomadic lifestyle. Wherever they go with their herds, Somalis tend to get along with the local inhabitants, which implies respect for the local culture. An estimated one million Somalis presently live abroad, and most have perfectly adapted to the new lifestyle. Many foreign business enterprises and universities employ Somalis.

A recent incident illustrates how well Somalis adapt to a new environment. At the Seattle-Tacoma airport, a supervisor in the personnel department told me that he prefers Somalis to any other ethnic group. "These fellows," he said, "are a cohesive lot. When one makes a mistake, the others correct it. When one is ill, the others fill in for him. They settle all of their problems themselves. A colleague of mine at another airport," he continued, "recently asked me to send him a team of 50 Somalis to be employed as security people, luggage handlers, administrators, cleaners, and what not."

What struck me most about Somalis abroad is that they immediately team up in the area where they find themselves living, irrespective of clan affiliation. They form, as it were, a new clan. But in large cities like London and Toronto, where there are many Somalis, they split up again along clan lines.

I have also met Somalis who resumed life among their kin in Somalia after living abroad. These generally pursue a lifestyle somewhat different from that of the "regular" Somalis. Obviously Somalis are capable of change when placed in an environment different from that of the village in which they grew up, but even those who never left the territory of their clan are accustomed to having foreigners around. For centuries, Arab and Indian traders and shopkeepers lived among them. They were able to peacefully co-exist with the Somalis because of the Somali custom that a foreigner must associate with a particular jilib under the patronage of a clansman. His patron guarantees his guest's safety and pays compensation to any victim should the guest violate the law.

Another objection sometimes raised against the freeport approach is that Somalia is not ripe for manufacturing and would do better to concentrate on improving its livestock operations, in which it has a great advantage. Fifty years of experience with production sharing tells a different story, however. Those agricultural countries that passed up the opportunity to "go industrial" have made minimal progress, whereas countries that took that opportunity have achieved a higher level of prosperity than those that chose any other path of economic development. Moreover, that higher level was reached much faster than were those lower levels. Even the critic who remains unimpressed by the well-documented experience of freeports may learn something—for the chief activity of two freeports in Jordan is cattle fattening.

On the Somali side, some might be tempted to call freeports of any description a new form of neo-colonialism. They would find it difficult, however, to substantiate such a charge. The freeport as envisioned would be altogether apolitical, and its management structure would have nothing in common with that of the former colonies. Nor would its managers have the backing of any government. Moreover, the freeport-clan's written constitution, consisting of all of the leases in effect at any given time, would give its managers only such *contractual* authority as might be required for the conduct of business. It would confer no power whatsoever to levy taxes or enforce any regulation that had not been mutually agreed to.

Many Somalis have bitter recollections of the colonial period, and these are sometimes rekindled upon meeting a foreigner. Colonialism was a vicious formula for "cooperating" with the Europeans, and its after-effects have been disastrous. Many hundreds of thousands of Somalis died in the turmoil caused by the governmental organisation the colonial powers left behind. Somalia has not been alone in this. Similar events have taken place in virtually every African nation. The leftovers from the colonial period have been like landmines buried in the political landscape of these countries. They are the main cause of the present insecurity in most of Africa. Somalia is the only country where the population has cast off the imposed colonial superstructure. Now it remains for Somalia to create a viable business environment. For this, Somalis will need foreign business people to assist in the development and management of freeports. Aside from being foreigners, these people will have nothing in common with the former colonisers. The true neo-colonialists today are the political activists who seek to establish a federal democracy in Somalia. Regardless of intentions, it is the advocate of democracy who is trying to divide Somalis once more into two classes, rulers and subjects—those who rule and those who are ruled.

At this point, I should address a commonly asked question. Is there not a more direct way to adapt Somali customary law to the needs of a global market economy? Could not a nationwide parliament directly legislate law to bring about the desired reforms? The problem is that, in clan societies even more than elsewhere, such parliaments are inclined to look to their own interests rather than those of the population at large. Political representatives, once elected, tend to forget the constituency they are supposed to represent. The African continent is rife with examples. Better to trust the spontaneous forces of Somali society. Left unfettered, the people themselves will bring about change in the law as more desired practices attain the status of popular custom.

All things considered, it seems likely that conditions are favourable for rapid growth in the customary law, and that one of the ways this might be expedited would be through the formation of a new clan that, in the beginning, would largely consist of foreign businesses and business people. It remains to be seen how such a new clan could be structured to be congenial to Somali traditional law and politics and also create a business environment that would attract professional and business people in adequate numbers from other parts of the world.

SPECIFIC CHANGES IN THE LAW
Having looked in some detail at one way in which the spontaneous growth of the customary law might be accelerated through economic

development, let us consider what specific changes in that law might be most desirable for creating a better business environment.

Sale of Land

Land will find its highest and best use when its owners are completely free not only to use it themselves, directly, but also to make any disposition of it through sale, rent, or other means. In many countries, this has only become possible with expanded recognition and practice of the concept of individual property. Individual property is the right to acquire, use, and dispose of something as one likes as long as one respects the equal property rights of others. When a person is publicly acknowledged to have such a right, that person is an owner. That is why important transfers of property in oral societies were always carried out publicly, in the presence of many witnesses, and today are posted as matters of public record. Only someone publicly acknowledged as an owner can make a contract, since only such a person can convey "quiet title"—a title none will contest. Indeed, by accepting title, a buyer implies respect for the title of every other owner. To participate in such arrangements is a natural right of all men. That is to say, it is part of the natural law, the natural order, the rationale of human social organisation.

As a practical matter, therefore, property is anything that can become the subject matter of contract. Land surely falls in this category. According to Somali customary law, however, land cannot be bought or inherited by any but clan members. Because this is an obstacle to maximising land use in an emerging market economy, landowners and the market in general are poorer than they would be without that restriction. A parallel can be noted in the rules of entail and primogeniture in Europe. When those restrictive rules surviving from an earlier time were abandoned in the early nineteenth century, the resulting freedom to buy and sell land was a major impetus to the production of wealth accompanying the industrial revolution.

The Somali restriction on the transfer of land is motivated by concern that outsiders may not respect the needs of the clan. This is a challenge not just for Somali clans but for any community: how to devise adequate and continuing means of land-use control that won't unduly restrict a buyer, while yet ensuring that he will conform in specific ways to the needs of those around him.

Basically, there are three options for controlling the use of land acquired by an outsider. One is to legislate controls. Any student of politics knows, however, that such control exposes the land user to many uncertainties associated with the political process. These include unpredictable elections, taxation, licensing of business activities, arbitrary regulations, unresponsive bureaucracies, propaganda and brainwashing of the population, bribery and corruption, and a general tendency of politicians to set people against one another. Any of these things will inhibit the productive use of land and depress land values.

A second option is for an owner to place specific use restrictions in the ownership deed, covenants that will bind subsequent buyers and be enforceable in the courts. Covenants have two weaknesses, however. Not only are they inherently rigid and difficult to modify to fit changing circumstances, they are difficult to enforce. Someone must devote time and resources to take a violator to court, and the logical person to do so is an adjacent landowner, since he is most affected. But he may not be able to devote the resources to see the matter through, he may not care, or he may be reluctant to confront a neighbour. Because of this, the tendency of people over time is to establish a political authority to enforce the deed restrictions and otherwise regulate land use—which brings with it the uncertainties and disadvantages mentioned above.

A third option is to keep the title intact and lease parcels of land instead of subdividing and selling them. If a contract is sufficiently long-term and contains a reasonable renewal provision, the land user will have secure access to the land. He won't be able to sell off lots, but he will be able to parcel them out by sub-letting, so long as the sub-leases are not inconsistent with his own. In the lease agreement, the lessor can specify any land-use requirement he or she deems important. Provided the agreement is well drawn by both parties, these obligations will be known and predictable. They will not be subject to the vagaries of a vote, they will be flexible, since they can be changed by agreement of the parties, and they will be readily enforceable by termination should either default. A clan or its members might therefore enter into long-term land leases with outsiders without losing control where it matters. This is the approach most consistent with traditional Somali law and least likely to become political.

Matters of major concern to most Somali clans include enforcement of prohibitions against murder and theft, preservation of the natural environment, and cooperation in matters of common benefit including joint defence. Any non-clansman acquiring land, therefore, should as a minimum be required to

- Observe the basic rules of the customary law and insure against any liability that might arise from a violation of the rights of others.

- Maintain his land and not let it run down to the point that it causes flood or pests or otherwise adversely affects neighbouring lands—and to insure himself against any liabilities he might incur under the law for failure to do so.

- Meet his share of any levies the clan might need to impose on landholders in time of war—and to insure himself against any inability to meet such obligations.

- Make voluntary contributions to the common pool in order to provide relief to others in time of natural calamity, or in order to build facilities perceived as benefiting all, such as roads, schools, or wells, and, failing to make any contribution to these, to forego any benefit from them.

Choice in Insurance

From the earliest formation of their nation, Somalis have understood the value of insurance. How else can we explain the custom from time immemorial that a person cannot be a member of the Somali nation unless insured against any liabilities he or she might incur from breaking the law? This custom must have evolved from the practise of some families providing such surety to their members, which worked so well that other families followed suit. In the end, those that did not were excluded from business and social intercourse. In keeping with the voluntarist character of Somali society, they would not have been punished by fines, but would simply have been boycotted by the families that did insure their members.

Somalia has no commercial insurance companies. Each individual insures with his or her own family. But this practice has consequences incompatible with natural rights. One is that a victim must share his compensation with his family. Another is that a successful entrepreneur is subjected to endless claims for charity by members of his jilib. These features of Somali society will likely disappear when Somalis begin to obtain insurance from independent companies. It might be advantageous, therefore, to invite insurance companies to do business in Somalia, giving Somalis the option thereby of insuring with outside companies instead of with their family.

Insurance within the extended Somali family has the further weakness that it does not cover commercial risks. But as independent insurance companies extend their business operations to Somalia, they will undoubtedly insure for many kinds of risk, including commercial. This will decrease the number of ties that connect Somalis to their clans, but it need not mean a reduction of social cohesion. On the contrary, many Somalis now flee their clans because the burdens are too onerous. Being relieved of surety duties and obligations may enable them to take more rather than less pleasure in the company of their extended family.

Saving and Investing
Saving and investing money is facilitated by banks, which pay interest on savings and attract creditworthy people in search of finance. Banks will make it easier for Somali entrepreneurs to obtain loans and raise equity capital. They will also make it more difficult for family members to pressure successful entrepreneurs out of their profits, especially if the banks keep their client accounts confidential. The presence of banks will profoundly change the present attitude of Somalis towards money. Such change will benefit everyone. It will make Somalia prosperous in ways that few can now conceive. Similar changes have occurred in nearby Dubai and the island of Mauritius, where rapid changes in the business environment have sparked great economic activity. What happened there can happen in any nation adopting a consistent freeport policy.

Status of Women
The natural rights of women will be better respected when their rights are spelled out, publicised, and enforced, and as the public

becomes better educated in the medical, psychological, economic, and judicial consequences of violating these rights. It is unfortunately beyond the scope of this book to enter into the many ramifications of this important topic.

Cooperation with Foreigners

Cooperation between Somalis and foreigners is crucial to the development of economic activity in Somalia. Foreigners now have little interest in cooperating because their natural rights are not sufficiently guaranteed. As discussed earlier, a step toward improving this guarantee would be to invite foreigners to develop freeports in Somalia so structured as to allow a smooth interface with Somali customary law and politics.

Documentation Centre for Jurisprudence

By collecting all of the major jurisprudence under Somali law and making it available to theoreticians and practitioners of that law, Somalis could enhance the quality of the law and facilitate the free assimilation of the various customary law systems into a coherent body of common law.

Coordinating Police Forces

Criminal investigation and enforcement of the judgments of the customary courts will improve greatly as clan institutions begin to make use of computers linked to one another and to Interpol.

As Somali law comes into closer alignment with natural rights, further weaknesses will surely be found and remedied. The same will hold true for the law of the Somali freeport-clans, although to a lesser extent since these will have the advantage of having been built from the start on natural law principles. Because the human capacity for endless innovation makes it impossible to foresee what types of conflict will arise and what types of settlement will best satisfy people's sense of justice, a perfect alignment will never come about. Hence the enterprise of perfecting the law is never-ending.

Notes

13. Bryce Bigwood (2002) suggests another area of change in the customary law, namely transferable restitution. Speaking of conditions in

Mogadishu, he writes, "The number one thing that needs to be taken care of .. is the security situation, both in terms of reducing petty and heinous crime and the spontaneous eruptions of rivalrous, battling militia. The easiest and quickest way to do this would be to get transferable rights to restitution implemented. Xeer is halfway to this concept, but the victors at court are expected to collect restitution themselves. It would take two subclans in Mogadishu to make a bilateral agreement to accept that rulings by their clan elders could be sold to third parties. Sections of the business community may be suggestible to this scheme. Minority ethnic Bantus, women, and foreigners may support this after it starts working (those who have low or no status in the clan system). If it works, more and more subclans will be making such deals, and it may become the dominant system." Transferable restitution is well known in other customary law systems, such as that of Iceland. – Editor SM

14. If successful, "new clans" might be replicated in different clan territories, each named after the host clan by substituting for "Somali" the name of that clan, e.g. the "White Samaron." –Editor SM

Chapter 12
Dangers

How could one persuade the Somalis with joy in their heart to revive a gigantic parasite that, incapable of defending the general interest and public good, was at best, during its short existence, a useless intermediary, a reducer of liberties, a producer of harassing regulation and an enemy of Somali traditions, and at worst a faceless predator systematically plundering the country and distributing its loot among the members of the dominant tribe?

—Christian Bader (1999:239)

The main threat to the continued growth and development of the Somali system of law and politics comes from those on all sides who would re-impose a central government and statutory law in the former territory of the Republic. The most commonly advanced arguments are that legislation is needed to strengthen and unify the customary law; form a nationwide judiciary, police, and military; develop the Somali economy, particularly its infrastructure; make treaties with foreign government agencies; and bring Somalia into the family of democratic nations.

A principal theme of this book has been that traditional Somali society has within it, and only needs time and freedom to develop, all of the social resources required for Somalis to meet their every need and, to the extent they may want to do so, to participate fully in the modern world economically, technologically, artistically, scientifically, and culturally.

The only one of the arguments named above that has not already been touched upon is the purported need for a central government to make treaties with foreign government agencies. To suggest that a nation can only conduct a foreign policy if it has a central government is to ignore the fact that the Somalis have long dealt with foreign governments and their agencies on a clan-by-clan basis. That began long before they were colonised, and it revived after 1991 when they dismantled their central government.

A common ministry of foreign affairs would pose a grave danger from the Somali point of view. Such a ministry would surely conclude treaties and engage in political deals that would eventually supersede or undermine the customary law. If in the future some of the clans perceive a need for a common policy, they will not need a common minister of foreign affairs to initiate, formulate, impose, and conduct it. They will be far better off appointing a private company as their common agent. It might be called, for example, Somali Foreign Services Ltd., and it could implement those foreign policies on which all of the clans agreed. Such a format would ensure that no clan would have to obey or pay the costs of a foreign policy with which it disagreed. This format would also ensure that no treaty would be ratified that would change or abrogate, against its will, any clan's customary laws.

The most common argument for a central government, however, is not grounded on practical considerations at all. It is ideological and alien to traditional Somali law and politics. It is the argument advanced repeatedly by the United Nations and foreign governments that a central government is necessary to bring Somalia into the "family of democratic nations."

At the constitutional conference held in Arta during the summer of 2000, the proposal to introduce democracy was prefaced by the argument that "Somalia has been isolated long enough and should now join the other nations in having a 'real' government." Not mentioned, of course, was the fact that "real" government means the end of customary government. The type of government proposed by the United Nations is incompatible with the highest principle of the Somali customary law, which is the right of all people to their life, liberty, and property.

Not only is the Somali system of politics and law, which I have characterised as a near-kritarchy, incompatible with democracy. In the Somali worldview, it is very much superior. The Somali system of law and politics is realistically geared to protecting every person's freedom. Democracy serves little more than to provide an easy life and guaranteed revenue for its operators and protégés.

Democracy is not even a viable option for Somalia. It functions, so far as it functions at all, in countries where political parties vie with each other for the popular vote; as long as parties alternate in controlling the government, the people do not rebel or secede. But when the electorate is composed of close-knit tribal, religious, linguistic or ethnic communities, the people invariably vote, not on the merits of any issue, but for the party of their own community. Automatically, the community with the greatest numbers wins the election, and the minority parties then put rebellion and secession at the top of their political agenda. That is nothing but a recipe for chaos. Creating multi-clan political parties is impossible in Somalia. It will remain so until the various clans have become little more than loose-knit associations or have been dispersed throughout the nation.

Proponents of democracy generally advance only one argument in defence of their system, and that is that it is superior to dictatorship. In that way, they avoid discussion of its other characteristics. They do that because they know that democracy regularly violates a number of fundamental rights, such as the right to defend oneself, to choose one's own court of law, to enter into mutually agreeable contracts with people of one's choice, to freely engage in economic activities of one's choice, to freely dispose of one's rewards for services rendered, to educate one's children, to leave and re-enter one's country, and to operate on open markets. Democratic governments violate those rights by maintaining a monopoly of all police and judicial services, conscripting people for their armies, levying taxes, Imposing passport and visa requirements, subsidizing one's competitors, and thousands of other restrictions on one's freedom—and all of this with one's own money, taken willy-nilly.

Those pushing for the introduction of democracy and statutory law in Somalia spare no effort to undermine Somalia's present system of law, politics, and economics. Hardly had Somalia's central government collapsed and been dismantled than a plethora of "state-builders" tried to revive it. Some of these were former officials of the Republic of Somalia, while others belonged to foreign governments or international agencies. The money spent on their state-building efforts over the past 14 years is conservatively estimated at more than three billion United States dollars. These efforts have been of several kinds. There were diplomatic efforts, then military efforts, then emergency aid coupled with economic and political development aid, and finally grants-in-aid for conducting and publishing research on social, economic and political issues.

On February 8th, 1998, at a conference of Somali politicians in Addis Ababa, it became clear to most observers that all of these efforts had been in vain, and that the Somali population was averse to the creation of a new central government. From that day, most Somalis have realised that their nation will go its own way and remain faithful to its indigenous political culture.

While the United Nations was busily trying to re-establish a central government in Somalia, a handful of sovereign political entities formed within the boundaries of the former Republic. The most active of these were Somaliland, Puntland, Benadir, Rahanweinia, and Jubaland. It is by no means certain how many more will eventually be created or how many will prove to be viable. They may easily fall apart or remain an empty shell over the coming decade. Whether these sovereign entities will ever associate politically will almost certainly remain an open question for a long time to come.

At a May 4, 1998 meeting in Rome, the Inter-Governmental Association for Development (IGAD), headquartered in Djibouti, took note of the refusal of the Somalis to go along with the proposals brokered by the internationally backed Egyptian government toward the end of 1997. It took a new tack, resolving to help strengthen "the civil society and local administrative structures of the Somalis in view of building up new Somali institutions through a bottom-up approach."

The IGAD has seven regular members and, more important, 21 associated members. The governments of Ethiopia, Sudan,

Uganda, Kenya, Eritrea, Djibouti and, supposedly, "Somalia" are the "regulars." Among its 21 associates are the United Nations, the United States, and the governments of Italy, France, and Britain. It was the Italians who pushed IGAD's associate members towards adopting a bottom-up approach. Despite its unanimous adoption, however, very few foreign diplomats had a clear idea of what they wanted to achieve in Somalia (Loan 1991).

The new IGAD policy has an obvious weakness in view of the fact that there are only two possibilities for political activity in Somalia. Either one tries to work toward establishing a European type of central government, or one favours the present indigenous type of multi-clan government. A mixture of the two was tried from 1960-1991 and failed. What the IGAD had in mind was to form mini-democracies at the village level and then try to cajole these into ever-larger units. This policy, of course, ran into much opposition from the local customary institutions. Both the elders and the religious leaders were well aware that the IGAD aims at completely changing the present structure of their society.

When it became clear that IGAD was getting nowhere with its new policy, the Government of Djibouti, strongly supported by Ethiopia, the United States, and the United Nations, made another "top-down" effort to establish a nationwide central government. It convened more than a thousand Somali elders and intellectuals at a constitutional conference in the Djibouti town of Arta. During the summer of 2000 it produced, after three and a half months of discussions, a constitution and a parliament quite like those with which the Somalis began their first post-colonial government. Understandably, most Somalis looked upon the Arta conference as the umpteenth effort of foreign governments to destroy the Somali system of politics and law.

One might well ask why the United Nations is so adamant in its efforts to re-establish a democracy in Somalia, especially since its founding Charter does not give that organisation a mission to promote democracy around the world. Certainly the founders of the United Nations were acutely conscious of the fact that Adolf Hitler had come to power by a democratic process. By the democratic elections of 1933, his Nazi party had obtained a sufficiently large following that he was asked to be the new prime minister. A year later, in a referendum to decide whether he should also become president, Hitler received 84.6 percent of the popular vote. This illustrates how readily a cunning demagogue can take possession of democracy's awesome political powers.

In fact, the United Nations' founding Charter mentions neither the term "democracy" nor any of its features, such as a division of the nation into rulers and ruled, political parties, periodic popular elections, majority rule, the rule of law, or the separation of powers. Rather, it looks to human rights as the principle that should guide all political activity. The idea that the United Nations should embrace democracy was not clearly articulated until 1948, when its General Assembly adopted the Universal Declaration of Human Rights. That document, filled with empty rhetoric and logical and economic contradictions, espoused a curious mix of real and imaginary natural rights (Van Dun 2000).

It must be stated clearly that foreign governments have solid, selfish motives for establishing a democratic government in the Somali-speaking realm. If kritarchy were to succeed, even in a place as remote from the main political centres of the world as Somalia, it could come to be viewed as an alternative to democracy. It might even spread elsewhere in Africa, leaving millions of politicians, together with their civil and military servants, seeking a job in the private sector. That would attract wide public attention, possibly endangering the privileges of powerful groups of government personnel and their protectors in parts of the world outside of Africa.[15]

The seriousness of the United Nations' threat against Somalia should not be underestimated. There are many arguments against democracy, just as there are many favouring kritarchy, and all are well grounded in logic and in economic research. The proponents of democracy are well aware of the many negative features of their system—which is why they must avoid comparisons with kritarchy. One way to avoid such a public debate is to forestall public awareness of kritarchy in the first place by offering development aid to Somali politicians who would promise to institute democracy. The well-funded international proponents of democracy constitute a threat of major proportions to the poor Somali nation. If they can find Somali activists willing to sell out the Somali nation, these democrats are willing and able to buy it.

Notes

15. A complete explanation of the persistent efforts of the United Nations to re-establish a taxing authority in Somalia might include concern for repayment of the $2.6 billion USD external debt (CIA 2004) stemming from the dictatorship of Siad Barre and owed presumably to the International Monetary Fund. John Perkins (2004) explains some of the political rationale for making large loans to impoverished countries in the first place. Recovery of these funds would not seem to be a major part of the explanation, however, since significantly more than that amount has already been invested in attempting to reestablish a central government in Somalia.

–Editor SM

Chapter 13
Summary and Conclusion

For any reform to be permanent and enduring, it must be based on and rooted in the principles of the aboriginal institutions.
—-John Mensah Sarbah (1864-1910), Ghanaian philosopher[16]

Most journalists describe Somalia as a lawless country. They began doing so fourteen years ago, when the Somalis dismantled their central government. I was intrigued, so I decided to have a look for myself. What I learned was that the Somalis are far from lawless. They have an elaborate indigenous law system that is basically sound, more so even than most legal systems in the world today. That came as a surprise. Who would have thought that an economically backward nation could have a legal and political system that was ahead of most other nations?

The United Nations is uneasy with the Somalis. It is not difficult to see why. Law and order in Somalia are not generated on the basis of democracy. The Somalis have no supreme court, no minister of justice, and no legislature. Nor have they a president or any other ministers. Yet they are not without laws or political institutions. What is more, virtually every Somali is knowledgeable about the law and active in politics. This is indeed puzzling. How do the Somalis generate law? How do they achieve order?

What I found was that the Somalis maintain a huge network

of hundreds, if not thousands, of mini-governments, each wholly independent of the others. These governments operate on a basic set of principles, many of which are harmonious with the concept of natural law. Indeed, but for a few exceptions, the Somali nation is structured such that it comes very close to what in philosophy might be called "the natural order of human beings."

With their nomadic lifestyle, the Somalis can't afford to have a big government. Theirs must be small, so small that it can be transported on the back of a camel. So they found an ingenious way to maintain law and order. Whenever a violent conflict threatened, the families of the opposing parties would ask their armed men to form a kind of *cordon sanitaire* around their quarrelsome cousins and create a balance of power. That would stop the violence and push these cousins towards settling their conflict with the help of mediators and arbiters. This method of 'freezing' conflicts gradually evolved into a custom of dispensing justice on the basis of property rights. The judges and policemen of this system are each time chosen ad hoc from among the extended family of the conflicting parties, which is why some observers call this system "familial government."

An attractive feature of this type of government is its approach to crime. Its only mandate is to compel criminals to compensate their victims. It does not punish criminals, which Somalis consider a waste of time and resources. The job of re-educating criminals is left to the respective families. A preventive feature is that every person is insured against any liabilities he might incur under the law. When a person causes damage to another person's life, liberty, or property, his entire family guarantees compensation.

Somalis also treasure freedom of speech, freedom of movement, freedom of contract, free trade, and respect for the property rights of others. Their judges and policemen do not maintain an office and therefore have no fixed costs. They charge only small fees for their services. Those seeking justice pay these themselves, obviating the need for a tax-levying bureaucracy. In this way, Somalis achieve a maximum of protection of their rights with an absolute minimum of government—one whose cost effectiveness is difficult to surpass. In fact, few nations exemplify so clearly the spirit of a truly natural, free, law-abiding human society as the Somali nation.

Can one call this multitude of independent families a nation?

The Somalis themselves have no doubts about this. Due to their respect for property rights and free trade, they can freely move among the various clans, conducting business, and contracting marriages in one another's territories. Consequently, the clans have come to enjoy many features in common: a language, poetry, music, religion, lifestyle, certain physical and personality features, and a long history. Moreover they are a growing nation, at present one of the largest ethnic groups on the African continent.

During the twentieth century, the Somalis were subjected to the heavy-handed policies of the colonial powers. These powers left a form of government behind that was at odds with Somali political culture. It took the Somalis 30 years to get rid of it and return to their pre-colonial political structure. Many problems arose in the course of this, but gradually the Somalis are resolving them. Foreign observers fail to understand what they are doing; they think the Somalis have been trying to establish a democratic government and constantly failing to do so. In reality, the chief aim of many Somalis is to clean their indigenous legal and political system of its foreign elements.

The vitality of the Somali people comes not from economic power, but from an amazing system of law that has left a strong imprint on the personality of each of its members. The British scholar I.M. Lewis noted the "formidable pride of the Somali nomad, his extraordinary sense of superiority as an individual, and his firm conviction that he is the sole master of his actions and subject to no authority except that of God." My own findings agree with this. But are these personality traits the reason why most foreign government agencies have failed to come to grips with Somalia?

During the past fifty years, the United Nations has systematically promoted democracy in Somalia. Yet nowhere does the United Nations founding Charter mandate such action. That document doesn't mention the word "democracy" or anything about it. Instead it calls for respect for human rights, which the founders of the United Nations, the Nazi conflagration fresh in mind, must have thought an alternative to democracy, not merely an adjunct of it. But within three years, the United Nations Assembly adopted a "Declaration of Human Rights" that embraced wholeheartedly the democratic system with all its awesome powers to restrict freedom and create privilege.

The Somalis were ruled according to the democratic system from 1960 to 1969. With their own eyes they saw how it divided their nation in two groups, those who rule and those who are ruled. The rulers and their protégés shamelessly violated the fundamental rights of the rest of the population in their urge to fill their pockets. In 1969, Somalis felt relieved when a dictator put an end to democracy. But they soon found they had their own Hitler, and they suffered badly during the 22 years it took to get rid of him. That is why Somalis prefer their own system, which is eminently suited to prevent the rise of a dictator. At first blush, this system looks primitive. But on taking a close look, we discover that it has much in common with the order implied in the founding Charter of the United Nations. Some political scientists aptly call that order a "kritarchy."

The United Nation's continuing effort to establish a democracy in Somalia suggests that its policy makers may not be wholly aware of democracy's many weaknesses. Central among these is the fact that it doesn't work in countries where the population is composed of close-knit ethnic groups and the only viable political parties are those formed along ethnic lines. In such a situation people always vote for their group's political party, and not on the issues. If a democratic government were established in Somalia, the various clans, each with its own clan-based political party, would try to take exclusive control of it. They would all have the same motive: to escape being dominated by politicians of another clan.

A democratic government has every power to exert dominion over people. To fend off the possibility of being dominated, each clan tries to capture the power of that government before it can become a threat. The scenario of what would happen if Somalia were to go democratic is the following. Initially, the government would be controlled by an alliance of several clans. Those clans that didn't share in the spoils of political power would realise their chances of becoming part of the ruling alliance were nil. Therefore, they would rebel and try to secede. That would prompt the ruling clans to use every means to suppress these centrifugal forces. Ultimately one of the ruling clans would eject its partners from the ruling alliance. In the end, all clans would fight with one another.

That scenario for the political developments in Somalia is all the more probable now for having already happened between 1960 and 1990. Also, it has some parallels in the political history of Europe, where virtually every nation has tried, during the past two millennia, to dominate the others. Beginning with the Romans, Europe has suffered under the imperialistic exploits of the Huns, the Franks, the Austrians, the English, the Spanish, the French, and the Germans. It took many centuries before their governments finally agreed to form a European Union, which is in fact a confederation with certain elements of a federation.

Having analysed the present system of politics and law in Somalia, I went on in this book to speculate in what direction it might possibly develop. My first question was whether the clans are a passing phenomenon or are here to stay. The day is not far off, I think, when independent insurance companies will make their appearance in Somalia. They will then take over the insurance burden of the clans and a large part of the litigation. Another development may be the establishment of freeports. That will not only give a tremendous boost to the Somali economy, it will put the Somalis in contact with a variety of other cultures and increase the level of tolerance.

These twin developments will undoubtedly change the nature of the clans. They will lose both their present function of "settlers of conflicts," and the will and the means to impose moral values such as charity and solidarity upon their members. That will be a fortunate development. Charity and solidarity are natural inclinations with most people. Practising them out of one's free will makes one virtuous, but being forced to practise them reduces one to the level of a slave.

So it appears that the clans will be less involved in conflict settlement and will exert less pressure on the moral choices of their members. But it is my guess that they will continue to be very active centres of political activity. This is so because the Somalis look to their clans as bulwarks against political tyranny. That is characteristic of African tribes. The main feature of their political philosophy is to preserve their society from the curse of political tyranny—and democratic majority rule is precisely a form of that tyranny.

The continuing omni-presence of the clans will have a major impact on the Somali political system, the development of which will indeed be influenced by the clans rather than by a multi-clan elite. Each clan will want to maintain its independence of the other clans. That will not hamper them in conducting foreign policy. Where two or more clans want to pursue the same policy, they can form a syndicate and put a private company in charge of its implementation. Eventually, co-ordinating agencies may develop through a process of trial and error. It would be premature to speculate on the form these could take, but whatever that form, no clan will ever let itself be outvoted by another clan. One can safely conclude, therefore, that the clans will never accept a federal system of government.

As for the future of Somali law, the Somalis are acutely aware that its development should have top priority. The law develops best and fastest when exposed to the hustle bustle of daily living. That is how the eleven weaknesses of this law described in Chapter 10 will gradually disappear. A documentation centre will probably emerge where law practitioners can access the jurisprudence of the various clans. This will stimulate the gradual unification of the many law systems into one body of nation-wide law. That body will have the same basic characteristics that one now finds in the laws of the different clans, to wit: everyone has access to it, anyone can try to improve it, and no one, least of all governments, will control it.

These speculations on the future of Somali society are accompanied by a substantial worry. In the background of Somali society lurk three monsters: anarchy, democracy, and dictatorship. Anarchy shows itself whenever the warlords find people willing to help them seek power over other Somalis. The monster of democracy will be let loose when the United Nations insists on majority rule as a prerequisite for United Nations recognition. The monster of dictatorship will show up when the United Nations promotes the idea of a central government in Somalia based on federal or confederate principles. In the eyes of the Somalis, any such political government would be the beginning of a dictatorship, so every clan would have no choice but to try to capture the presidency. Indeed, there could be no better way of starting an armed struggle among all the clans than by helping them become a federal or confederate state.

If, however, these three monsters can be kept quiet, it is fair to predict that the Somali nation will prosper. That prosperity will attract attention elsewhere in Africa, which has often been called "the lost continent." It is "lost" only because its nations have spent most of their energy trying to maintain political systems that are incompatible with their own culture. These systems were established by the colonial powers and are being perpetuated by the United Nations. The Somalis are the first nation to have rid themselves of their foreign political system. Because most African nations show great similarities with the Somali nation, the political experience of the Somalis during the past fourteen years is bound to influence political behaviour in the rest of Africa. The beneficial result of that may well be that the colonial time bombs that continuously explode on Africa's political landscape will finally be defused.

The Somalis have taken substantial steps toward a humane society. They transformed a simple method for stopping violence into an effective method for generating just laws. They created a law system that operates in ways similar to the worldwide communications system of the Internet. It would have been better had the United Nations left them alone, but that was not to be. The United Nations moved into Somalia with elaborate plans to develop that country. All it has to show after 50 years of trying is that more than a million Somalis fled their country and now live abroad.

The United Nations' biggest problem is that it doesn't understand that law and order can prevail without a central government, without a state. In order to come to grips with the concept of a stateless society, however, one must drop the notion that law is a command promulgated by politicians. That was the prevailing vision of law until the holocaust. The millions of victims of the Nazi regime were mostly brought to their death by people abiding by the "laws" of their government. That brought an old and almost forgotten truth back into the centre of the public debate about law, namely, that only those rules can be considered laws that conform to timeless criteria that have universal validity. The laws that governments enact do not meet that standard. That is, they do not meet that standard unless they respect the concept of property rights—and so far as they do meet that criterion they are superfluous, for then they are identical to the laws of nature. The universal laws of human society pre-exist political government and continue to exist in its absence.

The officials of Somali clan government respect property rights better than those of most other governments in the world. That is why the Somali system of law and order should be taken seriously. Left alone, it could develop into a full-blown kritarchy resembling in its external features the United Arab Emirates. It might even be called the United Somali Sultanates. It would not make sense, however, to attempt to pressure the Somalis into any such formula. Reconstructing their nation on the basis of the concept of property rights is no small challenge. It will take much patience.

Somalis recognise the proper nature and function of universal law, and they are willing to defend its principles with their lives. As such, they constitute a perfect illustration of the kind of society that the founding fathers of the United Nations might have had in mind. Much has been written since 1945 on the theory of law; less is known about the practise of achieving a free society. That is where the Somalis, with their fine sense of drama, are showing the way.

Notes
16. Langley 1991:98. Cited in Ayittey 1991: xxxvii.

Part III

Economic Development

Chapter 14
Prospects

Spencer H. MacCallum

POLITICAL STABILITY TODAY

When the Somalis effectively abolished their central government in 1991 and became a stateless nation, most international observers expressed fear that the country would fall into chaos. The world media still play on this foreboding theme. Most Europeans and Americans know—or think they know—that Somalia is in unrelenting chaos, ravaged by warfare, starvation and disease, the battleground of rival warlords such that people can neither put in their crops nor harvest them if they do, nor safely herd their animals. What could one expect of a country that has been without a central government for fourteen years?

Influenced by this near-mantra of the media, I was hopeful but sceptical when in 1997 Michael van Notten and his wife, Flory Barnabas Warsame, visiting from Somalia, told me the picture was sadly exaggerated. While there was some fighting and disorder in the southern port cities, they said, the over-all picture was different. Many Somalis were finding that the absence of a central government had its advantages. Somalia was more peaceful than it had been under the Republic, and people were becoming more prosperous.

The possibility that my friends might be right intrigued me so much that over the next few months I found myself looking for corroboration. It came from several places that year. First, a

Los Angeles Times article, "A Somali Alternative to Chaos," described the prosperity of the seaport of Bossaso in northeastern Somalia. Its beginning words were, "Near the tip of the Horn of Africa, a port city is booming, helped by a lack of clan warfare and the absence of a central government" (Simons 1997).

Under the Republic of Somalia, Bossaso had been a village. A few small fishing boats came into its port each day to offload fish. Occasionally a cargo vessel came in as well. Officials of the Republic crawled over these boats collecting taxes and demanding payments for supposed services and permits of every kind. After the demise of the Republic, however, control passed to the local community, and the port began to be managed on a commercial basis. A lively import/export trade developed that soon reached an estimated value of $15 million USD per year. Private enterprise provided essential public services such as trash collection, power, and telecommunications. In eight years, the population grew from 5,000 to 150,000. Parents and teachers put up schools for their children and built a university. In the absence of a government-run court system, the heads of the extended families of contentious parties settled disputes on the basis of customary law.

The next corroboration was a signed newspaper editorial in Addis Ababa, Ethiopia, entitled, "Does Somalia Really Need a Government?" There could be no doubt that the author, Mohamed Mohamed Sheikh (1997), was a qualified observer. Born in Somalia south of Bossaso, he had worked in Mogadishu as a radio reporter, then in the information services of various ministries and finally as a consultant with UNESCO. He wrote,

> The donor countries and international financial institutions which have much leverage over African governments and shape the destiny of the ordinary citizens in Africa through their development programmes are uneasy with the Somali experience which they perceive as dangerously contagious. In fact, the Somali experience is rather confusing for the ordinary minds. Who could imagine that Somalia exports today five times more than in 1989, the last year of which official estimates are available.
>
> ... The Somali economy functions as a perfect model of laissez-faire as conceived by Adam Smith. Government

> spending is reduced to zero and inflation is very low. The
> Somali shilling is freely convertible in the market and
> exchange rates are more stable than in most African
> countries. Telecommunications and air transport have
> made tremendous development during the last seven
> years.... Indeed, Somalia has no custom authorities and all
> goods are imported duty free. New schools and clinics are
> opening every day, offering their services to those who can
> afford to pay.

In the absence of statistics, I wondered, how did Mohamed
Mohamed Sheikh gain his information that Somali exports had
increased fivefold? We corresponded, and he explained how he had
personally carried out field research on the question, what assumptions
he had made and how he defended his conclusion. The
approximation sounded reasonable, even though rough.

A third bit of evidence was a lengthy report in the APC-EC
Courier of the Commission of the European Communities, Brussels,
from which the following extract is taken:

> The outside world's picture of Somalia has been distorted
> by the natural tendency of the foreign media to focus on
> bad news.
>
> In the absence of a central government, Somalia has
> fractured into dozens of different fiefdoms with all
> manner of competing and overlapping authorities. Peace
> reigns in most of the country. Regional and local
> governments have been able to resume working in many
> areas, albeit on a minimal basis.... Town and city markets
> contain a wide range of imported goods. We found
> entrepreneurs who were trading, providing services and
> manufacturing—filling the markets with consumer goods
> and providing much needed employment. They now
> provide many services normally associated with
> government. The lack of state structures means no
> bureaucratic interference. Somalis seem particularly well
> adapted to operating in such an environment.
>
> ... Somalis consider themselves born free. To them,
> the State equals registration, regulation, and restriction.
> Some might think this is a heresy, but many of the business
> people we spoke to believe that the absence of government

is an advantage. There are no central taxes to pay, no forms to be completed in triplicate, and no interference from government inspectors. (Homer 1997:46-66)

Added to these and other independent reports were those by French sociologist Roland Marchal, who on several occasions felt compelled to admit that, even in the south and in Mogadishu itself, things were not as bad as had been expected. For example (Marchal 1999:26):

> In many ways, the survival of Mogadishu is surprising. In 1991 political observers thought the capital could not survive without a government. It was on this assumption that the Italian diplomats launched their biased policy, which actually fostered rather than averted the crisis. When the United Nations pulled out in 1995, again, the worst was predicted.... But we have to admit that nothing like that happened.... No longer is there any government distribution of water and power. But the wells of the city were repaired, and the sale of water is providing jobs for hundreds of people. Generators have continued operating since the '80s. The only difference between then and now is that today the more fortunate can watch Indian movies with subtitles in Somali, or CNN, or Western movies, thanks to the aerials that have mushroomed in Mogadishu.

All of these and other reports lent credence to my friends' original remark that when the Somalis effectively dismantled their State in 1991, clan governance quickly filled the vacuum. Despite efforts of the Republic to eliminate Somalia's traditional judges and police from the political scene, clan government remained the government of choice for Somalis. According to my friends, this indigenous government, composed of traditional councils of elders and part-time police and law courts, had been quite effective during the previous seven years in keeping the peace in the rural areas. Many people, they said, uncritically describe this situation as anarchy whereas, in reality, it is government based upon natural law.

The experience of Bossaso is the rule throughout northern Somalia, and even in large parts of the south. Although exports from the southern coastal cities have dwindled to insignificance due to armed conflict, which continues to be fuelled by United Nations efforts to re-establish a central government, Peter D. Little (2003) reports extensively on the herding economy and cross-border trading in the south. He finds that herds in the south, which are predominantly cattle as opposed to camels in central and northern Somalia, are at pre-war levels or higher (37), and that overland trade with Kenya has more than doubled (18). "Losses due to cattle theft and insecurity are relatively low," he notes (103), consistent with his finding that transaction costs as indicated by transport costs and brokerage fees changed little between 1988 and 1998 (103-109). The pastoral economy in central and northern Somalia is equally robust, annual exports of small ruminants from the ports of Berbera and Bossaso exceeding pre-war levels (38). Indeed, Somalia's pastoral economy is stronger than that of neighbouring Kenya or Ethiopia (67).

Although Somalia is a global player in livestock production and trade, accounting for more than 60 percent of livestock exports from East Africa during the 1990s, an equal or greater source of income in today's economy are the substantial funds sent back home from family members living and working abroad in Europe, Canada, the United States, and elsewhere (37).

Little also reports at length on the Somali shilling, which continues to circulate despite the absence of a national treasury (138-147). Whereas its value declined more than 98 percent during the 1980s under the central government, it showed remarkable stability in the period 1991-1998.

Despite this encouraging picture of economic resilience in Somalia, recovery is far from complete. Militia rivalries continue in the south, anticipating a restoration of the central government. These often operate in open violation of the customary law. Not only have they disrupted much of the historically important symbiotic relationship between pastoralists and the towns (Ibid:45-64), but they are seriously compromising the traditionally strong network of inter-clan relations. While Somalia has greatly confounded the political pundits of the world, it is far from being completely restored to social health. Nevertheless, the healing process is far along.

Natural Resources and Business Opportunities

Concerns about the safety of doing business in Somalia deter many would-be investors. Such concerns reflect in part the strong media bias noted above. But they also reflect in large part uncertainty among Western businessmen about the art of negotiating in a traditional society. As compared with the costly but familiar process of obtaining licensing, franchises, and permits from a bureaucratic government, operating under customary law is uncharted territory. Visitors must learn to work within the clan system, starting by arranging a *marti* relationship with an *abbaan*.

A different discouragement to prospective investors since the September 11, 2001 attack on the World Trade Centre has been the largely American military threat. NATO General Tommy Franks charged that Somalis were harbouring Al Quaeda and threatened, by way of punishment, to bomb all Somali port facilities. This was restated as NATO policy in February and November of the following year, and again in 2003. No evidence of Al Quaeda in Somalia has been forthcoming to justify such threats, although warlords competing for foreign aid and weaponry from the United States periodically make such claims.

Despite these several causes of concern, Somalia's resources and opportunities are such that the international business community is already making overtures. A new Coca Cola bottling plant was recently completed at Merka, south of Mogadishu, and at least four airlines offer regular service between neighbouring countries and the cities of Borama, Bossaso, Burao, Hargeisa, and Mogadishu. Hargeisa boasts a new, 5-star Ambassador Hotel (www.ambassador-hotelhargeisa.com/).

Somalia is rich in deposits of copper, uranium, zinc, lead, talcum, bauxite, thorium, and rubies. Coal, emeralds, and gold are presently mined by traditional hand methods. Natural gas is indicated, and several companies located oil when they still held concessions under the Republic.

Its location on the equator makes Somalia well suited for launching commercial satellites into space, and the proximity of the oil-rich Arab Peninsula, especially its refineries in Aden and Dubai, would make rocket fuel relatively inexpensive.

Traditional enterprises include fishing, salt winning, animal husbandry, tanning, forestry, agriculture, horticulture, and tourism. Although the Somali potential for fishing is estimated at 300,000 tons annually, Somali waters have long been under-fished. At one place on the northern coast where the sea penetrates 15 miles inland, the brackish water would be suited to fish farming.

Southern Somalia has rich agricultural lands between the Jubba and Shabelle Rivers. Agricultural products that do well include coffee, mango, bananas, lemon, grapefruit, sugar, cotton, hides, and skins. These are all in demand in the markets of Europe, North America, and Asia, especially fresh fish, fruits, and vegetables. Production of dried fruits and vegetables might also be profitable.

Transport offers other possibilities. Aviation companies might transport fresh fish, fruit, and vegetables to Holland and Germany, returning with machinery and electronics, while dried fruit and vegetables could be transported as ocean freight. Ocean shipping is needed for transporting livestock to the Arab Peninsula.

Public Goods as an Economic Opportunity. In the absence of a State, a novel and important area of enterprise for Somalia is public goods. As E.C. Riegel (1978:75) astutely noted,

> There is profit in rendering service, and the boundaries of private and public service are not fixed. The extent to which private enterprise may absorb so-called public services depends solely upon the vision and initiative of enterprisers.

Economic activity is stimulated by completely free interplay between investors, entrepreneurs, and engineers. A government monopolizing any area of the economy impedes this interplay, if only by taxing away some or all of the savings that otherwise would be invested. A developing economy needs no taxation; the argument that only central governments can build roads, deliver mail, generate power, provide pure water, supply hospitals, manage schools, run telecommunications, issue money, fight contagious diseases, erect light houses at harbours, patrol neighbourhoods, provide justice, protect the environment, engage in charity, help the poor, advise consumers, and protect the country and its people cannot be defended. On the contrary, abundant evidence shows that when a democratic government engages in these activities it brings personal loss of freedom, lower quality of products and services, higher costs, and stagnant innovation.

A recent dispatch from Mogadishu by the Associated Press (Alexandra Zavis 2005) informs us that:

> Private companies providing power and running water to a few hundred households apiece have mushroomed across town. When Somalia still had a government, Faduma Mayow bought her water off a donkey cart for about $1.50 a barrel. It was expensive, sometimes contaminated, and never enough, said the mother of eight. Now Isaf Water and Electricity Supply has installed a faucet in her courtyard from which chlorinated water flows for less than half the price. The chlorine comes from UNICEF, but otherwise Isaf is privately funded. The same company powers lights and electric mixers at the family bakery, at 65 cents per outlet per day. "Before, we used to mix everything by hand," said Mayow's husband, Abdallah Kasim Mohamed. "So now that we have mixers, we are making big business." Isaf installs the cables and pipes as well as street lighting using neon strips wired to old lampposts.

Recent technological advancement removes any doubt that may ever have existed regarding the economic feasibility of private enterprise undertaking any or all of the tasks listed above.[17]

Somalia thus presents an unfettered opportunity for the private, entrepreneurial provision of "public goods," meaning every kind of service once monopolised by government agencies. In the absence of a central government in Somalia, all of these augment the spectrum of goods and services that can be offered in the marketplace.

Can that include national defence, some will ask? If Somalia continues to be a stateless society, as now seems likely, how will the inhabitants protect themselves from predatory incursions from other parts of the world? After all, defence has long been deemed to be the weakness of the stateless society, for it tolerates no standing military.

Such vulnerability was a valid concern historically and earlier, when the world knew only small, local economies. It explains the global displacement of traditional institutions by statecraft that we see today. But the advent of a world economy and advancing technology has changed the picture. Today such vulnerability of the stateless society is at best short-term.

The experience of Hong Kong gives us the reason for this change. The lesson to be drawn from that experience is that economic freedom under a classical-liberal rule of law allows rapid creation of wealth. Initially, Hong Kong seemed to have everything against it. It lacked all natural resources, had virtually no flat land area, and was 8,000 miles from its major markets. Added to this, it was overwhelmed in 1948 by a flood of political refugees that in thirty-six months had tripled its population. But a quirk of historical fate spared it the socialistic tide of its mother country, England. Enjoying relative economic freedom safeguarded by an unusually astute and able Financial Secretary in the 1960s, it moved in a few decades from a third-world economy to a gross national product the equal of any in the world. [18] It is clear from that experience that given not the merely relative economic freedom of Hong Kong, but *total* economic freedom, a stateless society in a comparable period of time could become so affluent and so advanced technologically that it would need fear no aggressor.

It is worth noting that, at such a time, the insurance industry, whose interest it is to protect persons and property, would doubtless become involved in a major way with guaranteeing public safety (Walker 2005). A recent work edited by economist Hans-Hermann Hoppe (2003) addresses the claim that only governments can provide defence.

Safety from foreign aggression nevertheless remains, at least in the short term, a serious concern for Somalia. The history of foreign interventions from colonial times to the present testifies to that. But even in the near term, Somalis have much going for them. Regardless of conflicts among themselves, the segmental clan system of the Somalis draws them together to show a united front when attacked.

Even without a standing military, Somalia has shown that it is not toothless when confronted with a common enemy.

STRATEGIES FOR ECONOMIC DEVELOPMENT

Road Building. A major development strategy for Somalia will be to open the hinterland of the Horn of Africa to the world's markets by building roads to that region and port facilities to serve the traffic that will surely follow. When Eritrea became independent of Ethiopia and the two governments assumed an attitude of mutual distrust, the vast hinterland became landlocked, dependent on the single port of Djibouti. Djibouti can only be reached by a bad road and an antiquated railroad, and its port facilities are both limited and expensive. The next nearest coast is Awdal, in Somalia.

The interior of the Horn has an under-served population of approximately 70 million people. That number is expected to exceed 100 million by 2020. African countries on average import 2,000 pounds per person per year by sea. Due to poor management of the port of Djibouti and the roads inland, however, Ethiopia imports only 20 pounds per person, leaving a shortfall of some 50 million tons in demand not being shipped.

Seen in this light, Somalia's 1600 miles of coastline becomes a major asset. An obvious strategy for Somalia will be to build roads to the interior and improve port facilities on the two sides of the Horn—on the Indian Ocean in the south and on the Gulf of Aden in the north. An improved port near Kismayo would lie within 600 miles of Nairobi. Coffee growers, frustrated with the congestion, corruption, and inefficiency of Mombassa seaport, could fly their produce to a well-run Somali port and bring back cars and electronics as return freight. Such a port could do more than open up the Ethiopian hinterland; it could become a major port for Kenya, Uganda, Rwanda, Burundi and Eastern Congo. A port and road system to the interior from Somalia's north coast, on the other hand, would open that same hinterland to the world's busiest shipping route—that connecting Singapore with Europe and America through the Suez Canal.

Jim Davidson (2003) recalls how in late 1995 he and Michael van Notten began to discuss prospects for doing business in Awdal:

We planned and had every intention of undertaking fishing,
tourism, road building and toll road operations, port
development, utility operations, mining development, and
import-export businesses in Awdal or off its coast. We
also considered opportunities near Kismayo, especially in
seafood, port operations, and satellite launch activities.
Michael showed me letters he had written on business
possibilities in the territory of the Wersengeli and
introduced me to friends from Sool and Sanaag. He
was inclined to share with me any interesting articles,
news stories, and essays he found on business activities
in Hargeisa, Mogadishu, Puntland, and elsewhere in
Somali lands.

They decided upon road building and formed the Awdal Roads
Company, incorporated in Mauritius. They planned first to improve
the road from Djibouti to Borama in Awdal and operate it as a toll
road, leasing the right-of-way from the Samaron Clan. Then they
would develop a port facility, also on land leased from the Clan, and
build additional toll roads linking the port with other parts of Awdal
and the hinterland. The existing road inland is an unimproved track
that is difficult at best in dry weather and impassable in wet. Improving
this road capacity and building new roads would make it economically
feasible to develop the port facility as a freeport.[19] The first part of
the plan, the toll road from Djibouti to Borama, has the approval
of elders of the Samaron Clan. In 2002, however, the Company
suffered a setback with the unexpected death of Michael van Notten,
its president and chief liaison with the Somali clan elders. After the
Afghan conflict, moreover, prospective investors were deterred by
the United States' extreme military posturing. Though temporarily
on hold, the Awdal Roads Company exemplifies the kind of
imaginative business enterprise that can be undertaken in Somalia.

Freeports. A second major development strategy has already
been discussed in principle in Chapter 11 and will be taken up
more fully in the following chapter with respect to its practical
application. This potentially powerful strategy involves
developing one or several freeports, both as a means of
accelerating the autonomous development of the customary law

and as a programme of economic development.

Notes

17. For discussion of ways in which advancing technology is undercutting the intellectual argument for government intervention in the economy, including especially the provision of "public goods," see Fred E. Foldvary and Daniel B. Klein, *The half-life of policy rationales: How new technology affects old policy issues* (New York University Press 2003). For a more broadly philosophic treatment of this question, see MacCallum 2003, "The Enterprise of Community," Journal of Libertarian Studies 17:4, Ludwig von Mises Institute, www.mises.org/journals.asp. –Editor SM

18. Christian Wignall, "The Champion of Hong Kong's Freedom." Unpublished paper dated 2003, concerning the career of Financial Secretary John James Cowperthwaite. Available from the author at <cwignall@pacbell.net>. Although Hong Kong's economic freedom was not total (e.g. it's housing sector is heavily socialised), it has enjoyed relatively greater economic freedom than anywhere else in the developed world. Two indexes of freedom (*The Index of Economic Freedom*, by Marc Miles et al, published by the Heritage Foundation, and *Economic Freedom of the World*, by James D. Gwartney et al, published by the Cato Institute, both in Washington) annually rank more than 100 countries according to their degree of economic freedom. These show unequivocally the strong correlation between economic freedom and prosperity. –Editor SM

19. A business plan for the Awdal Roads Company is available from Jim Davidson <davidson@net1.net>.

Chapter 15
The Freeport-Clan

Spencer H. MacCallum

Hong Kong had the advantage of a classical-liberal rule of law, without which any meaningful economic freedom would have been impossible. We saw in earlier chapters that Somali customary law protects persons and property and that, left alone, it might be expected to develop into a full body of common law capable of serving every need of a technically advanced society. This would provide for Somalia a rule of law such as made a prosperous Hong Kong possible. Customary law changes slowly, however, so in Chapter 11 we considered ways that the process might be accelerated. We looked at the potent catalyzing role that freeports might play in the growth of Somali law as well as in the growth of the economy.

Michael van Notten in the early 1990s married into the Samaron Clan and set about promoting economic development in the Awdal region of Somalia, founding and directing the Eastern Hararghe Development Agency. Influenced in part by Peter Drucker's writings and to a greater extent personally by Richard Bolin, dean of the *maquiladora* phenomenon in Mexico, he appreciated the economic leverage that freeports bring to poor countries. But in the absence of a central government, how could a freeport be promoted to investors and business people accustomed to relying on a central legislative authority to guarantee property and enforce contracts? On the other side, how could such an enterprise be integrated with traditional Somali politics and law—as would have to be done in order to attract a motivated work force from the local population, not to mention reassuring prospective investors?

At this point, his fellow clansmen made the pregnant suggestion noted in Chapter 11. They said that to develop and operate a freeport in Somalia, he should bring together his business friends and form a new clan. They should design their own set of laws for compatibility with Somali customary law so that differences that arose could be settled in traditional courts.[20] If the law of the freeport were made to dovetail with the customary law of the surrounding region, then businessmen locating in the freeport could operate with equal ease in Somali society and in the world market, while Somalis could readily come and go and interact in the freeport.

The challenge would be to design a law system and a social structure that could interface with both Somali customary law and the conventions and usages of the global business community. To move from this vague but tantalizing idea to a developed concept and business plan would be no mean task, but Michael van Notten was undaunted. Here, he felt, might lie the key to a breakthrough in the legal and economic development of his adopted land.

By a fortuitous circumstance, I met Michael van Notten in 1997 and brought to the task a project of my own having to do with the feasibility of developing a community in a stateless setting. It was a heuristic exercise of many years duration, involving the inputs of many different people. The object of the exercise was to design a means of providing privately, by purely free-market means without taxation, all of the public services of a community which, of course, a freeport would be.

Such a community would operate on a land-lease basis like any multi-tenant income property, examples being shopping centres, hotels, professional centres, and so forth. These were the prototypes. But the exercise envisioned a fully generalised community in which the master-lease form would set out all of the expectations between landlord and tenant and between each tenant and his neighbor in sufficient detail to make a viable community without recourse to statutory law. Coincidentally, during the same years that I had been pursuing this, Michael van Notten had been working at drafting a proposal for a legal system, consisting of an outline of natural law principles and their derivative natural rights, together with procedural rules for safeguarding those rights, that could serve a community in lieu of statutory law.

My leasehold structure had the drawback that it assumed, as a prior given, a sufficiently developed framework of common law to sustain a rule of law. Michael van Notten, on the other hand, had outlined a natural-law system but lacked a means of introducing it into a community. When we met, we critiqued one another's work, suggesting refinements. From our collaboration emerged an idea: introduce Michael's system of natural rights and procedural law into the freeport community by making it a matter of contractual agreement. A commitment by all parties to observe that rule of law could be a condition of the lease. Land lease thus afforded Michael a vehicle, while his outline gave me my needed rule of law. Together they suggested a package of social software that could generate a freeport-clan—a community governed as a kritarchy. Natural-rights scholar Roy Halliday (2002) wrote of the proposal that it

> comes as close as anything I have seen to establishing the framework for a civil society consistent with liberty and natural rights. The idea of incorporating a description of natural rights into the master lease for a proprietary community is brilliant. It satisfies both the strong natural rights advocates ... and the skeptics who believe rights are created by contracts. The lease contract provides a way to specify how rights are to be enforced.

A working draft of the master-lease form is set out in Appendix C, "Proposed Membership Agreement for a Freeport-Clan." The concept, however, can be explained as follows.

THE CONCEPT OF THE FREEPORT-CLAN

The freeport-clan is a proposed organisational structure to enable freeports to operate in a customary-law setting like that of present-day Somalia. Its form of government is a kritarchy. Freeport-clansmen resemble traditional clansmen in that each is united with his/her fellows in a well-understood web of relationships. The difference is that the web here is one of contract rather than kinship status. Freeport-clansmen become members not as an incident of their birth, but by participating in a rental or lease of land in which all parties to the agreement explicitly contract to observe the freeport law set out therein. Employees and day-visitors, not being tied into the system of land tenure, occupy a different category. Nevertheless, they also explicitly contract to observe the law during their stay, either in their agreement with their employer or, on entering the freeport, with the freeport leasing authority.[21] Their relationship to their employer or the leasing authority may be said to be more like that of a *marti* to an *abbaan* (guest and protective host) in Somali law.

Two Kinds of Law. The law of a freeport-clan, like that of any community, is of two kinds. There are rules and procedures applicable to everyone at all times and places (natural law), and there are rules and procedures specified in agreements between particular individuals and applicable to them alone (contract law). In the event of conflict, the former take precedence.

The land-tenure agreements (contract law) bind owners, residents, and visitors in a self-consistent network of relationships described in a cascade of subleases following the initial lease of land from the Somali host clan. To be consistent with the master-lease form and thereby valid, every lease, sub-lease, and sub-sub-lease, etc., requires a clear commitment by the contracting parties to a regime of natural law and procedural rules set forth in the master-lease form. The master-lease form thus brings together contract law and natural law in a single document. From this document is generated the written constitution of the community, which is the sum of all leases in effect at any given time.

Whereas contract law is whatever the contracting parties may agree to so long as it is not inconsistent with natural law, natural law principles and rules and the procedures for protecting and enforcing them are not as easily identified. They are the principles and rules of human social behavior that are essential to the functioning

of any society at any time and place. As such they must be capable
of being universalised. While we can discuss them in general terms,
precisely what they are has been the subject of speculation and de-
liberation by, among others, ethicists, moralists, legal scholars, and
social philosophers.[22] Humankind being part and product of the
natural world, it is only reasonable to assume that scientific method
ultimately will illumine the workings of human society and discover
the natural laws that operate there as elsewhere in nature.[23]

It is expected that the system of law here proposed will be
readily enforceable through a decentralised ("polycentric") justice and protection industry consisting of freely competing court
and police services. The land-lease structure of the community
resolves many common objections to the idea of competitive
police services, since all such competing services are thereby integrated into one and the same web of contractual relationships.
Should anyone refuse to acknowledge a court summons or judgment, including any investor in or officer of the community or
any member of a justice court or police, he will be in violation
of his lease agreement. Consequently, unless or until he redeems
himself, he will be subject to eviction, or banishment, losing
both figuratively and literally his standing in the community.

Two Contributions

Each of the two formulations of law that enter into the structure of the freeport-clan, that of contract law (the lease agreement) and that of natural law (the law principles enumerated
therein), has its independent history.

Outline of Natural Law. A practicing lawyer in the Netherlands, Michael van Notten first developed an interest in outlining principles of natural law in response to a competition in
which he took first prize. The competition called for drafting a
constitution for a classical-liberal community. Mentored by his
friend, Belgian legal philosopher Frank van Dun, and with the en-
couragement of other friends, he went on to work for some years
at teasing out a coherent formulation of a system of natural law.
Then, in Somalia, he found a customary law system in place that in
important ways resembled just such a system as he had come up

with. His outline of a system harmonised with Somali customary law as no legislated body of rules ever could. When in 1997 he formed a company with Jim Davidson to develop, among other things, a Somali freeport that called for its own law that would be compatible with Somali customary law, he already had in outline form a law system that he could use for that purpose.

Michael van Notten believed that natural law describes the voluntary, universal order of human society, that it originates in our life as reasoning human beings among our kind, that it acknowledges the right of every person to live a life governed by his own goals, judgments, and beliefs, and that it serves to prevent as well as to resolve conflicts among people. It stipulates that every person shall be free to make any disposition he likes of his own property and shall refrain from making any disposition of the property of others without their permission. It permits all activities that do not infringe upon the person or property of another. This law takes priority over all other principles and rules that shape human society, including rules legislated by parliaments or established by contract. Finally, it requires that its enforcement be pursued only in ways consistent with itself.

The natural law principles enumerated in the master lease, together with all contractual obligations freely undertaken by residents and visitors consistent with those principles, are the only law in the freeport-clan. Anyone is free to offer and perform police and judicial services, provided they follow the procedural rules, or protocols, spelled out in the membership agreement to protect the natural rights of the members.

The Agreement. The agreement itself, on the other hand, has a longer and quite different history. It was the culmination of an exercise in applied anthropology that I had conducted for more than a quarter-century. During most of that time, it had been known informally as the "Orbis" project—Orbis being one of a cluster of imaginary settlements in outer space. I promoted the exercise as a means of exploring how private contractual commitments might provide for community needs in the absence of a legislative government. Extrapolating from what is well known about clan societies, I had hypothesised that in contemporary society common or community goods no less than private should be able to be produced through the competitive market process in a manner fully consistent with normative property rights.

The exercise began in 1971 when Werner K. Stiefel, CEO of Stiefel Laboratories, commissioned me to draft, in exchange for a two-percent equity in the project, a master lease for a floating community which he intended to develop in international waters. He had experienced Germany in the 1930s and thought he saw the same dynamic of political democracy leading to similar results in the United States. Many whom he knew had escaped Germany by fleeing to the United States. But when the time came, he thought, where could people flee to from the United States?

Werner Stiefel's dream, which was inspired in large part by the philosophy of Ayn Rand, was to found a new country on the high seas, starting small but with the expectation that it would grow. Werner devoted millions of dollars of his personal resources to the project but eventually fell short of his goal. At that point, however, he encouraged publication of the master lease form, hoping that it would provide a stimulus to innovative thinking about the private provision of common goods. He only requested that it be described in a fictional setting that would not draw political attention prematurely to the concept of settlement on the ocean.

I distributed drafts of the Orbis lease form and invited criticism, and gradually it took on a life of its own. Several iterations were published. Over the next 30 years, like the open-source software for a free community that it was, it came to reflect the inputs of many different people.

The intellectual challenge of the Orbis project was to envision in a practical way how a hypothetical settlement, removed from all contact with earth's legislated laws, might be structured solely along lines of private agreements to meet all of the needs of its inhabitants. The reality of stateless society at the clan level is well known to anthropologists. That was the starting point. If statelessness is the normal mode at that level, I speculated, why not at the level of a more developed, market society? The reason we don't see it may not be that it contradicts any law of social organisation; it may simply have to do with the epoch in which we live, a function of evolutionary timing.

According to the hypothesis that began to form, humankind is navigating a transition from local cooperation based on kinship status to global cooperation based on contract and enabled by an evolving web of financial and many other supportive business institutions and a market pricing system (MacCallum 1997). It is common knowledge that times of transition, or change, are marked by instabilities and stresses. In the case of the transition just described, these manifest most poignantly as the dehumanising,[24] institutionalised coercions of various kinds that, taken together, we call "the state" and suppose to be normal for human society. But is it normal? Perhaps statelessness is normal for more developed levels of human organisation as it is at the lesser. Does the adult not develop in the pattern of the embryo? Since it has not been demonstrated that statelessness in a market economy is self-contradictory, and considering the accelerating rate of social change, an advanced stateless society cannot be excluded as a possibility.

Moreover, a broad range of empirical data in contemporary society goes a long way toward putting the burden of proof on those who would argue the inevitability of a state. For it suggests strongly that the private production and management of any and all common goods for a community of any imaginable size is technically feasible and potentially profitable. That body of data is found in the twentieth-century growth of multi-tenant income properties in real estate. What is significant about that growth is the fact that complex hotels, shopping malls, etc. resemble in important respects what we are accustomed to think of as communities and require the same sort of administration. A hotel, for example, maintains private and public areas including a landscaped lobby corresponding to a town square with shops and stores, distributes public utilities, provides artificial climate, physical security, and public transit, which happens to operate vertically instead of horizontally. The difference is that instead of being funded by taxation, these common goods are provided entrepreneurially for profit—quietly, effectively, and pleasantly.

A first step, therefore, in addressing the challenge of Orbis was to observe that all multi-tenant income properties have in common the fact that they are structured on leasehold. Instead of a development being fragmented and sold for a one-time capital gain, the owners keep the land title intact, parcelling it into usable sites by land-leasing. This lets the property be managed as a long-term, conservative investment for income. It creates what might be called an *entrepreneurial* community as opposed to a political one, a community in which an entrepreneur, standing behind his product, creates and maintains optimal human environment for the market he targets. As he succeeds in attracting customers, he builds land value as measured by revenue flow. His customers pay for the privilege of living and/or working in an environment they find conducive to the realisation of their particular goals. Ground rent pays the costs of the community administration and a profit besides.

Although it might seem novel, such a non-political community does not represent a fundamental departure from tradition. Growing from rootstock antecedent to the state, it retains the structure and much of the function of seigneurial and manorial forms of human settlement found in many parts of the lesser developed world. The difference lies in the circumstances of the management and the services it can offer. Instead of a small and localised kin group pursuing an inevitably mixed agenda, the management is a specialised firm operating competitively within the supportive institutional context of a global economy and pricing system.

Nevertheless, the question arises, "Isn't a government needed? Isn't some regulation of conduct required in an entrepreneurial community?" It is, of course, but it need not take the form of a taxing authority. Observe that the sum of the lease agreements in effect at any time is analogous to the written constitution of a traditional, political community. The difference is that here is a self-regulating system within a competitive market. Instead of legislated rules, private lease agreements, individually negotiated, set out not only each person's obligations to the community owners and theirs to him, but in all important particulars his and his neighbours' behaviour vis-a-vis one another.

Life in a large and complex entrepreneurial community would be highly decentralised; for such a community would resemble a complex molecule comprised of many different kinds of atoms.

Most land tenants would deal not with the primary lessor, but with any of a great variety of sub-lessors operating at various degrees of remove as the land continued to be parcelled into use. Moreover, short of conflicting with provisions in the master-lease form, agreements would be customised to suit many tastes. Adding to this potential for variety is the fact that buildings or other improvements could be separately owned; only the underlying land need remain in single title.

The challenge of the Orbis project, therefore, was to design some social software that, absent any possibility of falling back on statutory law, would anticipate each and every need and contingency of life in a complex community. The assignment turned out to be less daunting than might be imagined. It was simplified by the project's focus being upon *means* rather than upon any particular Utopian end. Human ends are infinite, limited only by the power of the human imagination, but effective means derive from constant principles that are few in number and involve the *how* of things on an abstract level. These principles partake of natural law, the rationale of nature, and are to be discovered through examining successful behaviour and what makes it so. Understanding what makes for successful social behaviour in any place and in any age was the genius of Michael van Notten and his mentor, Frank van Dun.

In 1997, for a small equity in Awdal Roads Company, Michael van Notten commissioned an application of the Orbis master lease form for a proposed Somali freeport. He had promoted the freeport idea among his Samaron clansmen, noting that, among their many advantages, freeports would enable Somalis to capitalise on their stateless tradition. World-class professional and business talent would be attracted to a setting that was free of the uncertainties, delays, and hardships associated with taxation and bureaucratic regulation.

The multi-tenant income property model, he realised, is well suited for a freeport-clan. Not only have most successful freeports been developed as land-lease communities rather than as subdivisions, but they can be developed on leased land. This is fortuitous, since Somali law is receptive to leasing land, even long-term, but does not entertain the idea of selling or otherwise permanently alienating land from the clan. Leasing has the further advantage of not tying up scarce capital needed for development and operations.

The multi-tenant-income-property model also has broad areas of congruence with traditional life in a clan society. The pervasive role of insurance in a multi-tenant income property, for example, finds functional parallels in Somali clan practice. In a shopping centre, moreover, the manager's concentrated entrepreneurial interest in the whole encourages and allows him to act as a facilitator rather than as a ruler—precisely as does the head of a traditional African village or clan.

FREE CITIES

Freeport-clans could function as latter-day "free cities" not unlike those of the late Middle Ages that gave rise to the modern era. Like those cities, which offered enterprising individuals a path out of feudal servitude, the freeport-clan would offer escape from oppressive governments or unduly restrictive practices in other parts of Africa and the world. As elements of its freer business environment spread by adoption to other clans, it would become easy for people to migrate to the Horn of Africa, adopt its language and ways, and become productive members of a new Somali society freed of both the aftermath of colonialism and the restrictive aspects of the clan system. Further, if people outside Somalia found it in their interest to agree to observe the law of one of the cities or a common law evolving from several of them, this would give rise to a trading nation based on a law that was entirely independent of place—a law resembling in this respect traditional Somali law, which is kin-based rather than geographically determined.

In marked contrast with the European model, the cities of the new Somalia would be free for these reasons:

- Community services and amenities would be provided in abundance and variety through exclusively proprietary means in a competitive market, for profit, without recourse to taxation.

- The community authority would exercise leadership that was interested yet impartial, since it would have a personal and business interest in the success of the community as a whole. Private interest and public interest would be aligned.

- The community authority would not exercise any police function, but would serve only as a facilitator in a role like that of a clan or lineage head in many stateless societies.

- A flexible system of land use control—land leasing—would allow incremental land use changes over time without eminent domain or other prejudice to property rights.

- A quantitative feedback in the form of land revenue would permit rational evaluation of plans and policies.

- The community would be served by a comprehensive, polycentric (non-monopolistic) police and justice system for the adjudication of disputes and protection of natural rights, a system agreed to individually and before the fact by every member.

- The economy would be freely competitive, with no coercive restraints on entry or trade, and it would be in the interest of the community management to keep it so.

If the "new Somalia" comes about, it will simply be an evolved version of traditional, pre-colonial Somalia. It will provide a navigational light in a world ravaged by political democracy, a beacon for a humanity that has lost its bearings.

Notes

20. Michael van Notten died without disclosing the author of this idea.
21. The envisioned freeport is not a subdivision in any of its forms, including condominiums, but strictly a multi-tenant income property. This is an important caveat since many people, unaccustomed to making the distinction, bracket these very different kinds of real property. The subdivision, to the extent it has any organisation at all, functions like a cooperative, whereas the envisioned freeport is a commercial property.

22. See, for example, Roy Halliday (2000).
23. For some pregnant suggestions on this subject, see Alvin Lowi, Jr., *Scientific Method: In Search of Legitimate Authority in Society*, unpublished   monograph   available   from   the   author (alowi@earthlink.net).
24. See, for instance, Butler Shaffer, "A Passion for Life," Chapter 55, *The Wizards of Ozymandias*, LewRockwell.com Ebooks.   http:// www.lewrockwell.com/ozymandias/

Appendices

Appendix A
Case Law

1. **The Pregnancy of an Unmarried Girl.** An unmarried girl became pregnant. Her parents felt hurt in their pride. The customary law once prescribed that parents of a pregnant but unmarried girl should receive compensation from the family of the man who had impregnated their daughter. But that rule changed a few years ago. The elders agreed that compensation would not be due if the girl had consented to the act.

    The judges in this particular case found that the girl had invited the young man to the house of her parents while they were away and had drawn him into her parents' bed. Therefore, the court found that the girl had consented and ruled that no compensation was due. However, the father of the pregnant girl had brought a second complaint. He claimed that the boy had violated the sanctity of his home. The court found this second complaint valid and condemned the boy's parents to pay compensation on that score.

    The case became widely known not so much because it marked a change in the law on "reputation," but because it was the pregnant girl's father who, years earlier, had proposed changing the law in this respect, and he was now once more in a position to refine the law on this point.

2. **The Murder of a Homosexual.** A boy who was reaching adulthood developed homosexual tendencies. He began to perfume himself and sought the company of other homosexuals.

He was living in Djibouti, a big town where the customary law was attenuated, so there was no scarcity of such company. For a Somali family, homosexuality is an abomination. Therefore, a brother of this boy decided to put an end to it. On a given evening he went to the street where homophiles were accustomed to meet and slit his brother's throat with a dagger. The Djibouti police searched for the murderer but could not find him. After a few days, however, the elders of the murderer and his victim went to the police and told them what had happened. They said they would deal with the matter under the customary law of the clan, whereupon the police closed its file on the case.[25]

3. **Destroying One's Own Property.** A clansman had given his shop in loan to his brother. The shop was located in the Republic of Djibouti, whose officials one day decided to allocate the shop to a woman from another clan. They instructed their police to remove the brother's merchandise and furniture from the shop and authorised the woman from the other clan to install herself in the vacant premises. The woman, however, realising that the clan of the previous occupant would never allow her to establish herself on the confiscated premises, paid him the equivalent of 250 U.S. dollars, which he accepted. He accepted the payment not because he intended to transfer the property title of the shop to the woman (after all, he had no such title to convey), but because he had suffered from no longer having a shop from which to make his living. The woman, however, thinking she was now entitled to occupy the premises, installed herself accordingly. Thereupon, the owner set fire to his property. The fire also destroyed a number of neighbouring shops. Total damages were estimated at 150,000 U.S. dollars. The owner was instantly apprehended by the Djibouti police and put in jail, whereupon his clan elders went to the police and argued that the case should be settled under the customary law. They added that if the owner were condemned under the law of the Republic of Djibouti, their clan would declare war on the clan of the woman who had pushed the Republic's officials to seize the shop for her. The court ruled that the case could be settled under the customary law, and the police released the owner. The clan

court later ruled that the owner had acted in self-defence and that no customary laws had been violated.

4. **The Execution of a Murderer.** The most successful and respected businessman in the city of Jigjiga was murdered. He was a merchant of qhat, a naturally occurring amphetamine stimulant that he bought in Jigjiga and sold in the towns of Borama, Hargeisa, Berbera, Burao, and beyond. This qhat is transported every day to Jigjiga in lorries, owned and driven by members of the Oromo nation, from the Chercher Mountains where it grows. In Jigjiga it is taxed by the Ethiopian government and then is sold to Somali merchants, who unpack, air, repackage, ship and sell it to customers in Somaliland. When the merchant in question started his business, there were at least two-dozen members of his clan engaged in the trade, each with his own vehicle. He soon realised that economies of scale could be achieved if one company handled the whole volume of qhat traded in Jigjiga.

Within ten years, this merchant had brought most qhat traders of the Jigjiga area together in his organisation. His profits were considerable, but so also was the number of persons demanding a share of those profits, since under Somali law a wealthy man is obliged to share his wealth with his neighbours and family members. The law is detailed on this. It stipulates what persons are entitled to receive something and when—which turns out to be any time a businessman concludes a profitable deal. This qhat merchant was paying approximately 50 Birr every day to some 150 people, representing that many households. In addition, he paid for the construction of a large mosque in his village of origin. Also, he regularly paid for the acquisition of tools and livestock by close family members. Should any clansman find himself in financial need despite these payments, he could always count on this man's support. To facilitate this distribution of his profits, he always had a judge at hand to arbitrate when he had to turn down a prospective beneficiary of his charity.

In addition to these parasites, who enjoyed the protection of the customary law, this merchant also had to deal with competitors and with predators such as highwaymen and politicians. He once said that the latter were relatively easy to deal with compared to his closest family members. Nevertheless, a highwayman from a neighbouring clan shot him to death while he was accompanying one of his lorries. The customary court constituted by both clans sentenced this highwayman to death. His clan captured him and delivered him to the court, whereupon its judges asked some federal soldiers to execute him as a convicted murderer. The soldiers recognised the validity of the customary verdict and did so on the same day.

5. **Theft of Vehicles Belonging to Clansmen of Another Nation.** Young men from a Somali clan had stolen three vehicles from members of the Oromo nation. The Oromo sent a delegation of three elders to the head of the "robber clan," asking for restitution. The head of this clan ordered his own jilib to return the vehicle its members had stolen and summoned two others to do the same, which they did. In addition, the clan head arranged a safe conduct thereafter for all Oromo vehicles entering his clan's territory. In his judgment, he stated that Somalis must respect their own laws when dealing with people from other nations.

6. **A Dignitary Commits a Crime.** An oday in Herigel had been condemned to pay twelve oxen where normally one would have been due, but he had refused. He was tied to a tree, after which the villagers began to slaughter his oxen. When six had been slaughtered, he promised to pay the compensation he had been condemned to pay. The remaining six oxen were then set free. This shows that when a dignitary such as an oday, imam, or ugaas violates the xeer, the penalty (*yake*) is higher than for an ordinary person.

7. **Murder of a Judge.** Two villagers of Sheddher had a boundary dispute over their land. They brought their dispute to their judges, who formed a court of law and established who was the real owner of the disputed area. The person who was denied ownership thereupon killed the judge of his opponent and fled

to the clan of his mother. He was given the death penalty in absentia, and his family was condemned to pay the usual 100 camels. Because his family was suspected of having facilitated the escape of the criminal, however, it was condemned to pay the camels within 24 hours and to serve as soldiers at the border of the clan's territory. After some time, the murderer resumed his usual activities of herding livestock and cultivating the land in his village. His jilib had paid the blood-price, so he was a free man again. But thereafter, members of his jilib watched him carefully for two reasons: to prevent him ever getting in trouble again and to prevent the family of the victim from seeking a belated revenge.

8. **The Missed Inheritance.** A woman was invited to visit her dying father, who told her that on his death she would inherit his house. When on his death she claimed title to the house, her oday told her that an Islamic court would decide the matter. The judge (*Kadi*) ruled that according to the customary law she was indeed entitled to inherit the house, but that according to Koranic law, only brothers and uncles could inherit, not the daughters and sisters of the deceased. If she claimed her right under the customary law, therefore, he would be obliged to damn her in the name of the Prophet. Consequently, the woman gave up her right to her part of the inheritance, not wanting to live the rest of her life with the social stigma of an outcast from the Islamic community. But she is still bitter about her fate, especially since the judge was the father-in-law of one of her brothers.

9. **Execution of a Rapist.** A ten-year-old girl was raped in Borama and instantly died. The rapist hid himself in the house of one of his clan's elders. When the girl's family came to arrest him, he tried to defend himself with a pistol. By mistake, he shot and killed the son of his host. When he was brought before a court of law, the father of the victim pleaded that the accused did not merit the death sentence because he had been a hero of

the 1988-1991 rebellion against the Ethiopian dictator Mengistu Haile Mariam. Moreover, he had been a member of the Samaron militia called the Horyaal Democratic Front. Nevertheless, he was sentenced to death and was executed the same day.

10. **The Third Wife.** A clansman wanted to marry a young girl. However, he already had two spouses, and his family was reluctant to pay still another bride's price. So he abducted the girl and brought her before an Islamic court, which dutifully married the two. The girl's parents felt 'dishonoured' and demanded compensation. The abductor's family now became obliged under the law to pay the bride's price to the family of the girl.

11. **Fraud.** A clansman wanted to marry a girl of another clan. The mother of the girl disliked his proposal but nevertheless consented, fixing the bride's price at 20 cows. When that price was paid, the mother said she opposed the marriage after all but would keep the cows. Because the clansman was an orphan, the mother of his fiancée had calculated that he would not be able to muster the support of his family to retrieve the animals. After a year had passed, the clansman finally secured the full support of his jilib, which then demanded restitution. A court was formed and rendered a verdict that the mother of the fiancée had acted fraudulently and that the cows had to be returned, including their offspring.

12. **Love and Justice.** An intelligent, lively, and beautiful woman married a man who had divorced his first wife. It was a happy marriage, and neither seemed to mind that no children were born of it. But one day they quarrelled. The husband took his dagger and mutilated his wife's face so badly that it was expected she would die. But she recovered, albeit with her face covered with ugly scars and one eye missing. To everyone's surprise, she begged her family not to demand payment of the blood price. Indeed, she offered to pay her family out of her own livestock that she had received as bride's-wealth (*yarad*). She even went

back to her husband, living with him happily for several years more until one day he took his dagger and, this time, cut his wife into dozens of small pieces. Her family took no action, respecting this woman's great love for her husband. But three years later, an opportunity presented itself for one of her cousins. He was driving his lorry when suddenly the murderer came into view. Not hesitating a moment, he ran over him, leaving him dead. The dead man's only son from his first marriage did not call for compensation. Everybody agreed justice had been done.[26]

13. **A Series of Murders Broken.** Someone murdered a man from a neighbouring clan. The clan of the victim reacted by killing a man from the murderer's clan, setting off new killings until three more men of the victim's clan had been murdered and two more of the murderer's clan. Finally, the elders managed to convene an inter-clan court of law that condemned the clan of the first murderer to pay the blood price for the first victim and to offer that victim's clan a nubile girl to seal a lasting peace treaty. That was accepted, but it posed a problem. What young man of the victim's clan would be willing to marry her? That was a hard question, because the woman was small and not very attractive. Finally the clan decided that a son of the jilib's head person should marry her, despite the fact that he was already engaged to a woman from another clan. The marriage was concluded and the young husband fathered a child with her, then divorced her and married the girl he loved. Many years later he became the chief of his clan, partly because as a young man he had helped secure peace between the two clans. His marriage to the nubile girl did in fact secure friendly relations between the two clans that lasted five generations and continues today.

14. **The State of Ethiopia Dealt with as a Clan.** In 1992, a year after the Tigraens took control of the Ethiopian government, some federal soldiers wantonly killed a Somali merchant near his village of Sheddher. Their reason was that he had refused to give them some of his merchandise, which happened to be qhat.

An hour later, the family of the victim killed two federal soldiers who happened to be passing through the village. The military commander of the Somali region thereupon ordered a punitive expedition and sent an entire platoon to Sheddher. On its arrival, the soldiers learned that the villagers could have killed several more federal soldiers that day but had not done so. They had acted according to their customary law, which stipulates that when someone of another clan murders a clansman, two members of that other clan will be killed. Shortly thereafter, a similar incident happened in the same territory, in the village of Lafaissa, where a federal soldier had sought refuge in a military camp after wantonly killing a Somali. The family of the victim went to a military camp in the nearby village of Herigel and killed two federal soldiers. The military commander in Harar chose to take no action against the clan and informed his soldiers that henceforth they had to respect the customary law. As a result, no more killings occurred in the territory.

15. **Collaboration with Government Employees.** Several times in 1999, Ethiopian federal soldiers in the Jigjiga area seized a vehicle from a Somali to pursue someone suspected of transporting contraband. To reduce the effectiveness of the soldiers, since smuggling did not violate the customary law, the elders decided that a Somali who allowed soldiers to take his vehicle would be considered an accessory to any outlawry the soldiers subsequently committed. For example, if a soldier were to kill a Somali smuggler, the family of the "collaborator" would be condemned to pay the blood price to the family of the victim.

16. **A Spy Put to Death.** A young widow married a second time. She had one male child from her first husband and several children, mostly boys, from her second. Her first husband was of a different clan than her second; therefore her first child was of a different clan than her other children. When her first child became an adult, a war broke out between the two clans. Thinking it was his duty to help his own clan, this son of the first marriage spied on the warriors of the clan in which he had grown up. It

was discovered, whereupon his younger half brothers killed him. The elders judged that the killing was justified and no blood price needed to be paid.

17. **A Republic or a Confederation of Clans?** The Republic of Somaliland had made a rule obliging all cattle exporters to send their cattle abroad through the seaport of Berbera. But when the exporters sent their livestock to Berbera, there was a problem. The clan in whose territory Berbera is located decreed that its own exporters should have priority. Whenever one of these was ready to load his livestock on board a ship, other exporters had to wait. The clan observed, quite correctly, that the customary law stipulated this. It held that at the wells of a given clan, the livestock of that clan always had priority over the livestock of other clans. This dispute led the parliamentary members of the Republic belonging to the same clan as one of the excluded exporters to quit the Parliament. Their reasoning was that if the customary law of the Berbera Clan could take priority over the rules of the Republic, then so should the customary law of all of the rest of the clans, and these customary laws all recognised the principle of free trade.

18. **A Particularly Heinous Murder.** A group of young men wounded and killed another by throwing hundreds of stones at him. The murder was considered so atrocious that the court condemned the families of the boys to pay 200 camels instead of the usual 100 to the family of the victim.

19. **Exclusive Use of Clan Territory.** A woman married someone from another clan who then came to live with her. They had children. When the couple died, the children inherited all of their belongings including the mother's land. According to the customary law, however, these children were members of their father's clan. That didn't bother the closest members of the mother's family, among whom the children, now adults, were living. Nevertheless, several years after the death of the parents, the elders of the mother's jilib ruled that her offspring should

leave the clan's territory with all their movables and join their own clan. They argued that for reasons of the clan's safety only members of the clan could hold land in the clan's territory.

20. **Meaning of Terms of a Contract of Sale.** A man wanted to buy a camel from someone from another clan. Having no ready money, he asked for some time in which to make the payment. It was agreed that he would pay as soon as it started raining. In the area where the seller and the buyer both lived, the rains always came by mid-March. However, this time the seasonal rains did not fall in March but earlier—in January. So the seller claimed his money two months earlier than the buyer had expected. The buyer refused and said that the phrase "as soon as the rains start falling" should not have been taken literally. The judges decided in favour of the buyer, who was allowed another two months.

Because this dispute occurred between people from different clans, it was decided by a court made up of judges from the clans of each of the parties but was presided over by a judge from a third clan. The case is remembered because it almost led to a war between the two clans, each of which had put its cavalry of approximately 500 horsemen on alert.

This raises the question of how verdicts are enforced. If the parties to a dispute are from the same clan, enforcement is a simple matter; the court calls upon all able-bodied men in the village and tells them when, where, and how to carry out the judgment. But when the parties belong to different clans, the court must tread carefully. In such cases it has no authority to order enforcement. Only the judge on the court on whose territory the verdict must be executed has that authority. He must convince his own clansmen that the verdict is fair and should be enforced.

21. **First Possession of an Elephant.** Two people claimed an elephant. The first had thrown his spear, but not hard enough to inflict a fatal wound, and the elephant had escaped. A few hours later, however, the elephant ran into another hunter. This time,

the elephant was severely wounded and subsequently axed down. The first hunter claimed ownership, saying the animal had become an easy target for any subsequent hunter. The second hunter maintained that, on the contrary, the elephant had still been full of energy when he speared and axed him down. The court found for the second hunter. It declared him to be the owner, saying the first hunter's spear was too light to have caused major damage. The verdict was remembered, not only because everyone thought justice had been done, but because the judge had given a poetic twist to his words, concluding the judgment with a verse:

> A small water point is not enough to quench his thirst;
> he needs a river.
> A small bush is not enough to give him cover;
> he needs a whole forest.
> Likewise a light spear is not enough to kill an elephant;
> quite a bit more is needed.

> *Durdur mooyee laas ma deeqo*
> *Duud mooyee daleed ma qariso*
> *Maroodi mogolo mooyee madde ma disho.*

22. **First Possession of a Watering Place.** Two herds of livestock converged towards the same well. One was a very large herd, the other a very small one. As every Somali knows, two herds cannot drink at the same time because the animals will start fighting. Consequently one of the herds must wait. Which one? The judge decided that the smaller herd must be given priority over the larger. He reasoned that if some animals of a small herd die of thirst, the owner may not be able to feed his family, whereas if some from a large herd die, the owner will still have plenty left to feed his family. Everyone thought it a wise decision. Subsequent judges followed the same reasoning, and the case became part of the Somali law.

23. **A Tax Revolt in the Ogaden.** During the 1920s and early 1930s, the Ethiopian government imposed taxes in the Somali territories known as the Ogaden. Many Somalis refused to pay,

even though some tax resisters were hanged in the public square of their village. In 1936, the Italians drove the Ethiopians out of the Ogaden. When the Ethiopians returned in 1945, they asked the ceremonial chief of the Samaron Clan to collect a "voluntary tax" from his people, and he agreed. A few days later, because he had violated the customary law, the Clan deposed its chief.

24. A Death Sentence Compensated. Two clansmen had been quarrelling over the ownership of a piece of land. A court of justice was formed. It heard the arguments and decided in favour of the defendant. That was so maddening to the plaintiff that, in a fit of rage, he killed one of the judges and fled abroad before he could be caught. A new court of justice was formed. It condemned the murderer to death. It also condemned the family of the murderer to pay compensation and a heavy fine. Both were promptly paid. After a year, the murderer returned to his village and resumed his life as a farmer and herdsman. The family of the murdered person then said that the death sentence was still valid and demanded that the murderer be arrested and executed. The court ruled, however, that compensation had been paid and that therefore the man could go and live where he wanted.

The murderer thereafter lived in his village, but not in the same way as before. His family made sure he didn't carry a weapon, and a brother or a cousin accompanied him wherever he went. This was to keep him from committing another crime and probably also to protect him from possible acts of revenge by the family of his victim.

Notes

25. Although incomplete because it does not reveal how the court dealt with the matter, this case is retained here because it shows the widespread acceptance of the legitimacy of the customary law. –Editor SM

26. While it might be thought this is not a "case," since no court was involved and hence no application of the xeer, it may be that the xeer was so abundantly clear in this instance that the family of the victim did not call for a court to be formed. –Editor SM

Appendix B
What is Kritarchy?

Frank van Dun

*The most distinctive contribution of Africa to human
history has been precisely in the civilized art of living
reasonably peacefully without a state.*

—Jean-Francois Bayart (1989:58)

Kritarchy is an ideal legal and political system most closely
approximated in the institutional structures of traditional
societies, especially those described by anthropologists as
"acephalous," "polycentric," or "stateless." Such societies are based
on customary rather than statutory law. This type of law fares poorly
under statutory regimes, and stateless societies have diminished
drastically in numbers with the spread of political states over the
past several millennia. Nevertheless, though endangered, societies
approximating kritarchies are far from extinct. Nor should they be
considered primitive. The Somali system of customary law Michael
van Notten describes in this book, for example, is not a curiosity of
some backward tribe. It is a living and highly developed juridical
system looking to the future rather than the past.

Somalia is unique in the world today for being free of even the
titular domination of a central legislative apparatus. The central
government of the Somali Democratic Republic was dismantled in
1991 when, after the ouster of dictator Siad Barre, no agreement

was reached on a successor. For more than a decade, Somalis have resisted the unremitting efforts of the United Nations and its supporters to re-impose that government. If they continue to be successful in their resistance, then it can be reasonably expected, as Van Notten argues in this book, that the Somali customary law system will evolve into a full body of common law capable of meeting every need of a developed, free-market society.

RULE OF LAW

Kritarchy as a form of government is based on equal justice for all, where justice is understood as adherence to the principles of natural law. Natural law is the body of principles underlying all spontaneous human social organisation. Implicit in these principles are certain universal natural rights of individuals, notably property rights, including rights in one's own person, and freedom of contract.

Its consistent adherence to the rules of justice under natural law distinguishes kritarchy from other political systems. Under this ideal, even courts of law, police forces, and other organisations concerned with the day-to-day maintenance of law are denied any power, privilege, or immunity not in conformity with natural law. That means that a police force in a kritarchy can lawfully use its weapons and coercive powers only to maintain the law, i.e. to defend or remedy violations of people's natural rights. It also means that, unlike their counterparts in the prevailing political systems of today's world, courts of law and police do not constitute and are not incorporated into a coercive monopoly. Anyone is entitled to offer judicial or police services to willing others. None can be forced to support any court of law or police force against his will. In short, in a kritarchy, judicial and police services are offered in a free market—which, in so far as exchanges of goods and services are concerned, is the natural law of the human world.

Because of its commitment to *equal justice for all*, a kritarchy does not know the usual political distinction between subjects and rulers. It lacks a government in the modern sense of the word, i.e. an organisation with coercive powers that claims both the obedience of and the right to use the labour or property of those living in the area over which it effectively exercises control. Governing and taxing people by public or private force is not among the functions of the political system of kritarchy. People are free to govern their own affairs, either individually or in voluntary association with others, which means that each, in governing his own affairs, is required to leave others free to govern theirs. In this sense, freedom is the basic law of a kritarchy.

It follows that a kritarchy can only exist in societies where, and for as long as, a commitment to justice is sufficiently strong to defeat the efforts of persons who would use unlawful methods such as aggression, coercion, or fraud to further their ends or to evade responsibility and liability for wrongs they have caused others. While it is theoretically conceivable that freedom could be maintained by nothing more than unorganised, spontaneous actions of self-defence, in a kritarchy the commitment to justice manifests in its political system, which guarantees a free market for the enterprise of justice.

Origin of the Term

The term "kritarchy," compounded from the Greek words *kritès* (judge) or *krito* (to judge) and *archè* (principle, cause), was coined in 1844 by the English author Robert Southy. In its construction it resembles terms such as "monarchy," "oligarchy" and "hierarchy." "Kritarchy" is mentioned, among other places, in *Webster's Unabridged Dictionary*, *The Oxford English Dictionary*, and *The American Collegiate Dictionary*. According to its etymological roots, a *kritarchy* is a political system in which justice (more exactly the judgment that seeks to determine justice) is the ruling principle or first cause. Similarly a *monarchy* is a system in which one person is supposed to be the ruling principle or first cause of every legal action, everyone else being no more than an obedient subject of the monarch. In an *oligarchy* a few persons (the oligarchs), acting in concert but without a fixed hierarchy among them, are held to be the source of all legal actions. In the modern system of parliamentary sovereignty, for example, members of parliament constitute an oligarchy and have equal standing within the parliament. However, the results of their deliberations and decisions are supposed to bind all people who, because of citizenship or residence, are considered subject to the state's authority.

If "monarchy" denotes rule by one person and "oligarchy"

denotes rule by a few, it is tempting to understand "kritarchy" as rule by judges. However, the use of the word "rule" should not mislead us into thinking that the rule of judges is like that of monarchs and oligarchs, and least of all that it is a particular sort of oligarchy.

Monarchs and oligarchs aspire to political rule, i.e. to being able to enforce on their subjects obedience to their commands, rules, decisions, and choices. In short, monarchs and oligarchs rule by a mixture of direct command and legislation. Judges, on the other hand, are supposed not to legislate but only to find ways and means of managing conflicts in a lawful manner. They do not seek to enforce obedience to their commands as such. Rather they seek respect for law, which is an order of things objectively given and not just anything that corresponds with whatever desires or ideals the judges may have.

Judges in a kritarchy have no subjects. In other political systems, judges have been incorporated as magistrates into a system of political rule and empowered to use coercive means to drag citizens and residents before their benches. Monarchs and oligarchs in those systems impose, or allow their servants (judges, prosecutors) to impose their rulings on those subjects on whom they want to impose their rulings. In other words, they "pick" their subjects (which is the root meaning of the Latin *legere*, from which the word *lex* for legislated or statute law is derived). In a kritarchy, judges do not choose which persons will appear before them. Instead, those people desiring to have their conflicts and disputes resolved by judicial judgment will "pick" their judge.

The distinctive characteristic of a kritarchy, therefore, is that it is a political system without the institution of political rule. If we think of it as "the rule of judges," we must remember that these judges enjoy no particular privileges or special powers. Kritarchy is not the rule of legislators, judges or any other category of privileged officials. It is simply the *rule of law*.

HISTORICAL APPROXIMATIONS

Examples abound, recent as well as historical, of kritarchy or near-kritarchy, and also of attempts to use constitutions and other charters to introduce elements of kritarchy as checks on the powers of states and governments. In many parts of the world, even though they derive their authority merely from custom and not from a conscious and explicit commitment to natural law, unwritten customary laws memorized by clansmen frequently provide strong support for the dispersal of power that characterises kritarchy.

At the end of the second millennium before Christ, the Hebrews lived in a system described in the biblical book of the Judges. Their "judges" were not judges in the technical sense of modern legal systems. They were influential, respected men who provided leadership and counsel without having power to coerce or tax. The history of Celtic and Germanic peoples both before and during their confrontation with Roman imperialism is replete with examples, as is the medieval period after the collapse of the Roman Empire in the West. Kritarchy was firmly established in medieval Ireland until the middle of the thirteenth century, and in Frisia into the sixteenth century. In the first half of the nineteenth century, European immigrants who settled in the Midwest and the Far West of North America developed their own brand of kritarchy. Clan societies in Asia and Africa adhere to some forms of kritarchy so far as they have not been submerged in the statist structures imposed by the colonial powers and taken over by indigenous political rulers in the post-colonial period.

While these historical realisations or near-realisations of kritarchy may suggest that it is a primitive political system, it should be borne in mind that most of them fell victim to conquest or to the firm hold on power established by military lords in times of war, who then turned ostensibly temporary structures for the mobilisation of men and resources into a permanent apparatus of political rule. It is certainly true that kritarchies are ill equipped to make or endure war for long periods of time. The vulnerability of kritarchies in the face of massive military operations is comparable to that of a small or technologically backward state confronting the might of a large or technologically advanced neighbour. This is a problem, however, that we can acknowledge without losing sight of what a kritarchy has to offer for more "normal" times.

DEMOCRACY

Democracy, despite some of its advantages over other forms of political rule, is nevertheless a system in which some presume to have the right to govern the rest regardless of their consent. As such, it is unacceptable from the viewpoint of natural law and is incompatible with the political system of kritarchy. Under a democracy people vote to determine which individuals will be their political representatives, and there is no fault in that. The central defect and, in fact, the irreparable defect of democracy is that it embodies the 'right' of the representatives to rule over those who did not vote for them as well as over those who did. It allows the elected rulers to violate the natural rights of people with impunity—at least if they do so in a properly legal way by specifying in advance and in sufficient detail how it should be done, by which magistrates or officers of the state, where people can complain if they feel their rights are improperly violated, and so forth. As in other systems of political rule, however much formal independence of the legislature and the executive the judiciary may enjoy, there is in a democracy no truly independent—*no non-governmental*—police or judiciary to which people can appeal. A democracy outlaws all independent sources of protection of natural rights as a matter of constitutional necessity, in order to make sure that no natural rights can be invoked against the legal rights of democratic rule.

Democracy is often presented as "government by consent," but that is never more than the consent of a majority and, as a rule not even that. As a political device, democracy was no doubt a great invention. Regular elections provide a rough mechanism for ensuring an alignment of rulers and a sizeable part of the subjects over whom they rule. Elections thereby help to prevent or minimise the violent confrontations and unrelenting repression and exploitation that are permanent risks in other systems of rule. Nevertheless, elections have no basis in natural law. To understand this, it suffices to ask how a person could lawfully authorise another to do what he himself has no right to do. The question is pertinent because, to repeat, democracy is a system of political rule in which there is a distinction between the rulers and the ruled, and between the legal rights of the rulers and those of the ruled. If you attempted to do to your neighbours what a democratic government does to its citizens, let us say, tax them, fix their hours of work, force them to send their children to schools of your choice, or accept the money you have printed, you would very likely end up in jail. No democracy allows you to do such things. Nor does it allow you to undertake these activities in conspiracy with others. But it does allow you to have someone else do them in your name and on your behalf! All you have to do is to vote for your "political representative."

To deny anyone the natural right to withdraw his consent, moreover, makes a nation a closed community to which one is assigned by birth and for life: a life sentence. The inability to withdraw consent—to secede—except by permission of the government itself makes a farce of the whole idea of consent.

But the great mystery of democracy is that "representatives" are vested with powers the people who empowered them are not and should not be allowed to exercise. More fundamentally, in a democracy every voter is assumed to have a right to decide who should control the coercive monopoly and rule everyone else in the state. That becomes obvious in the unlikely scenario where only a single voter shows up at the polls. His vote then decides which party should take over parliament and the government, as if he were an absolute monarch picking his counsellors and ministers.

CONSTRUCTIONS OF ARTIFICIAL LAW

Leaving no room for the idea that human beings are natural persons in a natural world, current legal and political ideologies make any man or woman an artificial being, a "citizen," whose very essence is defined and created by the legal rules of the state to which he or she belongs. Within the state, human beings have no rights except in so far as some legal authority regulates their existence and freedom. That is why the United Nations' Universal Declaration of Human Rights, in its Articles 6 and 15, names "a legal personality" and "a nationality" among the things people have a right to. From the point of view of the Declaration's underlying philosophy, a legal personality and a nationality, in a word, "citizenship," are desirable because they are the necessary conditions of legal existence in the state. Without them a person is a nobody. Once we substitute the perspective of legal rule for that of natural law, we must admit that what a person has a right to do or to call his own depends, not on what he is or does, but on his status in the legal order in which he happens to find himself. He becomes an artificial person in an artificial order, like a piece of wood that is assigned different "rights and duties" depending on whether it is used in a game of chess, checkers, or backgammon.

The glorification of such artificial legal orders is common in contemporary legal and political thought, where fiction seems invariably to triumph over reality. These orders are based on artificial or imaginary distinctions and on the neglect of or disregard for natural distinctions. Some of them arbitrarily or systematically refuse to acknowledge certain persons as persons at all. Others define some or all persons as being in some or all respects a "part" of others, to which they are therefore said to belong. Some go so far as to define human beings as parts of non-existent imaginary or fictitious persons. In fact, however, natural persons are never "parts" of other natural persons or legal fictions. They may become members of some association or society, and in that sense become "participants" in its activities, but that does not imply that they are thereby mysteriously transformed in mere "parts" of a person—nor does it imply that the association is a person in its own right.

No matter what the philosophical pretensions behind the constructions of artificial law may be, they all share a common practical implication. They deny the freedom and equality of certain human beings. These artificial constructions cannot hide the fact that from the perspective of law some people either do not exist at all or exist only in so far as they are "represented" by others. Thus, by denying natural law and the natural distinctions that constitute it, they conjure up an idea of law that makes the non-consensual 'government' of one person by another seem "lawful."

It should be sufficiently clear by now that natural law is not a question of idle speculation, but of natural fact. In this sense a kritarchy is a political system based on respect for the facts of the human world. Respect for natural law is therefore an objective category of human action. Human actions that respect law are lawful and therefore just. Those that do not are unlawful and unjust.

JUSTICE

Justice in the general sense is the art or skill of acting in conformity with law, with due regard for the rights of other persons. In the particular "technical" sense it is the art or skill of discovering rules, methods, and procedures that effectively and efficiently provide for the defence and, if need be, fortification and restoration of the law of the human world. The discovery, refinement, and systematisation of such rules, methods, and procedures are the proper field of jurisprudence as a rational discipline.

In an evolved kritarchy, jurisprudence is the business of specialists—jurists—who supply their skills in an open market to individuals and organisations. In more complex societies, they render this service primarily to courts of law, police forces, and other organisations involved in enforcing observance of natural law and helping people make their actions conform to the requirements of justice. As noted before, in a kritarchy neither the courts of law nor the police forces have any legal monopoly. Their clientele and membership remain free to shift their demand from an unsatisfactory to a hopefully more satisfactory supplier of justice. Consequently, courts of law and police forces in a kritarchy have a strong economic incentive to avoid using violence or other coercive means to, say, compel a person to appear in court, unless they have good reason to believe that he is guilty as charged, is obstructing the course of justice, or is not insured to cover his liabilities.

Not being above the law, the courts and police forces of a kritarchy always run the risk, should they deprive others of their rights when justice does not require it, of being charged with unlawful behaviour in another court. That other court might be a competitor or a group of competitors. It might also be a parliament, i.e. a representative body that acts as a public guardian of the law. Such a parliament would sit only as a court of law, however; it would not have the power to govern or to make laws that restricted anyone's rights. However, it could be an effective agent of justice, for instance by convincing the public that the courts of law or police forces it convicts are not worthy of the public's trust, or by convincing other organisations of justice to enforce its verdicts against recalcitrant convicts. Because they need the consent of all parties if they wish to avoid the risk of using violence against an innocent person, the courts in a kritarchy must offer adequate guarantees of competence and impartiality. They must do so in order to elicit the cooperation of the accused and defendants as well as to assure the plaintiffs and claimants, who initiate the proceedings, that their verdicts are unlikely to be contested in another court. Short of seeking a monopoly by the violent elimination of its competitors, an organisation of justice has no alternative but to build up a solid reputation for justice.

Working out details, conventions, and protocols for an operational and efficient system of justice is no mean task. Like every other significant practical undertaking, it requires knowledge of the general principles of law as well as experimentation with different types of organisation for supplying justice. It is the task of applying entrepreneurial creativity to recombine available social, technical, administrative, and financial resources and skills to improve the prospect for effective justice. It is not likely that this task can be carried out with any consistency within the stifling confines of a legal monopoly. On this conviction, the case for kritarchy rests.

Frank van Dun, born 1947 in Antwerp, Belgium, studied law and philosophy at the University of Ghent. His Ph.D. dissertation in 1982, *The Fundamental Principle of Law* (in Dutch), attracted the attention of Michael van Notten, who used it to develop his own views on freedom and law into a framework of thought and action for his libertarian projects. Prof. van Dun teaches legal theory, philosophy of law, fiscal theory, and logic at the universities of Ghent and Maastricht. In addition to many papers on those subjects, he has published two books in Dutch, one on Utopias (*The Utopian Temptation*, 1997, with Hans Crombag) and another on fiscal practices (*Man, Citizen and Fisc*, 2000).

Appendix C
Proposed Membership Agreement for a Freeport-Clan

Spencer Heath MacCallum
Michael van Notten

Following in the spirit of the Orbis exercise described in Chapter 15, readers are invited to critique both the substance and wording of this master-lease form. If what follows seems complex or overly detailed, it is because, lacking a vast body of legislative and administrative rules to fall back, upon any written agreement must anticipate every possible contingency. This is truly open-source social software, hence by its very nature a work-in-progress. If you can identify areas that need attention, or suggest ways to simplify or make this proposal more practical, please share your thoughts by contacting the editor, Spencer MacCallum, at sm@look.net. All suggestions will be acknowledged, and the authorship of those that are adopted will be fully credited in the document unless the author prefers to remain anonymous.

I. WHEREAS SOMALI FREEPORT SERVICES ("SOFREE"), a private company not affiliated with any government or government agency and owning a 499-year leasehold from the Samaron Clan on the entrepreneurial community known as Newland Freeport (hereinafter called "Newland"), is in the business of developing, maintaining, and promoting the growth of optimal human environments in Newland conducive to leisure and/or business activities, and of sub-leasing to its customers exclusive sites giving full access to and enjoyment of the same as members of Newland, and

WHEREAS JOHN JOHNSON ("DWELLER") desires membership in Newland for the purpose of residing and/or pursuing business or leisure activities there,

NOW THEREFORE SOFREE, for consideration set forth below, conveys for a renewable period of 99 years to DWELLER, his heirs and assigns, subject only to the terms and conditions of this agreement, full membership in Newland including equal access with all other members to its common areas and facilities and, in addition, exclusive occupancy of that space, known as [a complete property description follows].[27]

II. SOFREE Further Covenants and Promises:[28]

A. To guarantee DWELLER quiet possession of his leasehold and the freedom, subject only to the terms and conditions of this agreement, to make full and undisturbed use of that space and of Newland's public areas and facilities.

B. To behave toward DWELLER and all persons in Newland in a manner consistent with the "Outline of Natural Rights and Obligations" appended to and made a part of this agreement and, most specifically, not to impose any tax or permit anyone to impose any tax on the person or property of DWELLER or of anyone else in Newland.[29] The word "tax" shall mean any imposition of any levy, fine, or assessment other than as provided for by the terms of this or other agreements voluntarily entered into.

C. To secure from anyone entering Newland for whatever purpose, who is not party to a lease or rental agreement, his or her written agreement to abide while in Newland by the law of Newland as described in the procedural rules set out in Section (IV.J.3) and the "Outline of Natural Rights and Obligations" appended to and made a part of this agreement.

D. To exercise due diligence in securing the safety of all persons and property in Newland. To this end SOFREE shall, as a minimum:

  1. Disseminate information concerning:[30]

     a. Health and safety.

     b. Insurance.

     c. Technology for the abatement of nuisance effects such as noise, smoke, vibration, noxious gases, odours, glare, heat, fire, explosive hazards, traffic, and waste effluent.

     d. Private means of dispute resolution.

  2. Foster the growth and development of freely competitive judicial and police services in Newland consistent with the "Outline of Natural Rights and Obligations" appended to and made a part of this lease and to the procedural rules in Paragraph (IV.J.3).[31]

  3. Reimburse uninsured losses resulting from fire, theft, or bodily injury suffered in Newland's public areas, or in DWELLER'S private area when said fire, theft or attack originated outside that area and was not caused by negligence of DWELLER or his tenants, guests or invitees, provided DWELLER has

apprised   SOFREE beforehand of any unusual amounts of property in his possession and has taken reasonable precautions for its safety.[32]

E. To assist the public in making informed land-use decisions in Newland by, among other things, collecting and disseminating pertinent marketing statistics and related data.[33]

F. To grant no franchises or licenses for doing business in Newland.

G. To conduct its business in a manner calculated to maximise its overall capitalised ground-lease revenue in Newland.[34]

H. To ensure and build good-neighbourly relations by behaving responsibly as a landholder within the territory of the Somali host clan, this including but not limited to

1. Taking strict precautions against any kind of environmental degradation of neighbouring lands,
2. Volunteering contributions to the common pool to provide relief in time of natural calamity,
3. Volunteering contributions to the common pool to build facilities perceived as benefiting all, such as roads, schools, or wells and, failing to make such contributions, to forego any benefit from them.

I. To have at all times sufficient insurance coverage or available reserves to compensate DWELLER for any loss or inconvenience DWELLER might suffer as a result of SOFREE violating any term of this agreement.[35]

III. DWELLER Covenants and Promises to SOFREE:

A. To pay to SOFREE or its successors the annual ground

rent of the leasehold, exclusive of improvements thereon, half to be paid on the first of January and half on the first of July of each year, or as otherwise agreed by both parties.

B. To behave toward SOFREE and all persons in Newland in a manner consistent with the "Outline of Natural Rights and Obligations" appended to and made a part of this agreement.[36]

C. To exercise diligence, at home or abroad, not to create a nuisance for, or to endanger the health, safety, or property of, other members of the Newland community, including their tenants, guests, and invitees.[37]

D. To be adequately insured against any possible liability for loss or injury that he or his tenants, guests or invitees might cause to others.[38] This shall specifically include but not be limited to losses or injuries resulting from his violating any part of this agreement, with particular reference to Paragraph (III.C).[39]

E. To be adequately insured against loss of his life, property, or earning capacity due to fire, sickness, accidental injury, or acts of God, including natural disasters and the effects of war.[40]

F. To purchase any insurance required by this agreement only from firms domiciled in Newland and carrying the highest certification from a major consumer rating service, and in all such policies to name SOFREE as co-insured.[41]

G. To scrupulously avoid using or threatening physical force against any person at any time or place, for any reason, if adequate peaceful means of dealing with the problem can be found.[42]

H. To be responsible at all times for the actions of his tenants, guests or invitees as if their actions were his own.[43]

IV. SOFREE and DWELLER Further Agree and Commit:

A. That the individual signatories to this agreement have authority to commit to the fulfilment of the terms of this agreement the full faith and credit of any affected organisations whom they may represent or by whom they may be employed, if such there be, and shall be personally and individually responsible for the consequences of their actions in Newland. They shall have no protected status before the law by virtue of their membership in or employment by any organisation.[44]

B. That this leasehold shall be DWELLER'S property to sell, sublet, encumber or otherwise deal with as he sees fit, subject only to the terms and conditions of this agreement and to SOFREE'S approval, which shall not be unreasonably withheld. If this leasehold is to be transferred to another party or parties, then this original agreement shall be returned to SOFREE with the proposed transfer endorsed thereon. Upon approval, SOFREE will issue a new agreement to the transferee. In the event DWELLER rents or sublets any or all of his space, his agreement(s) with his tenant(s) shall not be inconsistent with this agreement.

C. That the rent for the site herein leased shall be _____ per annum, and that this rent shall be revised every five years to the then current market value of the site, less a ____ percent reduction to DWELLER as a preferred tenant. Market rental value shall be appraised by three disinterested parties selected as follows: SOFREE and DWELLER each choosing one of three persons named by the other and the third to be selected by those two.

SOFREE and DWELLER shall then each submit to the panel of three their independent appraisals of the rental value of the site for its highest and best use, together with supporting evidence. The panel shall study the appraisals and choose one or the other, as it stands, without modification.[45] SOFREE shall make its leasing records freely available to assist the appraisal process.[46] Should DWELLER fail to select an appraiser within 30 days after SOFREE has submitted three names to him, then SOFREE shall be free to make the choice for him. Should either party fail to submit an appraisal, then that of the other will obtain.

D. That if rent payments fall into arrears for ___ days, DWELLER shall incur a late penalty of ___ percent of the balance due, and that after ___ days of arrears SOFREE shall be entitled, upon 24 hours written notice, to terminate this lease and resume possession.[47] In such event, SOFREE shall first return any rental balance pro-rated to the date of the written notice. Compensation for DWELLER'S fixed improvements shall be established in the manner set out in Paragraph (IV.C), above.

E. That this agreement may be modified or terminated at any time by mutual consent, provided, however, that any modification shall be subject to the appended "Guidelines for Letting and Subletting." Either party acting alone may terminate this agreement upon appropriate notification of the other, as follows:

1. DWELLER shall be free to terminate this agreement and quit the leasehold without further liability for rent under any of the following circumstances:

   a. Upon six months written notice, in which case the removal or sale of any improvements shall be DWELLER'S responsibility.

b. Upon 30 days written notice following violation
or neglect by SOFREE of any of the terms of
this agreement, including especially any act or
threat of violence upon DWELLER, his tenants,
guests or invitees, by SOFREE or any of its
appointed agents, or their entry on the premises
without DWELLER'S express permission, or
the imposition of any tax upon the person or
property of DWELLER, his tenants, guests or
invitees. In the event of such termination,
SOFREE shall:

1) Return any rents paid ahead by DWELLER,
pro-rated to the date of the complaint, and
shall compensate DWELLER for the value
of his site improvements as ascertained in
the manner set out in Paragraph (IV.C),
above.

2) At its own cost safely transport DWELLER
and anyone else residing at the time on
DWELLER'S premises, together with their
personal belongings, to any place of their
choosing.[48] If this cost exceeds that of
transportation to DWELLER'S point of
origin before coming to Newland,
DWELLER shall pay the difference.

2. SOFREE shall be free to terminate this agreement
and resume possession of the leasehold under any of
the following circumstances:

a. Upon 24-hours written notice following
DWELLER'S failure to payrent in full for a
period of 30 days after it has become due and
payable. In that event, the compensation for
DWELLER'S fixed improvements shall be
established in the manner set out in Paragraph
(IV.C), above, and shall be paid to DWELLER

by DWELLER'S successor, if such there be within a year, and otherwise by SOFREE.

b. At the end of any negotiated lease period, following at least one year's prior written notice, in the event of repeated complaints by other residents of disturbances of the peace. Provided, however, that in the absence of any further complaints, the notice shall have no effect.

F. That provisions in this or other leases entered into in Newland by SOFREE or by DWELLER that do not accord with the "Guidelines for Letting and Subletting" attached hereto and made a part of this lease, or that conflict with any provisions of this lease not specifically exempted by said Guidelines, will be null and void. Further that, except for such provisions as may be deleted or modified in accordance with the Guidelines, every lease, sublease, sub-sublease, etc. in Newland will carry every provision of this lease.

G. That disputes with any member of Newland that cannot be resolved informally by the disputing parties, including disputes over the terms of this lease or its performance, shall be settled by a mediator or, failing that, a neutral arbitrator in conformity with the "Outline of Natural Rights and Obligations" appended to and made a part of this agreement, and with the procedural rules in Paragraph (IV.J.3) below.[49]

H. That disputes with anyone outside Newland that cannot be resolved informally by the disputing parties shall be settled as in (IV.G) above or, if this is unacceptable to the other party, SOFREE and DWELLER will diligently seek a different, mutually agreeable means of resolving the dispute.

However, disputes involving a Somali, regardless of his or her clan affiliation, shall be settled by mediation or, failing that, by an arbitration panel of two or more judges, an equal number chosen by each of the disputing parties. Both the law of Newland and that of the clan in question shall apply. In case of a conflict of laws, a compromise shall be found. Should the judges be unable to agree on a verdict or on selecting a tie-breaking judge, the judges or one of the parties shall request the Center of the International Convention for the Settlement of Investment Disputes between States and Nationals of Other States (ICSID) adopted in Washington DC, USA, on March 15th, 1965 to appoint a judge, who will then act as their chairman.

I. That any contract either might make with persons outside Newland shall contain an arbitration clause specifying a mutually agreeable means of dispute management that will be binding on the parties.[50]

J. SOFREE and DWELLER do further agree with respect to safety and justice that

1. DWELLER may offer and perform police services for anyone in Newland, provided he has the sanction of an impartial third party prior to or immediately following the event, and then only:

- at the request of a person whose rights have been violated,
- against the person who violated them,
- for the sole purpose of remedying such violation,
- with the least violent means available, and
- only until the violator agrees to comply.

And that DWELLER, performing such services, shall be liable for his actions as if he were acting for himself alone.

2. DWELLER may offer and perform judicial,

mediation, and arbitration services for anyone in Newland. When acting in the capacity of a judge, he shall render judgments on questions of law and rights only on the basis of facts as presented, irrespective of the litigants' opinions, achievements, family, or physical characteristics, and shall only recognise obligations that are consistent with natural rights. DWELLER shall at all such times be responsible for his actions as if he were acting in his private capacity.

3. When acting in such a protective or judicial capacity, DWELLER shall observe the following procedural rules or protocols. These rules are intended to be a starting point in the search for effective means of defending and enforcing the list of natural rights appended to this document. It is recognised that while natural rights are unchanging, our knowledge of them together with procedures for defending and enforcing them are subject to continual improvement. Hence police and judges in Newland shall be free to specify more detailed rights, obligations and procedures, provided they are not inconsistent with those set out in this agreement.

   The "Outline of Natural Rights and Obligations" appended at the end of this agreement and the procedural rules listed below shall be capable of amendment at five-year intervals by the unanimous recommendation of SOFREE and a panel of five judges who have practiced continuously in Newland for more than five years and earned during each of those years the highest certification from a major consumer rating service. The minimum procedural rules required of anyone residing in Newland and performing protective or judicial services shall be these:

1. Anyone accused of having violated a person's natural

right shall be presumed innocent until judged guilty by a court of law. Until then, he is entitled to

1.1 Agree with the plaintiff on initiating, interrupting, or terminating any litigation before a judge of their choice.

1.2 Refuse to submit to a judge who has denied his request for a jury.

1.3 Be informed, in writing and in a language which he understands, of the nature and reason for the charges against him.

1.4 Try to refute those charges (pleas of ignorance of the law shall not be accepted).

1.5 Be assisted and represented by counsel of his choice and to keep his communications with that counsel confidential.

1.6 Resist interrogation, decline to supply evidence against himself or his organisation, and refuse confession.

1.7 Be given a trial without undue delays, in the location where the violation occurred, and be granted a public session of the court.

1.8 Reject procedural and evidentiary rules that infringe upon his presumed innocence.

1.9 Inspect the evidence brought against him and cross-examine his accusers and their witnesses.

1.10 Have his own witnesses testify under the same conditions as the witnesses against him.

1.11 Present his defence in writing, elucidate his defence

orally at his trial, and be allowed adequate time for the presentation of his defence.

1.12 Receive a transcript of the trial's proceedings and verdict.

2.   Anyone arrested shall be

2.1 Informed immediately of the reason for his arrest, his right to remain silent, and the possible consequences of making statements, and instructed in writing and in a language that he understands of the nature and reason for the charges against him.

2.2 Given proper food, clothing, shelter, and accommodation as well as immediate access to legal advisors and the opportunity to post bail.

2.3 Spared all forms of cruel or inhumane treatment.

2.4 Brought without undue delay before a grand jury or impartial court of law, failing which he is entitled to immediate release.

2.5 Released from detention when the court finds the charges lacking in credibility or when sufficient guaranty has been given to insure that he will appear at the trial and obey the judgment, and his release would not unduly hamper the investigation.

2.6 Permitted to receive mail and visitors.

3.   Anyone convicted of having violated a natural right is entitled to

3.1 Be informed, in writing and in a language which he understands, of the reasons and evidentiary grounds for his conviction.

3.2 Appeal against his verdict and have its interpretation of the law reviewed by a separate court.

3.3 Avoid forcible execution of his verdict by complying voluntarily.

3.4 Avoid any punishment in the form of imprisonment.

3.5 Avoid any corporeal punishment.

4. No one judged by a court of law shall be put in jeopardy again for the same activity, except upon appeal by the plaintiff to another court.

5. Anyone falsely arrested, unduly detained, or mistakenly convicted shall be compensated by the responsible parties.

6. Any person in clear and present danger is entitled to use force to

6.1 Defend his rights against immediate attack or stop an attack in progress.

6.2 Arrest his attacker in the act.

6.3 Seize his attacker's assets whenever they risk disappearing before a police or judicial agency can secure them as a bond for his liabilities.

6.4 Conserve proof or evidence, provided that a judicial agency certifies, either before or immediately afterwards, that: (1) the proof or evidence is or was at risk of being lost and (2) the least violent means available will be or was used.

7. Anyone who believes his natural rights have been violated is entitled to

7.1 Initiate proceedings against the violator in a court of arbitration.

7.2 Halt such proceedings and suspend or stop the execution of any verdict in his favour.

7.3 Appeal from a verdict of acquittal that does not state the reasons For the acquittal.

7.4 Appeal from the verdict in appeal when it overturns the original verdict.

7.5 Have a court's interpretation of the law reviewed by a separate court of arbitration.

7.6 Have these entitlements exercised by an agent if he is not able to exercise them himself, or by his heirs if he has died.

8. A parent whose child's rights have been violated is entitled to seek justice on the child's behalf. If the violator is one of its parents or legal guardians, the child's insurance company or nearest relatives are entitled to bring suit.

9. Unless the litigants agree otherwise, the costs incurred by the courts for dispensing justice, as well as any litigation costs of the litigants, shall be borne by the defendant if convicted, and by the plaintiff if the defendant is acquitted.

Guidelines for Letting and Subletting

[These guidelines will provide for modifying certain provisions of this agreement such as IV.C and D (rent terms) and IV.E (termination) to fit the particular circumstances of a sublease, or omitting certain lease provisions inappropriate for subleases, for example II.G (requirement to operate as a business).]

Outline of Natural Rights and Obligations

PREAMBLE: Natural law describes the voluntary, universal order of human society. It originates in our life as reasoning human beings among our kind. It acknowledges the right of every person to live a life governed by his own goals, judgments, and beliefs, and serves to prevent as well as resolve conflicts among people. It stipulates that every person shall be free to dispose of his own property and shall refrain from disposing of the property of others without their permission. It permits all activities that do not infringe upon the person or property of another. This law takes priority over all other principles and rules that shape human society, including rules legislated by parliaments or established by contract. It requires that enforcement only be pursued in ways consistent with itself. Under the disciplines of profit and loss, supply and demand, and peaceful competition in the free market, means of enforcement can be expected to continually improve.

In order to safeguard the freedom of all who visit or dwell in Newland, Somali Freeport Services has undertaken as set out below to identify the principles of natural law and their derivative rights and obligations. As a prerequisite to entering this Freeport, every person shall agree to this law and at all times be adequately insured or self-insured against any liabilities arising under it. These natural law principles and all contractual obligations consistent with them and freely undertaken by dwellers and visitors shall be the only law in Newland. Anyone in Newland is free to offer and perform police and judicial services (IV.J.1,2). The procedural rules, or protocols, required of police and judicial workers in defending and enforcing the rights of residents and visitors to Newland are listed in Paragraph (IV.J.3) above.

Principles of Natural Law

Fundamental Rights
Everyone is free to:

- form and hold his own opinions,
- use his body as he sees fit,
- have as his property anything not belonging to another,
- make and perform agreements with others of his choosing; and
- defend these freedoms.

Fundamental Obligations
Everyone has a fundamental obligation to honour the rights of others by refraining from:

- claiming or pretending to be or represent another person without his explicit or implicit consent,
- using or threatening use of force against peaceful persons, or
- disposing of other people's property without their permission.

Remedies
Anyone who violates someone's natural rights has an obligation to
- cease such violation,
- return any property thereby alienated to their rightful owner,
- make restitution for losses suffered.

Such a person loses, to the benefit of his victim and to the extent required for remedy, his right to dispose of his property until payment is made or agreed upon.[51]

Should the rights violator and his victim fail to agree on whether a violation of natural rights occurred, what property was alienated, who was the rightful owner, or the nature and extent of losses inflicted or suffered, these things can be determined by an impartial arbiter.

Natural Rights Deriving from the Above
From these fundamentals, the following non-exhaustive list of natural rights is derived:

Everyone is free to:

1. Live peacefully according to his beliefs.

2. Express his thoughts and opinions in his own language and manner.

3. Travel and reside in any geographic region and freely move in and out of it with his possessions, provided he poses no physical danger to the persons or property of others and abides by any rules that the proprietors, if any, have announced to visitors.

4. Enjoy the privacy of his home, business, effects, and communications.

5. Create a family and raise his children according to his own insights.

6. Assemble with any others and to join or resign from any voluntary association.

7. Offer his services to people of his choice.

8. Break any employment contract as long as he honours its severance conditions.

9. Undertake any economic activity, including the adjudication or enforcement of natural rights, and to keep any rewards earned therefrom.

10. Sell, buy, lease, rent, lend, borrow, inherit, retain, or give away property by mutual agreement, and to repossess stolen property.

11. Develop his land, waters and air, and any material in them, and
    prevent others from spoiling or polluting them.

12. Keep and bear arms.

13. Defend himself forcibly when his rights are in clear and present danger, subject to his personal liability for his actions.

Rights not listed herein shall be upheld only if they are consistent with the principles listed above. Insults and defamatory acts violate natural rights only if they damage the victim's property.

Children

Children are immature persons. Brought into the world by the actions of others (their parents), they have a claim on those others to care for them until they become mature persons—that is, until they are sufficiently developed to care for themselves. If the parents neglect or are unable to care for their child, the child or others acting on its behalf may seek a guardian who will assume parental responsibilities.

A child enjoys the same freedom as an adult person except for restrictions imposed by its parents or guardians for its own safety, health, and development, or to control the child's actions for which they are liable towards others.

A child becomes an adult when it reaches sufficient maturity. At least until then, its parents or guardians are responsible and liable for its actions towards others. However, contracts concluded between a child and an adult are at the risk of the adult party and not at the risk of the child's parents or guardians.

Parents or guardians may extend the time of their responsibility and liability for the young adult's actions. They may do so unconditionally or upon acceptance of a commitment by the young adult to fulfil the conditions they specify. His failure to honour that commitment ends their responsibility and liability. A young adult may release his parents or guardians from their responsibility and liability for his actions by, implicitly or explicitly, indicating his willingness to assume responsibility and liability for his own actions.

Force

Anyone is free to use force to defend his fundamental rights or to remedy their violation, subject to his own liability for excessive force or avoidable property damage. This freedom can be exercised individually or by organising defensive police forces, including military forces, subject to the limitation just stated, which applies to all uses of force against persons.

Governance

Anyone is free to associate with others by entering into a contract to create an association dedicated to the pursuit of mutually agreed goals by mutually agreed means and methods. No such contract is valid, however, that infringes the natural rights of third parties, nor is any part valid that infringes the natural rights of the members by attempting to regulate where regulation is not explicitly called for in the contract.

No person can be considered a member of an association except by his explicit agreement to abide by its rules and regulations. Nor is anyone obliged to contribute labour or other assets to an association unless the contribution is part of the membership agreement.

Whatever the form and style of governance to which members of an association agree, the government of the association has no authority over the persons or property of non-members. Nor has it any authority over the persons or property of its members beyond that ceded to it individually by them in their membership agreement.

Outside the limits of the authority ceded to them by the members of the association, and in all their dealings with non-members, governing officers and personnel have no powers other than those accruing by right to all human beings—nor are they exempt from the obligations that accompany the rights of every human being.

Legislated rules that infringe upon the natural, voluntary order of human society are null and void, while those that are compatible with that natural order are binding only on those who knowingly and voluntarily endorse them.

Notes

27. While this sub-lease specifies a term, there is no reason why there need be a fixed date of termination. Of course, a sub-lease cannot have a term longer than the lease from which it derives. An individual might choose a very long or even a perpetual lease for the psychological sense of permanent membership in the community, contingent only on observance of the lease terms. Leases for 999 years are commonplace in English-speaking countries, as are perpetual leaseholds in many parts of the world even though not now recognised under Anglo-American statutory law.

28. Emalie MacCallum points out the aptness here of the word "promise," defined by Webster as "a declaration that gives the person to whom it is made a right to expect or claim the performance or forbearance of a specified act." But note that at English common law, a mere promise without consideration establishes no right for the claimant.

29. SOFREE and Dweller (Dweller in III.B) mutually promising to behave in a manner consistent with the appended "Outline of Natural Rights and Obligations" enables an operating system of law to be introduced into the community from the outset with each and every member committed to it by specific contractual agreement. This is important if the freeport is to interact with Somali customary law from the beginning. Courts will of course be free to interpret and apply it in accordance with accepted practice in the community, and Paragraph (IV.J.3) provides for periodic review.

30. A basic service of SOFREE will be to ensure that up-to-date technical information about the "how" of community living is readily and easily available to everyone in the community. One reason for this is that the membership/lease agreement does not specify the types of prohibited behavior that might endanger others or be a public nuisance, since this would call for policing—inspections and enforcement—by SOFREE. As the community owner, SOFREE is so much a large bullfrog in the pond that it is

politic to avoid or minimise situations that could lead to confrontation with other members. Instead, the landholder takes the initiative. He covenants (III.C) to exercise all due diligence to avoid endangering others. Should a dispute arise among members, it will go first to mediation and then to arbitration (IV.G), and a private arbitrator will determine whether one or another member acted contrary to the spirit of the lease agreement. If the arbitrator finds against the landholder, SOFREE will be free to act at its discretion on that information which, by then, will be public knowledge. The issue will turn partly on the question of whether the defendant was sufficiently informed to have acted differently.

31. The late Michael van Notten prepared the outline of natural rights and obligations and the list of procedural rules to be observed in their enforcement that are incorporated in this lease. Their inclusion in the lease enables a body of law to be introduced into the community that will be enforceable on SOFREE and all others in Newland through the lease agreement. Day visitors will agree upon entering to be bound by this law during their stay.

32. This provision has long precedent at common law, where an innkeeper is held to be insurer of the safety of persons and property of his guests.

33 This clause, extending the public-information services provided in Paragraph (II.D.1), seeks to facilitate spontaneous order in community growth. The assumption is that most inappropriate land-use decisions result from inadequate information and that where information is available, the nonconforming uses will be small enough in number and extent that they will be able to be tolerated. Thus SOFREE will promote a process of dispersed, or polycentric, community planning. It will assist existing and prospective leaseholders to make rational land-use decisions by seeing that they have the widest possible access to all relevant information, including not only economic data, but inputs from neighbors who may, for example, be anticipating changes in their own uses, and from architects and planners.

34. The ultimate protection for members is that SOFREE will be operated as a business and hence more rationally than it might otherwise. If it were operated for any other reason—ideological, charitable or whatnot—there would not be this protection. The impersonal, rational pricing mechanism of the market process is the ultimate safeguard of justice in a civilized community. The rental income from a proprietary community affords a quantitative measure of its success as a community and a yardstick by which to

evaluate proposals. It introduces into community planning a degree of rationality hitherto lacking; for it offers in principle a quantitative measure and feedback for ascertaining whether and by how much any given project adds to or subtracts from the "common good" understood as the attractiveness (marketability) of community membership.

It should be noted that this requirement (see appended "Guidelines for Letting and Subletting") need not and probably would not appear in subleases in Newland since, besides the usual residential uses and non-profit organisations such as churches and benevolent societies, Newland would afford a secure environment for groups to lease land on which to establish communes and intentional communities of diverse kinds.

35 This was suggested by a similar provision in the constitution of Ciskei, South Africa, and is intended as a further protection against tyranny, the main protection being the business nature of the public enterprise (II.G). This provision bonds SOFREE to perform its promises to the members, in effect insuring the constitution of Newland.

36. This commits DWELLER in all his conduct, including occasions when he might perform judicial, military, or police work in the community. It thus constrains judges and police by contract to follow specific procedural rules and to respect the natural rights of community members with whom they deal.

37. This would include actions not only within Newland, but also while traveling abroad, actions that might compromise the security of the Freeport or be considered provocative by one or more political governments of the world, leading them to take actions contrary to the interests of the Freeport community. In other words, members would have to observe the strict political neutrality of Newland. "Reasonable behavior" would be the criterion or test.

38. John Yench, of Long Beach, California suggested this and the following insurance clauses to eliminate the need for SOFREE to conduct health and safety inspections and policing, making these instead the proximate responsibility of the insurers even though the ultimate responsibility rests with SOFREE as landlord. Should insurance be denied or canceled and not picked up by another carrier, the leaseholder would find himself in default of his lease, at which point SOFREE would become involved.

39. DWELLER here insures his word as SOFREE does its word in (II.H). This provision shifts from SOFREE to the insurance provider(s), in whose interest it now is, the burden of inspections

and policing with respect to security (see III.C and accompanying footnote). The insurance providers in turn are monitored by consumer rating services (III.F). To complete this picture, no one, rating services included, escapes the eye of the equities market.

40. This clause insures the member against loss of membership from inability to pay rent because of accident, injury or other calamity and against him or his dependents becoming a burden on the community. It also protects creditors and contractual partners.

41. Because insurability is the foundation stone on which the security of Newland rests, it is essential that firms relied upon be real and reputable. Emalie MacCallum suggested consumer rating as an alternative to SOFREE maintaining a list of approved companies. The market process would then decide, whereas to require approval by SOFREE would be tantamount to licensing and hence in restraint of trade.

42. The test is reasonable behavior. This explicit rule (the only clause inserted in this lease solely by reason of a personal philosophical preference of the writer) confers a psychological and cultural benefit in Newland: By removing any and all violent action from the category of "right and justified" behavior and viewing it instead as a failure, however necessary it might have seemed in the perceived absence of alternatives the individual is challenged to look for peaceful means of resolving differences. The assumption is that there are always peaceful solutions, the challenge being to find them. While such an assumption cannot be proved, it is like the scientist's working assumption that the universe is rational and understandable. It is defensible because it is a productive assumption—*productive of discovery*. Physical harm inflicted in any situation is tragic. However, the person unable to avoid inflicting it is no more to be condemned than the unsuccessful seeker after scientific truth. He is rather to be viewed with compassion for his shortcoming in a situation that brought tragedy to a fellow human being and that may also have imposed liabilities on himself. It is hoped that this view will become a part of the cultural outlook of Newland.

As for SOFREE itself, it has a contractual obligation to make Newland safe for its members. If Newland or any part of it is threatened and SOFREE can think of no alternative but to use force to protect it, then it is incumbent upon SOFREE to use force. But this will be looked upon not as right and justified behavior but as unavoidable because SOFREE knew of no other way to handle the situation. It will be looked upon as improper means and, as such, will establish no precedent for the future. The individual or firm that meets threatening situations by innovating peaceful means of handling them will be admired and will enjoy an improved market position. SOFREE might even offer a periodic prize conferring public prestige on him who displays the greatest ingenuity of this kind.

Far worse, of course, would be for SOFREE to fail its responsibility of protecting life and property in Newland. Mahatma Gandhi's pragmatic injunction comes to mind: "He who cannot protect himself or his nearest and dearest or their honour by nonviolently facing death, may and ought to do so by violently dealing with the oppressor. He who can do neither of the two is a burden. He has no business to be the head of a family [read "community"]. He must either hide himself, or must rest content to live forever in helplessness and be prepared to crawl like a worm at the bidding of a bully" (Young India, November 10, 1928).

43. Konrad Godleske, of Portland, Oregon notes that this principle is strong in Japan, as is the tradition of having a guarantor co-sign for almost anything considered important. It is similar in function to clan-based collective responsibilities in customary law. DWELLER has insurance protection, of course, but his insurability will suffer and his premiums accordingly rise if he is careless or neglectful.

44. This clause recognises the lack of strict accountability of managers to owners in the traditional statutory corporation, which owing to the collectivisation of authority is lacking individual responsibility, personal liability, and proprietary interest. This can result in irresponsible behaviour on the part of management. Accordingly, prospective corporate tenants may find it necessary to adjust their contract with their agent. SOFREE itself may want to organise in other ways than a corporation, perhaps as a limited partnership. For a careful consideration of this question, see an unpublished paper by Alvin Lowi, Jr., "An Entrepreneurial Corporation," available from the author at alowi@earthlink.net.

45. The late Dr. F.A. Harper, of Atherton, California, suggested this form of arbitration, especially suited to cases where the facts are not in dispute. It has the virtue of bringing the parties closer together in their respective claims rather than farther apart, as happens in an adversarial system where each takes an extreme and opposite position in the hope that eventual compromise will favor him. Here, each party makes his proposed solution as close to the other party's claim as possible in the hope that it will become the decision in the case.

46. Suggested by Dan Sullivan, Pittsburgh, Pennsylvania.

47. Property management experience teaches that rent collections need handling promptly and strictly. Not only is it not a favor to a tenant to allow him to get into arrears, but it tends to create an unmanageable situation. The tenant is not without options: advance arrangements might be made for later payment; the leasehold might be financeable in the mortgage market; other loans might be available; or insurance might play a role. The writer in a special situation once renegotiated the rent retroactively over the preceding year for a good tenant, gaining the tenant a month.

48. This clause is responsive to a comment by David Friedman at a time when the initial assumption of the Orbis project had yet to be amended to make Orbis one space settlement in a cluster of settlements, thereby subjecting it to market competition. Friedman's concern was that the possibly high cost to a tenant of leaving a settlement remotely situated might tempt the proprietors to unilaterally raise rents, thereby in effect imposing a tax. This paragraph underwrites DWELLER's return transportation in such case. However, for SOFREE to violate its agreement in the first place, especially with competition factored into the equation, would be tantamount to relinquishing its business, so that in practical terms the likelihood would be remote. SOFREE would also face insurance cancellation or raised premiums, and its mismanagement would be an invitation to others to acquire controlling interest with a view to enhancing or restoring its profitability.

49. We can reasonably expect that in response to demand in a free-market situation, arbitration companies will come into existence and offer a complete line of dispute handling services competitively priced. A malefactor who refused a call to arbitration would lose the judgment by default. If he ignored the judgment, his insurer would pay restitution to the injured parties and then doubtless revoke his policy, putting him in violation of his lease. Unless he could find another qualified insurer, which might be difficult, he would soon find himself on his way out of Newland. If he were considered dangerous, the consortium of insurance companies presumably would have ways of dealing with him since they would have the most at stake in preserving the safety of life and property in Newland. By the same token, the consortium could be expected to join SOFREE in conducting a defense of Newland in the unlikely event of military threat.

The past two decades have witnessed a growing interest in polycentric, or non-monopolistic, legal systems. A useful introduction and guide to the literature is Tom W. Bell (1991). Valuable work not mentioned by Bell includes Randy E. Barnett (1998), Bruce L. Benson (1990, 1998), A.S. Diamond (1975), Bruno Leoni (1961), Francis D. Tandy (1896,62-78), and William C. Wooldridge (1970).

50. In the interest of foreign trade and cultural relations, Bruce L. Benson suggested that SOFREE and DWELLER should commit in the lease to seeking, in the event of a dispute with anyone outside Newland, a method of resolution agreeable to both parties. He pointed out that in the absence of such a provision outsiders might be reluctant to trade with Newlanders, resulting in Newland becoming isolated. Godleske adds that this provision would also lessen any danger there might possibly be of organised military aggression against the Freeport.

51. One who (willfully) invades the property domain of another places himself willfully under the jurisdiction of his victim for as long as he refuses to withdraw from the victim's domain, to restore the status quo ante or an equivalent condition, and to compensate for the losses the victim incurred while the invasion lasted and the costs he made in the endeavor to end it and get full restitution. – Editor FvD

Appendix D
A Practical Guide to
The Spelling of Somali

Mauro Tosco

Until 1972, Somali was for all practical purposes an unwritten language. In the past, Arabic script had occasionally been used, especially by Muslim scholars and for writing religious poetry, but this practice never gained a wide circulation. In the period between the two World Wars, an educated Somali of the Majarteen clan, Cusmaan Yuusuf Keenadiid, developed an indigenous script, generally referred to in the scientific literature as "Osmania." This script gained a somewhat limited circulation, especially in the central parts of the country, and several specimens of private letters and documents handwritten in Osmania have been recovered. Nevertheless, the script was unfit for printing, and was moreover somewhat connected with the clan of the author. After years of intense discussions, the military regime that came to power opted in 1972 for the Latin alphabet.

In the Somali national orthography, many signs have approximately the same value they have in English and other languages: "b", "d", "f", "g", "h", "k", "l", "m", "n", "s", "t", "w" and "y". One may note that "t" and "d" are pronounced further forward in the mouth than their English counterparts, and rather like in Spanish. "g" and "s" always have the "hard" pronunciation heard in English *garden* or *sack*, not the "soft" one of *gentle* or *those*. "r" has generally a "strong," rolled sound, and is always pronounced, also at the end of a word. "**j**" has the same value of English *j* in *John* or *banjo*; but it may also be pronounced voiceless, as English *ch* in *church* or *catch*. Also "**sh**" has the same value of English *sh* in *shame* or *ship*.

The difficult sounds are those written "**c**", "**x**", "**q**", as well as those rendered by the combinations "**dh**" and "**kh**". The signs "**c**" and "**x**" have very peculiar values in Somali, not at all similar to those of the same signs in other languages, and their use may seem confusing. Moreover, the sounds they represent are probably the most difficult to foreigners: both are pharyngeal, i.e., made by a constriction deep in the throat, in the area technically called pharynx. As a leading phonetician put it, "the best way to induce the pharyngeal compression is to activate what is called the 'gag' reflex. Unless the reader is exceptionally insensitive he can do this by sticking a finger into his mouth so that it touches, or merely approaches, the uvula, the red tip hanging down at the end of the palate, in the centre of the back of the mouth. The extreme convulsive contraction of the pharynx that this induces is the starting point from which to develop a milder, less intense, contraction" (Catford 1988:100). "**c**" is voiced, and sometimes difficult to perceive; interestingly, it is often transcribed as ʿ (an apostrophe) or even left unnoticed. E.g., the common Muslim male name written **Cali** in Somali corresponds to what is often written ʿ*Ali* or even simply *Ali* in English.

Its voiceless counterpart is "**x**", which "is like a heavily aspirated *h*, quite like the sound made when breathing on glass or metal to polish it" (Saeed 1987:17). Interestingly, it is often transcribed with a double *h*; thus, the Somali customary law which is the subject of this book, **xeer**, is often rendered as *hheer* in Western publications.

"**q**" is technically called an "uvular:" it is similar to "**k**" or "**g**", but with the tongue retracted further back in the mouth.

The sound written "**dh**" is "made like a *d*, but the tip of the tongue is curled back so that the tip touches an area in front of the hard palate" (Saeed 1987:16). Most speakers pronounce it as *r* within a word or at its end.

"**kh**" is relatively uncommon (only occurring in words borrowed from Arabic); it is similar to, but stronger than, Scottish *ch* in *loch*, or the Spanish *jota*.

Somali vowels may be short or long; long vowels are written by doubling the sign for the single vowels; thus, "**aa**", "**ee**", etc. The Somali vowels are the five "cardinal" ones; readers familiar with Spanish can take the Spanish vowels as a suitable guide.

"**a**" generally resembles the vowel heard in English *gun*; long "**aa**" is somewhat similar to the sound heard in *father* or *calm*.

"**e**" is approximately as English *pen, dress,* while "**ee**" has no counterpart in English.

"**i**" is similar to the vowel found in English *pen, fell* and long "**ii**" to the vowel of *fleece* or *beam*.

Long "**oo**" is similar to the vowel in *thought* or *law*, while short "**o**" has no direct correspondent in English.

"**u**" is similar to the vowel of *foot, good,* and "**uu**" to that of *goose, loot.*

Finally, stress (or tone) falls on the last or penultimate (the last but one) syllable, depending on such complicated factors as the gender (masculine or feminine) of the word, and also its position in the sentence and its grammatical role.

References

Catford, John C.
  1988   *A Practical Introduction to Phonetics.* Oxford: Clarendon Press.
Saeed, John I.
  1987   *Somali Reference Grammar.* Wheaton, MD: Dunwoody Press.

Mauro Tosco is Associate Professor of African Linguistics and Somali Language at the University of Naples "L'Orientale" in Naples, Italy. His main field of activity is the investigation of the Cushitic languages of the Horn of Africa. His publications include a grammar of the Somali dialect Af-Tunni (Cologne 1997), of the Dahalo language of Kenya (Hamburg 1991), and of the Dhaasanac language of Southwest Ethiopia (Cologne 2001). He is currently working on a description of Gawwada (Ethiopia) and on a book on language variety, minorities, and the role of governments in suppressing them. His views on language diversity and language policy were published recently in "The Case for a Laissez-Faire Language Policy," *Language & Communication*, 24:2 (2004), pages 165-181.

Appendix E
Somalia—A Brief Chronology

Egyptians, Romans, and Byzantines traded on the Somali coast. The latter called Awdal "Adulis." Chinese historians in the eleventh century speak of the Hawiye in the Mogadishu area. The first known appearance of the name "Somali" was in a hymn celebrating the victories of the Abyssinian king Yeshaq (1414-1429) against what later became known as the Sultanate of Awdal. In the sixteenth-century, Arab historian Shihab ed Din described Somali clans in his account of Ahmed Guray's devastating war against Abyssinia.

Somalis today number nearly 11.5 million, mostly leading a nomadic life herding livestock over the semi-arid lands of the Horn of Africa. Their territory measures approximately a million square kilometres, which is about twice the size of France.

Until the construction of the Suez Canal, Somalis had little contact with Europe. Then France, Italy, England, and Ethiopia were prompted to occupy Somali territory. They failed to penetrate the rural areas, however, where nomads continued their daily life undisturbed by foreign influences.

In 1947, the United Nations split the Somali nation among five countries. The population today is distributed approximately as follows:[52]

1. Former Italian Somaliland (200,000 square miles, 5.5 million population), now split among several political entities
2. Former British Somaliland (68,000 square miles, 1.9 million population), now called the Republic of Somaliland

3. Former French Somaliland (5,790 square miles, 0.25 million population), now called the Republic of Djibouti
4. The Ogaden and Western Awdal (142,500 square miles, 4 million population), now called Ethiopia's Autonomous Somali Region
5. Northeastern District of Kenya (10,000 square miles, 0.45 million population)

In 1960, former British and Italian Somaliland were consolidated into the Republic of Somalia. But 31 years later, following an impasse over who should succeed the deposed Siad Barre, the Somali clans of that combined region took the unprecedented step of allowing the government to collapse, effectively dismantling it. Fearing that other African nations might follow that precedent and become stateless as well, the United Nations during the decade of the 1990s spent more than three billion dollars on diplomatic, military, and humanitarian ventures attempting to re-establish a central government in the former territory of the Republic. Thus far, the Somalis have resisted such interventions. They dislike the concept of a central government, and many think that not having a central government may be a step toward reuniting the Somali nation.

Since time immemorial, Somalis have organised their society on the basis of a customary law called "xeer" (pronounced *hhèèr*). Left alone, the xeer has the potential of evolving into a full-fledged system of common law system capable of handling all of the complexities of a fully modern society. Unfortunately, foreign governments are continually intervening in Somali affairs. Their main reasons are to protect:

* The shipping route through the Suez Canal and Red Sea
* The world's prevailing political system, consisting of a tax authority enforced by a monopoly of defence and policing and legitimised by democratic voting
* The geo-political division of the Somali nation into four parts (after the 1960 merger of Somaliland and former Italian Somalia)
* Access to Somalia's mineral wealth, particularly uranium.

CHRONOLOGY

1862   France established rule over the region now known as the Republic of Djibouti, where it still maintains a military presence.

1869   The Suez Canal opened.

1870   Egypt established rule over today's Somali Region of Ethiopia and Harar. Withdrawing in 1884, it resumed an active interest in the area in the 1950s.

1884   Britain established rule over the northern and southern territories, now known as the Republic of Somaliland and the Northeastern Province of Kenya.

1885   Ethiopia established rule over the territories now called the autonomous Somali Region of Ethiopia.

1889   Italy established rule over numerous territories including what are now Puntland, Benadir, Digil & Mirifle, and Jubaland.

1947   The United Nations split Somalia five ways, rejecting a British proposal to unify the territories.

1954   In a unilateral action, Britain as a colonial power ceded Western Awdal, Haud, and Ogaden to Ethiopia.

1960   Departing British and Italians consolidated their former British and Italian Somalilands, establishing the Republic of Somalia under a constitution stipulating that the government should "promote by legal and peaceful means the reunion of all Somali territories."

1969   Brig. General Mohamed Siad Barre overthrew the Republic of Somalia and established a Marxist dictatorship, a Soviet client state which he renamed the "Democratic Republic of Somalia."

1972   A written Somali language was codified, and literacy became widespread.

1976   Djibouti gained independence from France, but French paratroopers intervened to "restore order."

1978   Siad Barre declared war on Ethiopia. The Soviets backed Ethiopia, whereupon Barre became pro-Western. Barre lost the war and his credibility with Somali citizens. Rebellion began in the north.

1988-89   A series of attacks in Berbera led to a government massacre of 30,000 civilians.

1991   Siad Barre's administration collapsed, and the government was dismantled. Clan fighting and widespread famine ensued.

1992   A United Nations army occupied Somalia to expedite humanitarian aid and impose a democratic government.

1993   The United Nations trained thousands of Somalis for jobs in a proposed new central government. Attack by the United States military on a peaceable assembly of Somalis incited violence.

1995   Acknowledging failure of its mission, the United Nations political and military personnel withdrew, leaving some specialised agencies behind.

1996   The United Nations Research Institute for Social Development (UNRISD) began meetings with local leaders to promote democratic ideology.

1998   The United Nations supported Inter-Governmental Association for Development (IGAD) attempted a "bottom-up" approach to building a democratic central government in Somalia.

2000   The Government of Djibouti, backed by the United Nations and the United States, formed the nucleus of a democratic government for Somalia called the Transitional National Government (TNG).

2002   The Inter-Governmental Association for Development (IGAD), backed by the United Nations and the United States, convened a National Peace and Reconciliation Conference at Eldoret, Kenya—the 14th effort by the United Nations and its supporters to unify Somalia under a democratic, Western style government.

2004   The Reconciliation Conference reached agreement on a "national government" for Somalia; the African Union authorised Ethiopia and four other East African nations to deploy 7,500 troops in its support.

A more detailed treatment of Somali history can be found in Maria H. Brons (2001) and I.M. Lewis (1961).

Bibliography

Somali Customary Law and Society

Ayittey, George B.N. *Indigenous African institutions.* Ardsley-on-Hudson, NY: Transnational Publishers, 1991.

Bader, Christian. *Le Sang et le Sait: Breve Histoire des Clans Somali.* Paris: Maisonneuve et Larose, 1999.

Bayart, Jean-Francois. *L'Etat en Afrique.* Paris: Fayard, 1989.

Bigwood, Bryce. "Ancap Mog: So Close Yet so Far." *Anti-State.com*, 2002, http://anti-state.com/article.php?article_id=205.

Brons, Maria H. *Society, Security, Sovereignty and the State in Somalia: From Statelessness to Statelessness?* Utrecht: International Books, 2001.

Burale, Ahmed Sheikh 'Ali Ahmed. *Xeerkii Soomaalidii Hore.* Mogadishu: Akadeemiyaha Dhaqanka, 1977.

Burton, Richard. (1856) *First Footsteps in East Africa.* Dover Publications, 1987.

Casanelli, Lee V. *The Shaping of Somali Society: Reconstructing the History of a Pastoral People, 1600-1900.* Philadelphia: University of Pennsylvania Press, 1982.

Cerulli, Enrico. "Il Diritto Consetudinario della Somalia Italiana Settentrionale." *Bolettinodella Società Africana d'Italia* anno xxxviii (1919). Naples.

Colucci, Massimo. *Principi di Diritto Consuetudinario della Somalia Italiana Meridionale.* Firenze, 1924.

Compagnon, Daniel. "Somalia: Les limites de l'ingerance 'humanitaire.'"*LÉchec politique de l'ONU* in *Afrique Politique* (1995): 195-196.

Davidson, Jim. Personal communication to Spencer H. MacCallum, 2003.

Drysdale, J.G.S. "Some Aspects of Rural Society Today." *The Somaliland Journal* (1955).

Horner, Simon. "Somalia: A Country Report," *APC-EU Courier* (Commission of the European Communities in Brussels) no. 162 (March-April 1998).

Iye, Ali Musse. "Le Verdict de L'Arbre, Le Xeer Issa, Etude d'une Democratie Pastorale." Djibouti: n.p., 1990.

Kapteyns, L. "Gender Relations," *The International Journal of African History* (1995).

Langley, J. Ayo, ed. *Ideologies of Liberation in Black Africa, 1856-1970.* London: Rex Collins, 1979.

Lewis, I.M. *A Pastoral Democracy: A Study of Pastoralism and Politics among the Northern Somali of the Horn of Africa.* Oxford University Press, 1961.

Lewis, I.M. "Lineage Continuity and Modern Commerce in Northern Somaliland." *In* Bohannan, Paul and George Dalton, eds. *Markets in Africa.* Evanston: Northwestern University Press, 1962.

Lewis, I.M. *Blood and Bone: The Call of Kinship in Somali Society.* Trenton, NJ: Red Sea Press, 1997.

Little, Peter D. *Somalia: Economy Without State.* Bloomington: Indiana University Press, 2003.

Mirreh, Abdi Gaileh. *Die Sozialökonomischen Verhaltnisse der Nomadischen Bevölkerung im Norden der Demokratischen Republik Somalia.* Berlin: Akademie-Verlag, 1978.

Mohamed Mohamed Shiekh. "Does Somalia Really Need a Government?" (Signed editorial). Addis Ababa, Ethiopia: *The Sun,* August 28, 1997.

Noor Muhammad. "Civil Wrongs under Customary Law in the Northern Regions of the Somali Republic," *Journal of African Law* 8, no. 3 (1967): 157-177.

Noor Muhammad. *The legal system of the Somali Democratic Republic.* [Pages 70-88, 115-119, 287-288]. Charlottesville: University of Virginia Press, 1972.

Pirone, M. "Leggende e Traditioni Storiche dei Somali Ogaden." *Archivio per l'Antropologia e l' Etnologia* LXXXIV (1954). Florence.

Samatar, Abdi Ismail and Ahmed I. Samatar. *The African State: Reconsiderations.* Westport, CT: Heinemann, 2002.

Simons, Anna M. "A Somali Alternative to Chaos." *Los Angeles Times,* July 9, 1997.

Sorens, Jason P. and Leonard Wantchekon. *Social Order without the State: The Case of Somalia.* Working paper, Council on African Studies. New Haven: Yale Center for International and Area Studies, 2000.

Van Notten, Michael. "From Nation State to Stateless Nation." *Liberty* 17, no. 4 (April 2003): 27-32.

Van Notten, Michael. Various draft writings: "Aims of a Project on the Somali Customary Law," May 30, 1999 (1 page); "International Conference for Assistance to Refugees in Africa (ICARA)," May 16, 1999 (1 page); *The Juno File,* no date (80 pages); "Reaffirmation of Somali Nationhood." February 5, 1997 (2.5 pages); "Rebuttal of an Open Letter on the New War between

Ethiopia and Eritrea," December 25, 1998 (under pen name Wilbur Black); *Ten Memoranda and Drafts on Somali politics,* no date; "Which Political System for the Somalis?" November 15, 1998 (1 page); "Why Awdal is so Shockingly Poor," May 7, 2002 (under pen name Frank Douglas Heath).

Van Notten, Michael (under pen name Graham Green). "Laissez Faire in Africa."*Economic Government Group,* 1998, http://www.econgov.org/articles/index.shtml.

Van Notten, Michael (under pen name Graham Green). 1998 "Toward a New Country in East Africa." *Economic Government Group,* 1998, http://www.econgov.org/articles/toward.shtml.

Van Notten, Michael (under pen name Graham Green). "Why Stateless?" *Economic Government Group,* no date, http://www.econgov.org/articles/toward.shtml.

Van Notten, Michael (under pen name Graham Green). "Somali Customary Law." *Economic Government Group,* no date, http://www.econgov.org/articles/toward.shtml.

Van Notten, Michael (under pen name Graham Green). "Fines under the Xeer (Customary Law) of the Darod Tribe." *Economic Government Group,* no date, http://www.econgov.org/articles/toward.shtml.

Van Notten, Michael (under pen name Graham Green). "Somalijskie Prawo Zwyczajowe." *Libertarianizm.pl.* http://www.libertarianizm.pl/green.html.

Van Notten, Michael (under pen name Frank Douglas Heath). "Whither Somaliland? Tribal Society and Democracy." *Somaliland Forum,* 2000. http://www.somalilandforum.com/articles/whither_somaliland.htm.

Wright, A.C.A. "The Interaction of Law and Custom in British Somaliland and their Relation with Social Life," *Journal of the East African Natural History,* 1942: 66-102.

Zavis, Alexandra. "Authority-Free Somalia Makes Modern Gains." *Seattle Times,* The Associated Press, 25 February 2005.

General

Anderson, J.N.D. *Colonial Office: Islamic Law in Africa* [pages 40-57, 114]. Kent: Fangorn Books, 1954.

Anderson, J.N.D., ed. *Changing Law in Developing Countries.* Praeger, 1963.

Barkun, Michael. *Law without sanctions: Order in Primitive Societies and the World Community.* Yale University Press, 1968.

Barnett, Randy E. *The Structure of Liberty: Justice and the Rule of Law.*Oxford: Clarendon Press, 1998.

Bell, Tom W. 1991 "Privately Produced Law." *Extropy* 3, no. 1 (Spring 1991). [Since reprinted and available from Libertarian Alliance, 25 Chapter Chambers, Esterbrooke Street, London SW1P 4NN.]

Benson, Bruce L. *The Enterprise of Law: Justice without the State.* San Francisco: Pacific Research Institute for Public Policy, 1990.

Benson, Bruce L. *To Serve and Protect: Privatization and Community in Criminal Justice.* New York: New York University Press, 1998.

Berman, Harold J. *Law and Revolution: The Formation of the Western Legal Tradition.* Harvard University Press, 1985.

Bower, Bruce. "Ancient mariners: Caves Harbor View of Ancient Egyptian sailors." Science News 167:19 (May 7, 2005). Page 294.

Bozeman, Adda B. *Conflict in Africa: Concepts and Realities.* Princeton University Press, 1976.

Central Intelligence Agency (CIA). *The World Fact Book.* Washington DC 2003. http://www.cia.gov/cia/publications/factbook/geos/so.html.

De Jasay, Anthony. *Against Politics.* London: Routledge, 1997.

De Jouvenel, Bertrand. *On Power: The Natural History of its Growth.* Indianapolis: Liberty Fund, 1993. [Original in French: *Du Pouvoir: Histoire Naturelle de sa Croissance.* Génève: Les Éditions du Cheval Ailé, 1945].

Diamond, A.S. *The Evolution of Law and Order.* Westport CT: Greenwood Press, 1975.

Foldvary, Fred E. and Daniel Klein. *The Half-Life of Policy Rationales: How New Technology Affects Old Policy Issues.* New York University Press, 2003.

Friedman, David D. *Law's Order" What Economics Has to Do with Law and Why It Matters.* Princeton University Press, 2000.

Fuller, Lon. *The Morality of Law.* Yale University Press, 1964.

Gwartney, James D. and Robert A. Lawson. *Economic Freedom of the World: 2004 Annual Report.* Washington, D.C.: Cato Institute, 2004.

Halliday, Roy. *Enforceable Rights: A Libertarian Theory of Justice.* (2000)http://royhalliday.home.mindspring.com MYBOOK.HTM [Also published on microfiche as *Peace Plans 1687, 1688* by Libertarian Microfiche Publishing, Box 52, Berrima NSW, Australia, 2001.]

Halliday, Roy. Email message December 17, 2002 to Spencer H. MacCallum. Quoted by permission.

Hoebel, E. Adamson. *Law of Primitive Man: A study in Comparative Legal Dynamics.* New York: Scribner, 1968.

Hoppe, Hans-Hermann, ed. *The Myth of National Defense*. Auburn, AL: Ludwig von Mises Institute, 2003.

Kendall, Frances and Leon Louw. *After Apartheid: The Solution for South Africa*. San Francisco: Institute for Contemporary Studies Press, 1987.

Leoni, Bruno. *Freedom and the Law*. Princeton: Van Nostrand, 1961.

Lester, J.C. *Escape from Leviathan*. London: Macmillan, 2000.

Loan, Albert. "Institutional Bases of the Spontaneous Order: Surety and Assurance." *Humane Studies Review* 7, no. 1 (Winter 1998).

Lowi, Alvin, Jr. *Scientific Method: In Search of Legitimate Authority in Society*. San Pedro, CA: Unpublished monograph available from the author (310) 548-8457 <alowi@earthlink.net>).

Lowi, Alvin, Jr. "An Entrepreneurial Corporation." San Pedro, CA: Unpublished paper available from the author (310) 548-8457 alowi@earthlink.net).

MacCallum, Spencer H. *The Art of Community*. Menlo Park, California: Institute for Humane Studies, 1970.

MacCallum, Spencer H. 1971 "Jural Behavior in American Shopping Centers: Initial Views of the Proprietary Community." *Human Organisation* 30, no. 1 (Spring 1971): 3-10.

MacCallum, Spencer H. "The Quickening of Social Evolution." *The Independent Review* 2 no. 2 (fall 1997): 287-302.

MacCallum, Spencer H. 2001 "Land Policy and the Open Community." *Laissez Faire City Times* 5 no. 2 (January 8, 2001), San Jose, Costa Rica.

MacCallum, Spencer H. "The Enterprise of Community: Market Competition, Land and Environment." *The Journal of Libertarian Studies* 17 no. 4 (fall 2003).

MacCallum, Spencer H. "Planned Communities without Politics: Finding a Market Solution to the Economic and Social Problems of Common-Interest Development." Unpublished paper available from the author (sm@look.net).

Machan, Tibor, ed. *Individual Rights Reconsidered*. Stanford: Hoover Institution Press, 2001.

Marchal, Roland. "Mogadiscio tra Rovine e Globalizzazione" [Mogadishu between Ruin and Globalization]. In *Afriche e Orienti*, no. 2 (1999): 20-30.

Miles, Marc and Edwin J. Feulner, Jr., Mary Anastasia O'Grady, Ana Isabel Eiras, and Asron Schavey. *Index of Economic Freedom, 2004*. Washington, D.C.: Heritage Foundation, 2004.

Peden, Joseph R. "Stateless Societies: Ancient Ireland." *The Libertarian Forum* (April 1971).

Perkins, John. *Confessions of an Economic Hit Man.* San Francisco: Barrett-Koehler 2004.

Riegel, E.C. *Flight from Inflation: The Monetary Alternative.* Los Angeles: The Heather Foundation, 1978.

Smith, Tara. *Moral Rights and Political Freedom.* Lanham, MD: Rowman & Littlefield, 1995.

Tandy, Francis D. *Voluntary Socialism.* Denver: Tandy, 1896 [62-78].

Van Dun, Frank. *Het Fundamenteel Rechtsbeginsel: Een Essay over de Grondslagen van het Recht* [The Fundamental Principle of Law]. Antwerp: Kluwer rechstwetenschappen, 1983.

Van Dun, Frank. "Human Dignity: Natural Rights versus Human Rights." In Roos, N. and P. van Koppen, eds. *Liber Amicorum.* Maastricht: Metajuridica Publications, 2000. [Subsequently published in the *Journal of Libertarian Studies* 14 no. 4 (Fall 2001): 1-28.]

Van Notten, Michael. "Enterprise Zones in Europe." *The Orange County Register,* July 1982.

Van Notten, Michael. "Encouraging Enterprise: The Belgian Experience." *Economic Affairs* (July 1983).

Van Notten, Michael. "D-Zones met Zuigracht." *Economisch Statische Berichten* (March-April 1983).

Van Notten, Michael. "Foretakssoner mot Byrakrati, Ideer om Frihet." *Norvegian Magazine* (February 1984).

Van Notten, Michael. "Make Governments Compete for People." *Economic Affairs* (July 1984).

Van Notten, Michael and Richard Bolin. "The Case for Export Processing Zones." *The Wall Street Journal,* European Edition, October 24, 1986.

Walker, Bill. "Insuring Your Future." *LewRockwell.com,* April 19, 2005. http://www.lewrockwell.com/orig5/walker7.html.

Wignall, Christian. "The Champion of Hong Kong's Freedom." Unpublished paper available from the author at cwignall@pacbell.net. 2003.

Wooldridge, William C. *Uncle Sam, the Monopoly Man,* Chapter 5, "Voluntary Justice." New Rochelle NY: Arlington House, 1970.

About the Author

Que notre Dieu accueille son Paradis éternel. Je suis vraiment touché la disparition de M. Michael van Notten que j'ai considéré comme mon père. Il était courage, intelligent, sincère, expérimenté et connaisseur de mon peuple.
—M. Houssein Djama

Michael van Notten was born on 8 December 1933 in Zeist, the Netherlands. He graduated from Vossius Gymnasium in Amsterdam in 1953 and served two years as 1st Lieutenant in the Royal Cavalry. In 1960 he graduated from Leiden University in law and was admitted to practice in Rotterdam. In 1959, Michael and Tina van Roijen married. They had four daughters, Marina, Henriette, Isabelle and Ariane.

Michael dedicated his life to promoting human dignity and freedom. In particular, he sought to help bring about a separation of law and justice from the realm of politics. He gained many admirers for his writing and his dedication to ideals.

In 1962 he joined the New York law firm of Shearman & Sterling, where he served for a year-and-a-half before moving to Brussels to join the legal staff of the Directorate of Cartels, Monopolies, Dumping and Private discriminations, of the European Economic Community, or "Common Market." In this post he was an ardent champion of free trade. In the mid 80s, he directed the Institutum Europaeum, a Belgium-based policy research organisation, promoting the concept of "D-zones," or freeports, for economic development in the Netherlands, Belgium, and developing countries.

With Hubert Jongen, Michael co-founded in Holland in 1975 the Libertarian Centre, one of the first liberty groups in Europe. During its early years, Michael was active in almost all libertarian activities including publishing the Dutch libertarian newsletter "de Vrijbrief" ("Freedom Letter," now in electronic form as "E-VRIJBRIEF"). At about this time he became active in the Mont Pelerin Society. In 1982 he made a major contribution to the first world convention of the International Society for Individual Liberty (ISIL), arguing strongly and successfully that ISIL should not be organised politically with voting for representatives, committee structure, or bureaucracy, but as an entrepreneurship, a privately run business. He continued to have an important role in succeeding conventions.

In or around 1990, Michael discovered Somalia and became interested in the possibility that it might develop in the modern world as a stateless society. He remarried in 1991, this time to Flory Barnabas Warsame, cousin of the chief of the Samaron Clan in Awdal. For the next twelve years he studied Somali customary law and promoted the economic development of the region. He formed a non-governmental organisation (NGO) in Ethiopia's Hararghe, a region ethnically Somali and traditionally known as "Western Awdal." His Eastern Hararghe Development Agency built water retention facilities, dug wells, obtained farm equipment, imported hospital equipment, and on two occasions took Somalis to the United States to study advanced methods of raising cattle in Arizona's desert that could be applied to the semi-arid lands of Awdal. A special project was to develop in Awdal a complete fishery and fish processing industry.

In 1995, Michael and a business associate, Jim Davidson, began detailed plans for an Awdal Free Port on the Gulf of Aden, southeast of Djibouti. Five years later they incorporated the Awdal Roads Company in Mauritius to build a toll-road that would connect the Free Port with Ethiopia, thereby opening up a trading area of 70 million population in Ethiopia and the highlands of Awdal—the great hinterland of the Horn of Africa. He explored economic development opportunities in every part of Somalia.

As these plans were beginning to mature, Michael saw a new window of opportunity for promoting freedom in The Netherlands with Pim Fortuyn's entry into politics. He thought this new opposition movement might be open to Libertarian ideas. Following Mr. Fortuyn's untimely death, he tried to work with the politicians of his party, promoting among other things a plan to employ in his ports, fisheries, and roads projects a large number of Somalis who had to return or wished to return to Somalia—a programme that would have cost a fraction of the current development aid. The Prodos Institute awarded Michael posthumously its Dutch Capitalism award as an acknowledgement of his activities in Holland. Michael spoke eight languages, including two Somali dialects. He was keenly interested in analysing the intricacies of clan politics and travelled fearlessly in war-torn Somalia, which gained him the nickname among the ex-pats in Mogadishu of "Bullet-proof Michael." In recognition of his marriage with Flory, Somalis even from neighbouring clans such as the Isaaq would call him "seddi," or "brother-in-law."

Michael delighted those who knew him with his always understated humour. He took enormous pleasure in the company of his family and, especially, his eight grandchildren. He was a world traveller, resourceful, an architect of great plans, unafraid to dream. Invariably he was an inspiration to his friends. He died in Nimes, France, of a chronic heart condition on June 5th, 2002, at 68 years of age.

Index

INDEX OF PROPER NAMES